Exemplary Science: Best Practices in Professional Development

Robert E. Yager, Editor

NATIONAL SCIENCE TEACHERS ASSOCIATION

Arlington, Virginia

NATIONAL SCIENCE TEACHERS ASSOCIATION

Claire Reinburg, Director
Judy Cusick, Senior Editor
J. Andrew Cocke, Associate Editor
Betty Smith, Associate Editor
Robin Allan, Book Acquisitions Coordinator

ART AND DESIGN, David Serota, Director
PRINTING AND PRODUCTION, Catherine Lorrain-Hale, Director
  Nguyet Tran, Assistant Production Manager
  Jack Parker, Electronic Prepress Technician

NATIONAL SCIENCE TEACHERS ASSOCIATION
Gerald F. Wheeler, Executive Director
David Beacom, Publisher

Library of Congress Cataloging-in-Publication Data
Exemplary science: best practices in professional development / Robert Yager, editor.
   p. cm.
  Includes bibliographical references and index.
  ISBN 0-87355-256-3
 1. Science—Study and teaching—Methodology. 2. Science teachers—Training of. I. Yager, Robert
Q181.E83 2005
507'.11—dc22
                2004030525

Contents

Implementing the Changes in Professional Development Envisioned by the National Science Education Standards:

Where Are We Nine Years Later?

Robert E. Yager, Editor
University of Iowa

Nine years have elapsed since the 1996 publication of the National Science Education Standards (NSES) (NRC 1996). The critical issues in science education now are these: How far have we progressed in putting the vision of the NSES into practice? What remains to be done? What new visions are worthy of new trials?

The four monographs in the NSTA Exemplary Science Monograph series seek to answer these questions. The monographs are *Exemplary Science: Best Practices in Professional Development* (the book you are reading), *Exemplary Science in Grades 9–12: Standards-Based Success Stories* (currently available); *Exemplary Science in Grades 5–8*; and *Exemplary Science in Grades PreK–4* (the latter two books are in development).

How These Essays Were Chosen

The series was conceived in 2001 by an advisory board of science educators, many of whom had participated in the development of the National Science Education Standards. The advisory board members (who are all active and involved NSTA members; see p. xv for their names) decided to seek exemplars of the NSES *More Emphasis* conditions as a way to evaluate progress toward the visions of the NSES. The *More Emphasis* conditions provide summaries of the NSES in science teaching, professional development, assessment, science content, and science education program and systems. (See Appendix 1 for the six *Less Emphasis/More Emphasis* lists.) The board sent information about the projected series to the NSTA leadership team and to all the NSTA affiliates, chapters, and associated groups. A call for papers on exemplary programs also appeared in all NSTA publications. In addition, more than a thousand letters inviting nominations were sent to leaders identified in the *2001–2002 NSTA Handbook* (NSTA 2001–2002), and personal letters were sent to leaders of all science education organizations.

After preliminary responses were received, the advisory board identified teachers and programs that it felt should be encouraged to prepare formal drafts for further review and evaluation. The goal was to identify 15 of the best situations in each of four areas—professional development and grades 9–12, 5–8, and PreK–4—where facets of the teaching, professional development, assessment, and content standards were being met in an exemplary manner.

The most important aspect of the selection process was the evidence the authors of each essay could provide regarding the effect of their programs on student learning. This aspect proved the most elusive. Most of us "know" when something is going well, but we are not well equipped to provide real evidence for this "knowing." Many exciting program descriptions were not among the final titles—simply because little or no evidence other than personal testimony was available in the materials forwarded. The 16 professional development models that make up this monograph were chosen by the NSTA advisory board as the best examples of models that fulfill the *More Emphasis* conditions of the Professional Development Standards; each has had a clear, positive impact on student science learning.

The History of the National Science Education Standards

Before discussing the contents of this book at greater length, I would like to offer a brief history of the National Science Education Standards.

Most educators credit the National Council of Teachers of Mathematics (NCTM) with initiating the many efforts to produce national standards for programs in U.S. schools. In 1986 (10 years before the publication of the National Science Education Standards), the board of directors of NCTM established a Commission on Standards for School Mathematics with the aim of improving the quality of school mathematics. An initial draft of these standards was developed during the summer of 1987, revised during the summer of 1988 after much discussion among NCTM members, and finally published as the *Curriculum and Evaluation Standards for School Mathematics* in 1989.

The NCTM standards did much for mathematics education by providing a consensus for what mathematics should be. The National Science Foundation (NSF) and other funding groups had not been involved in developing the math standards, but these groups quickly funded research and training to move schools and teachers in the direction of those standards. Having such a "national" statement regarding needed reforms resulted in funding from private and government foundations to produce school standards in other disciplines, including science.

NSF encouraged the science education community to develop standards modeled after the NCTM document (1989). Interestingly, both the American Association for the Advancement of Science (AAAS) and the National Science Teachers Association (NSTA) expressed interest in preparing science standards. Both organizations indicated that they each had made a significant start on such national standards—AAAS with its Project 2061 and NSTA with its Scope, Sequence, and Coordination project. Both of these national projects had support from NSF, private foundations, and industries. The compromise on this "competition" between AAAS and NSTA leaders led to the recommendation that the National Research Council (NRC) of the National Academy of Sciences be funded to develop the National Science Education Standards. With NSF funding provided in 1992, both NSTA and AAAS helped to select the science leaders who would prepare the NSES. Several early drafts were circulated among hundreds of people with invitations to comment, suggest, debate, and assist with a consensus document. A full-time director of consensus provided leadership and assistance as final drafts were assembled. Eventually, it took $7 million and four years of debate to produce the 262-page NSES publication in 1996.

There was never any intention that the Standards would indicate minimum competencies that would be required of all. Instead, the focus was on visions of how teaching, assessment, and content should be changed. Early on, programs and systems were added as follow-ups to teaching, assessment, and content.

The NSES volume begins with standards for improved teaching. That chapter is followed by chapters on professional development, assessment, science content, and science education program and systems. Content was placed in the document after the other three for fear that placing it first would invite a focus only on what should be taught—almost relegating teaching, staff development, and assessment to "add-on" roles. The major debates, however, centered on what should appear in the content chapter.

It is interesting to note that the early drafts of the National Science Education Standards did not include any mention of professional development. It was only when the final draft was about to be offered to the leadership in the National Academy of Sciences that a section on professional development was added. This addition came in response to the argument that such visions for the continued education of teachers would be needed if any significant use of the Standards, any improvement of existing teachers, and any improved ways of preparing teachers were to be realized. They were added as a way of ensuring that the science teaching standards would be central in the preparation of new teachers and the continuing education of all inservice teachers.

The Four NSES Goals for School Science

An exemplary professional development program must prepare teachers to implement the four NSES goals for school science, which are to educate students to be able to

Goal 1. experience the richness and excitement of knowing about and understanding the natural world;

Goal 2. use appropriate scientific processes and principles in making personal decisions;

Goal 3. engage intelligently in public discourse and debate about matters of scientific and technological concern; and

Goal 4. increase their economic productivity through the use of the knowledge, understanding, and skills of the scientifically literate person in their careers (NRC 1996, p. 13).

Let us look at each of these goals and consider how far along we are to meeting them in today's science classrooms.

Goal 1. For many educators, the first goal is the most important since it ensures that every student will have a firsthand, personal experience with the whole scientific enterprise. This means exploring nature with the natural curiosity that all humans enjoy. It means asking questions, identifying the unknown, proceeding to knowing—even if what results is a personally constructed answer or explanation that might be wrong in terms of current science academy notions. What matters is that personal curiosity sparks an original question.

Unfortunately, science educators sometimes define science as the information found in textbooks for K–12 and college courses or the content outlined in state frameworks and standards. Such definitions omit most of what George Gaylord Simpson (1969) described as the essence of science. Simpson held that five activities define science:

1. *asking questions about the natural universe; i.e., being curious about the objects and events in nature;*
2. *trying to answer one's own questions; i.e., proposing possible explanations;*
3. *designing experiments to determine the validity of the explanation offered;*
4. *collecting evidence from observations of nature, mathematics calculations, and, whenever possible, experiments carried out to establish the validity of the original explanations;*
5. *communicating the evidence to others who must agree with the interpretation of the evidence in order for the explanation to become accepted by the broader community [of scientists].* (Simpson 1969, p. 81)

These five activities are rarely carried out in schools. Science students seldom determine their own questions for study; they are not expected to be curious; they rarely are asked to propose possible answers; they seldom are asked to design experiments; and they rarely share their results with others as evidence for the validity of their own explanations (Weiss et al. 2003).

Overall, one could argue that "real" science is seldom encountered or experienced in most science classrooms. The typical focus is almost wholly on what current scientists accept as explanations (Harms and Yager 1981; Weiss et al. 2003). Competent science students only need to remember what teachers or textbooks say. Most laboratories are but verification activities of what teachers and textbooks have indicated as truths about the natural world. There is seldom time for students to design experiments that could improve human existence.

Goals 2, 3, and 4. The other three goals from the Standards focus on experiences in school science that affect the daily lives of students, helping them to make better scientific and societal decisions and leading them to increased economic productivity. Regrettably, these three goals are rarely approached, realized, or assessed in typical classrooms by typical teachers. Information that would help in realizing these goals is not offered in texts, teacher preparation efforts, or programs for inservice teachers. If we want science concepts and skills to be used in making personal decisions, we are going to have to deal with ideas of how these goals can be achieved. In *Understanding by Design,* Wiggins and McTighe (1998) provide ideas about what needs to be done—in particular, what evidence we need to collect to be sure we have met Goal 2 (i.e., using appropriate scientific methods and principles for making personal decisions). We cannot stop with the idea that students seem to know certain concepts and can perform certain skills. We need to expect evidence for learning to include practice with the concepts and skills in actually making decisions in daily living.

Regarding Goal 3, educators must focus on involving students in public discourse and debate in school, as well as in the outside community. Where do they actually use what is in the curriculum and what teachers teach? A whole new way of viewing content, instruction, and assessment is needed if this goal is to be realized. Goal 4 may be the most difficult to achieve and to assess. In some ways it is further from daily life and the immediate community than the other goals. It focuses on future economic productivity, possible career choices, and the use of concepts and processes that are often given short shrift in today's science classroom.

Professional Development and the Standards

Professional development is about ensuring that teachers continue to grow and improve. Professional development forces us to look at the acts of teaching and to discuss the effects of these acts on student learning. We have to be sure that learning does result and that it is learning with understanding and potential use—not merely an indication of students' ability to remember, repeat, and recite.

Professional development programs must not only help teachers meet the 14 *More Emphasis* conditions of the Professional Development Standards, but they must also assist teachers to implement the 9 *More Emphasis* conditions of the Science Teaching Standards and the 7 *More Emphasis* conditions of the Assessment in Science Education Standards (see Appendix 1 for these *More Emphasis* conditions).

Professional Development Challenges and Solutions

Professional development providers need to be familiar with how content strands are organized across K–12 curriculums and how major concepts and processes are seen and used in concert. Professional development initiatives must focus on science as inquiry and on how science teaching also can result in inquiries about teaching. If we focus too acutely on a single scientific discipline, and exclude concepts from other disciplines, problems result.

Another serious issue is that schools too often spend funds on general workshops with leaders from general education backgrounds. The workshops are presented to all teachers in a building or district, without regard to the likely impact of implementation on teaching, curriculum, or student learning. In addition, staff development efforts often present an abundance of suggestions for reform—too many to be carried out over a relatively short period of time.

Furthermore, professional development programs are often structured solely as a summer workshop or institute. Even those lasting over multiple weeks focus only on "more science study," with little attention paid to how new information and insights can be used successfully to promote more and better student plans. Recent evidence suggests that work with inservice teachers should be extended to plans for actual changes to be tried during the following academic year. Teachers should have opportunities to practice "evidence collecting" to determine the impact of what they have learned in the summer workshop or institute on their students (Weiss et al. 2003). Evidence suggests that inservice work is more effective the longer it is sustained—over three, four, or even more sequential years.

Among issues on the college level is the fact that although 50 semester hours of course work in science certainly indicates a strong background in traditional science, it is no indication of someone's ability to teach. And too often, science methods courses are taught in the same way that science is taught: Instructors define terms, provide lists of ways to teach, offer their own ideas, and expect students to take notes and repeat what they say for tests. This approach is no better than what typically happens in science classrooms and laboratories. We have learned more about how people learn in the last decade (see, e.g., Bransford, Brown, and Cocking 1999) than can be considered in a single, three-semester-hour methods course.

Conclusion

The 16 exemplars described in this monograph provide very creative ideas with all kinds of evidence that progress is being made toward carrying out the visions of the NSES. They each illustrate important contexts for assisting with the preparation of new science teachers and for assessing the continual growth and development of inservice teachers. Staff development should always be planned so that teachers become enthusiastic about the NSES and are ready to implement their visions.

About the Editor

Robert E. Yager was an active contributor to the development of the National Science Education Standards. He has devoted his life to teaching, writing, and advocating on behalf of science education worldwide. Having started his career as a high school science teacher, he has been a professor of science education at the University of Iowa since 1956. He has also served as president of seven national organizations, including NSTA, and been involved in teacher education in Japan, Korea, Taiwan, and Europe. Among his many publications are several NSTA books, including *Focus on Excellence* and *What Research Says to the Science Teacher*. Yager earned a bachelor's degree in biology from the University of Northern Iowa and master's and doctoral degrees in plant physiology from the University of Iowa.

References

Bransford, J. D., A. L. Brown, and R. R. Cocking, eds. 1999. *How people learn: Brain, mind, experience, and school.* Washington, DC: National Academy Press.

Harms, N. C., and R. E. Yager, eds. 1981. *What research says to the science teacher, vol. 3.* Washington, DC: National Science Teachers Association.

National Council of Teachers of Mathematics (NCTM). 1989. *Curriculum and evaluation standards for school mathematics.* Reston, VA: NCTM.

National Research Council (NRC). 1996. *National science education standards.* Washington, DC: National Academy Press.

National Science Teachers Association (NSTA). 2001–2002. *NSTA handbook.* Arlington, VA: NSTA.

Simpson G. G. 1969. Biology and the nature of science. *Science* 139: 81–82.

Weiss, I. R., E. R. Banilower, R. A. Crawford, and C. M. Overstreet. 2003. *Local systemic change through teacher enhancement; Year eight cross-site report.* Chapel Hill, NC: Horizon Research.

Wiggins, G., and J. McTighe. 1998. *Understanding by design.* Alexandria, VA: Association for Supervision and Curriculum Development.

Acknowledgments

Members of the National Advisory Board for the Exemplary Science Series

Hans O. Andersen
Past President of NSTA
Professor, Science Education
Indiana University–Bloomington

Charles R. Barman
Professor, Science and Environmental
   Education
Indiana University School of Education
Bloomington, IN

Bonnie Brunkhorst
Past President of NSTA
Professor
California State University–San Bernardino

Rodger Bybee
Executive Director
Biological Sciences Curriculum Study
   (BSCS)
Colorado Springs, CO

Audrey Champagne
Professor
State University of New York
Albany, NY

Fred Johnson
Past President of NSTA
Consultant
McKenzie Group
Memphis, TN

Roger Johnson
Professor
University of Minnesota
Minneapolis, MN

Mozell Lang
Science Consultant
Pontiac Northern High School
Pontiac, MI

LeRoy R. Lee
Past President of NSTA
Executive Director
Wisconsin Science Network
DeForest, WI

Shelley A. Lee
Past President of NSTA
Science Education Consultant
Wisconsin Department of Public Instruction
Madison, WI

acknowledgments

Gerry Madrazo
Past President of NSTA
Clinical Professor, Science Education
University of North Carolina, Chapel Hill

Richard J. Merrill
Past President of NSTA
University of California, Berkeley

Nick Micozzi
K–12 Science Coordinator
Plymouth Public Schools
Plymouth, MA

Edward P. Ortleb
Past President of NSTA
Science Consultant/Author
St. Louis, MO

Jack Rhoton
President, NSELA
Professor, Science Education
East Tennessee State University
Johnson City, TN

Gerald Skoog
Past President of NSTA
Professor and Dean
Texas Tech University
Lubbock, TX

Emma Walton
Past President of NSTA
Science Consultant
Anchorage, AK

Sandra West
Associate Professor, Science Education
Southwest Texas University
Canyon Lake, TX

Karen Worth
Senior Scientist
Education Development Center
Newton, MA

Assistant Editors at the University of Iowa

Suzanne Butz
Kris Dolgos
Brian J. Flanagan
Nancy C. Rather Mayfield

A Collaborative Endeavor to Teach the Nature of Scientific Inquiry:
There's More to Science Than Meets The "I"

Valarie L. Akerson
Indiana University

Deborah L. Hanuscin
University of Missouri

Setting

Built in 1959, in Bloomington, Indiana, Arlington Heights Elementary School is one of the oldest of the 14 elementary schools in the Monroe County Community Schools Corporation. The school serves about 300 students in grades K–6, the majority of whom are white. Approximately 29% qualify for free or reduced lunches. Arlington's faculty includes classroom teachers, resource/inclusion teachers, and certified instructors for music, art, and physical education. The school has an ongoing partnership with Indiana University (IU) and hosts a number of preservice teachers for their early field experiences and for student teaching. With the recent adoption of the Indiana Academic Standards for Science and the upcoming inclusion of science on statewide assessments, the school identified professional development in science as a need the university could address.

Professional Development Program

The professional development program created in response to this need, Learning Science by Inquiry, focuses on helping teachers promote scientific literacy. The vision of science education outlined by the National Science Education Standards (NSES) (NRC 1996) includes the development of scientifically literate students who can experience the richness and excitement of learning about the natural world and also apply what they learn about science to a wide range of personal and social decision-making processes. Central to this goal is an understanding of the nature of science—that is, the values and assumptions inherent in the construction of scientific knowledge (Lederman 1992).

The National Science Education Standards indicate that effective professional development should provide long-term, sustained support, collegial work with both peers and staff developers, and a variety of activities. We developed the Learning Science by Inquiry program specifically to target the content standards of inquiry, subject matter related to the nature of science, and understanding the role of prior knowledge in assessment. We planned professional development activities to meet the NSES Teaching and Professional Development *More Emphasis* conditions (NRC 1996, pp. 52, 72) that include teachers as members of a collegial community and teachers as both reflective practitioners and producers of knowledge about teaching; we also

Table 1. Targeted *More Emphasis* Conditions From the National Science Education Standards Aligned With Professional Development Activities in the Learning Science by Inquiry Program.

More Emphasis Conditions	Learning Science by Inquiry Professional Development Activities
Professional Development Standards • Long-term, coherent plans • Variety of professional development activities • Staff developers as facilitators, consultants, and planners	• 18-month-long program • Many activities: monthly workshops, collaboration with facilitators and peers, on-site support • Staff developers plan program in consultation with school administration and teachers, facilitate teacher progress
Content and Inquiry Standards and Assessment Standards • Implementing inquiry as instructional strategies, abilities, and ideas learned • Learning subject matter disciplines in the context of inquiry, technology, science in personal and social perspectives, and history and nature of science • Assessing to know what students do understand	• Teachers participate in inquiry and observe inquiry instruction in their own elementary classrooms • Teachers focus on inquiry and the nature of science in the context of elementary science content • Teachers learn assessment tools for becoming aware of their students' prior science content knowledge—student science journals, KWL charts, observation/inference charts, student observation records
Professional Development Standards and Teaching Standards • Collegial and collaborative learning/ teacher as a member of a collegial professional community • Teacher as intellectual, reflective practitioner/ producer of knowledge about teaching/ source and facilitator of change • Selecting and adapting curricula	• Teachers work with each other to enhance the science program by sharing ideas, providing feedback, presenting their work at state science teacher conferences • Teachers create change in their instruction, in students' knowledge; teachers reflect on their practices together, with facilitators, and individually • Teachers adapt existing curricula to focus on inquiry and the nature of science

helped program participants select and adapt curricula. The features that have been critical to the success of our program include sustained efforts over multiple academic years, collaboratively developed workshops, and on-site support for teachers. Workshops provide time for teachers to learn new information, discuss their current practices, and develop goals for their teaching. The alignment of each of these aspects with the NSES *More Emphasis* conditions that were used in designing the program are outlined in Table 1 and discussed in detail in the sections that follow.

Teachers in the Program

Of the 14 classroom teachers at Arlington Heights Elementary School, 6 participated in the program. We focus on 3 teachers in this paper: Kathy, Andrea, and Melissa. None of these teachers had specialized science training or any particular affinity for science; however, each recognized science as her weakest instructional area and expressed a desire to improve as her primary motivation for joining the program. We are showcasing these particular teachers because they represent the grade levels of participants in the program, and their results are typical for all teachers in the program.

Kathy, who has taught kindergarten for 29 years, teaches morning and afternoon classes of 18 students each. Andrea has five years of experience at the first-grade level and currently teaches 18 students in a self-contained classroom; she is also responsible for teaching science to all first-grade classes. Melissa is a new sixth-grade teacher, and her first year as part of this program was the first year she was responsible for teaching science. She teaches 36 students in a self-contained classroom.

Unique Features of the Program

The structure of the program, which was based on and reflects the *Changing Emphases* outlined in the NSES, was important to the success of the teachers as they implemented changes and developed their understanding of the nature of science and of scientific inquiry. The following sections will describe the program's unique features.

Monthly Workshops

Teachers attended a series of monthly half-day workshops during the school years. Based on conversations with faculty, during which needs and concerns were identified, the IU teacher educators designated topics for the initial year of the program (January–May). In the following year of the program (August–May), we selected workshop topics in cooperation with the teacher participants. (Workshop topics are listed in Table 2.) The involvement of qualified instructors who have used techniques successfully with students is critical to the success of professional development efforts (Loucks-Horsley, Hewson, and Love 1998). Guest speakers with appropriate levels of expertise were employed to lead workshops 1, 5, and 8. The IU teacher educators, who were former elementary teachers, facilitated the remainder of the workshops. Guest speakers and program staff used classroom vignettes and anecdotes from their own classroom experiences with teaching inquiry and the nature of science to help teacher participants visualize the strategies being presented.

Table 2. Monthly Professional Development Workshops

Workshop Topic	Month/Year of Workshop
1. An Introduction to the Nature of Science (NOS)	January 2002
2. Conducting Scientific Inquiry	February 2002
3. Assessing Inquiry Learning	March 2002
4. Strategies for Adapting Curricula to Be Inquiry Based	April 2002
5. Looking at Where Inquiry and NOS Fit Our Curricula	May 2002
6. Goal-Setting for New School Year	August 2002
7. Modifying Existing Curricula/Collaborative Planning	September 2002
8. Using Children's Literature to Teach NOS Elements	October 2002
9. Modifying Existing Curricula/ Collaborative Planning	November 2002
10. Presentation at HASTI (Hoosier Association of Science Teachers, Inc.) Conference	February 2003
11. Accessing Materials Inexpensively	March 2003
12. Debriefing/ Reflecting on Goals and Successes	May 2003

The workshop series was designed with the assumption that teachers benefit from inquiry experiences grounded in the same pedagogical principles they are expected to implement with their own students and that a change in teachers' conception of the nature of science teaching and learning happens over an extended period of time, not through "one-shot" workshops (Loucks-Horsley, Hewson, and Love 1998; NRC 1996). An introductory workshop included opportunities for teachers to reflect on aspects of scientific inquiry such as those in the National Science Teachers Association (NSTA) position statement on the nature of science (NSTA 2000), which emphasizes the importance of certain concepts—for example, that scientific knowledge is simultaneously reliable and tentative, relies on empirical evidence, is influenced by both existing scientific knowledge and the sociocultural context of the scientist, and does not rely on a universal, step-by-step scientific method for investigating phenomena. The nature of science is also emphasized in NSES Content Standard G, focusing on science as a human endeavor (K–8) and the nature of science (5–8). This introductory workshop provided a framework through which teachers could reflect on the view of science apparent in the workshop activities that followed. Having teachers participate in inquiry science has been shown to help them conceptualize inquiry learning and implement it (Kielborn and Gilmer 1999). Our second workshop involved teachers in a guided inquiry investigation of antacids to determine which was "best."

Teachers wanted to be sure that their change in instruction improved their students' learning; thus, the third workshop focused on assessment strategies. We helped teachers understand the role of prior knowledge in inquiry and also develop strategies for assessing students' ideas before, during, and after instruction. Class discussions and science journals were used to track students' ideas over time and identify their changing understandings.

Because teachers' existing curricula did not recognize the importance of teaching science as inquiry, a necessary step was supporting teachers in adapting their materials for classroom use. As teachers participated in the program, they were better able to critique curricula in terms of the activities included and the images of scientific inquiry portrayed. Two workshops were devoted to adapting curricula. Teachers revised the focus of their lessons to accurately and explicitly discuss aspects of the nature of science.

With the initial curriculum adaptation completed, teachers at the goal-setting workshop raised new topics, such as how to effectively integrate science instruction across the curriculum; ways to access necessary materials for teaching science; and an expressed desire to share their successes with other teachers. These questions formed the basis for future workshops. In the spring of 2003, teachers presented their work at the state conference of the Hoosier Association of Science Teachers, Inc. (an NSTA affiliate), and at the end of the 17-month period we held a final session to reflect on successes and future instructional goals.

Collaborative design of both the professional development topics and on-site support was based on the NSES Professional Development *More Emphasis* condition wherein staff developers serve as facilitators, consultants, and planners, rather than as educators. We also addressed the NSES Professional Development *More Emphasis* condition of viewing teachers as members of a collegial professional community. By focusing on inquiry and the nature of science, our program reflected the changing emphases on content and inquiry, shifting from a view of "content as the standard of understanding" to "content as the context for understanding the science community" (Sullenger 1999, p. 25). Our program placed more emphasis on implementing inquiry as an array of instructional strategies, abilities, and ideas to be learned and on learning subject matter disciplines in the context of inquiry, technology, science in personal and social perspectives, and the history and nature of science.

On-Site Support

One of the benefits of the on-site mentoring visits (designed in light of the NSES *More Emphasis* recommendation for a variety of professional development experiences) was the ability to tailor professional development to the individual teacher's changing needs over the duration of the program. While some concerns were common to all teachers in the program, individuals encountered unique challenges in implementing inquiry in their respective classrooms. Program staff engaged in (a) modeling inquiry-based instruction in the teachers' classrooms; (b) providing instructional support by co-teaching inquiry-based lessons; (c) observing and providing feedback to teachers on their instruction; and (d) assisting teachers in adapting curricula, accessing materials, and designing assessments for use in their classrooms. We will illustrate the effectiveness of the program on three participants' instruction and knowledge of science in the vignettes that follow.

Kathy's Story: Building on Her Strengths

After 29 years of teaching kindergarten, Kathy retains her enthusiasm and love for teaching, as well as the desire to improve her practice. Though she favors teaching reading and language arts, recognition of science as her weakest area of instruction motivated her to join the program. She views science at the primary level as building a foundation for future science learning. In addition to using her science textbook, she tries to locate activities related to her students' interests. However, she notes it is difficult to find science materials that are developmentally appropriate for her kindergarten students. As a result of the program, she believes her science instruction has changed for the better, particularly in her ability to adapt science lessons to focus on inquiry and to emphasize the nature of science to her students while building on their prior knowledge.

Though initially Kathy held a view of science as "truth," through ensuing discussions with colleagues, together with reflection on her own ideas, she came to understand the role of creativity and subjectivity in science as the way in which existing theories and scientists' own prior knowledge and experience influence the production of scientific knowledge. Kathy also now understands the way in which those findings are tentative, or subject to change with new evidence or interpretation. One of the activities designed to help participants reach these understandings was a reading and discussion of *Earthmobiles as Explained by Professor Xargle* (Willis 1991). This book discusses transportation on Earth from the viewpoint of aliens. The inferences made by the alien professor, while consistent with his observations, seem comical to readers, whose own perspectives are informed by their experiences with transportation. By recognizing that interpretation of data could vary based on the researcher's perspective, the creative aspect of meaning-making became clear to the participants. As Kathy explains, "Scientists use their creativity to interpret the meaning of data collected and to form opinions regarding the results of experiments."

As the Standards indicate, one of the important understandings about scientific inquiry students should grasp is that scientists develop explanations using observations (evidence) and what they already know about the world. Kathy has helped her own kindergarten students

Kathy uses the book *Seven Blind Mice* to introduce observation, inference, and subjectivity to her class.

understand this idea, as well as other aspects of the nature of science, including the distinction between observation and inference. Workshop 8 focused on ways to emphasize the nature of science through children's literature. Using the technique modeled by the children's literature workshop facilitator, Kathy used the book *Seven Blind Mice* (Young 1992) to illustrate that the white mouse is better able to identify the "something" in the book both because she collects more data *and* because the inferences made by the other mice give her prior knowledge. Kathy asked her students to relate how the white mouse made her inference as to how scientists go about their work and how their background knowledge influences those inferences. Asking students to discuss how the activity of the mice in the story was "like what scientists do" is an appropriate way to explicitly relate science activities to the nature of science for kindergartners. NSES Content Standard G, History and Nature of Science, indicates that K–4 students simply should recognize science as a human endeavor. As suggested by the facilitator of Workshop 5, Kathy did not use the word *empirical* with her kindergartners but rather emphasized *data* and *evidence* as ways that scientists both learn and make explanations about the world.

Though she had frequently used literature with her classes, this was her first use of literature to emphasize aspects of the nature of science to her students. The internalization of ideas presented throughout the professional development was apparent in her subsequent teaching approaches, where again she often related her new ideas about teaching science, building on her strengths in language arts instruction. Though she already brought with her a wealth of knowledge for teaching kindergarteners, Kathy made tremendous strides in teaching science as inquiry and in emphasizing the nature of science in her science lessons.

Andrea's Story: Assessment Practices for Inquiry and the Nature of Science

Andrea has taught first grade for five years. As a primary teacher, her first and foremost goal for science teaching is encouraging curiosity and enthusiasm for science in her students. Her assessment practices in science reflect this goal and include affective as well as cognitive outcomes. From her participation in the program, Andrea recognizes the subjective aspect of science and acknowledges the impossibility of a science without bias. She realizes that scientific knowledge can change with new evidence, or the interpretation of old evidence, and she can accurately describe the distinctions between observation and inference and between theory and law, indicating that her content knowledge of the nature of science is now in line with NSES Content Standard G, History and Nature of Science.

Andrea has readily incorporated new assessment techniques into her teaching practice, including assessment of students' understandings of the nature of science elements. During a lesson in which students would eventually observe signs of life on their playground, Andrea first held a class discussion. She asked students to predict the kinds of life they might see. She then asked them whether they would see all the life forms that lived on the playground during their investigation. She encouraged the students to think about the evidence they would see that different life forms were on the playground, in the absence of directly observing them (e.g., bird droppings, animal tracks). Andrea recorded student responses on chart paper prior to their investigation. Students brought their science journals to the playground, where they recorded observations and listed inferences—and evidence—about what lived on the playground.

Andrea monitors students as they record observations and inferences in their student science journals.

During the lesson debriefing, Andrea asked students to share their observations of the kinds of life on the playground, along with the evidence they had for the existence of that life. She helped them recognize that they did not have to directly observe the animal, but could find evidence that would lead them to infer that the life existed. During this lesson, Andrea was successful in assessing students' understandings of the distinction between observation and inference, together with the empirical nature of science, by using two modeled strategies—individual student journals and whole-class charting of observations and inferences. In her current teaching approach, Andrea always asks her students to relate what they are doing to scientists' work by asking, "How is what you are doing like what scientists do in their work?" This question again focuses specifically on NSES Content Standard G, History and Nature of Science—science as a human endeavor—for grades K–4. Andrea is able to assess students' content knowledge of science as well as their understandings of inquiry and the nature of science, employing the methods of assessment she uses as a result of participation in the professional development program.

Melissa's Story: Shifting from "Cookbook" Science Activities to Inquiry

Melissa teaches in a sixth-grade self-contained classroom. As a relatively new teacher, she is enthusiastic and eager to develop a repertoire of science teaching ideas and strategies. She initially tended to rely on the adopted text series to plan science lessons, but she found this approach insufficient for accomplishing her goals. Many of the "cookbook" science activities in the series required little more to complete than skill in following directions. As the Standards indicate, "when a textbook does not engage students with a question, but begins by assigning an experiment, an essential element of inquiry is missing" (NRC 2000, p. 28). Melissa wants her students to go beyond the experiments outlined in the textbook and to formulate their own questions and devise ways to answer those questions.

While many of Melissa's views of the nature of science were aligned with those outlined by the Standards, the activities of her text series did not provide her students with opportunities to develop these understandings themselves. For example, Melissa understands the subjective nature of science, stating, "Scientists' backgrounds influence how they interpret data." Similarly, she is able to describe the tentative nature of science and how theories can change with new evidence. She recognizes that no universal "scientific method" adequately characterizes scientific investigations. Her text's prescribed step-by-step activities fail to capture the complexity of science and can direct students' attention to one right answer and one way of finding out that answer, rather than helping them develop the ability to think critically and logically (NSES Content Standard A, Science as Inquiry). Interactions among the teachers in the program as they grappled with these ideas, and with how to teach these ideas to their students, helped all the teachers reconceptualize the scientific method as "science as inquiry with multiple methods."

For Melissa, helping her students to generate and refine questions—and to develop experiments of their own to answer those questions—was an important step in helping them take ownership of the task and develop their abilities to conduct scientific inquiry, which she found was recommended by NSES Content Standard G, History and Nature of Science (grades 5–8). A successful strategy for implementing inquiry for Melissa has been to use the "cookbook" activities to serve as a springboard for students' inquiries. This strategy was developed collaboratively by teachers during one of the curriculum adaptation sessions of the program. After her students have completed the experiment in the textbook, Melissa asks them to brainstorm variables that might affect the outcome of the experiment, formulate a testable question, and design inquiries to test the effects of those variables.

Once students collect data, Melissa helps them develop explanations for the evidence. At Melissa's invitation, the program director taught a model lesson to her students that focused on the skills of observation and inference using students' own interpretations of a presented scenario. The students were given an organizer to categorize their responses as "observation" or "inference." Understanding this distinction helps students evaluate the explanations proposed by classmates in determining which inferences are valid, given the observations they made, a step also recommended by Content Standard G (grades 5–8). Melissa continued to use this organizer to reinforce students' conceptions of this distinction during investigations of other topics.

Melissa works with a team of students to brainstorm ways their experiences at the Challenger Center relate to the work of scientists.

Melissa's efforts to help students understand the nature of science have focused on helping them connect their experiences in science class to the experiences of scientists. On one occasion, she took her class on a field trip to the NASA Challenger Center in Indianapolis. As part of their simulated mission work at the center, the students engaged in pre-mission activities and on-site science inquiries in the context of a mock Challenger mission. In the field trip debriefing lesson, Melissa asked students from each science team to record examples of how what they did during their mission was like what scientists do. She used categories collaboratively generated by the teachers for use in their classrooms (make a plan, investigate, predict, consider personal perspectives, infer, observe, create, collect data, classify, analyze, interpret, organize, ask questions, research). By sharing their experiences in a mock scientific exploration, communicating the science content they learned, and reflecting on how their experiences compare to the ways scientists go about their work, Melissa's students have developed a much richer understanding and appreciation of the scientific endeavor.

Evidence for Success

Teachers in our program made important changes in their views of the nature of science, their instructional practices, and their abilities to adapt curricula to emphasize inquiry and the nature of science. We tracked the effectiveness of the professional development program in helping the teachers accomplish these changes. Data collection and interpretation helped us plan additional professional development workshops and on-site support. Thus, the design of the professional development program was modified to meet teachers' needs as the data were collected and analyzed (Bogdan and Biklen 1998). Data for tracking the teachers' success included

- field notes written by program personnel at each workshop;
- videotaped sessions of teachers and program personnel teaching inquiry lessons;
- transcripts of interviews of teachers as they watched videotapes of their inquiry lessons;
- teacher responses to the Views of Nature of Science questionnaire (VNOS-B) pre and post, to determine changes in conceptions of the nature of science;
- teacher responses to the Views of Scientific Inquiry questionnaire (VOSI);
- e-mail and verbal communications between the program personnel and teachers regarding successes and difficulties associated with inquiry teaching; and
- teachers' descriptions of their lesson adaptations as they prepared them for a presentation at the state science teachers' conference.

To analyze the data, a comparison was made between the pre- and post-VNOS-B and VOSI questionnaires to track teachers' understandings of the nature of science elements and of scientific inquiry. Classroom observations, video-simulated interviews, e-mail and verbal communications, descriptions of lesson adaptations—we used these methods to note changes in instruction and to evaluate the success of the program.

Summary

Teachers participated in a long-term professional development program, designed in accordance with the National Science Education Standards, that enabled them to experience science as inquiry, to confront and change their own ideas about the nature of science, and to develop strategies for teaching science as inquiry while emphasizing the nature of science to their own students. A key feature of the professional development that enabled the teachers to change their science teaching was providing them with time, in terms of both the length of time of the program (17 months) and release time to explore, learn, and discuss changes in their teaching. This element has been identified as critical to the success of professional development programs (Loucks-Horsley, Hewson, and Love 1998; NRC 1996). The success of these teachers shows the importance of the *More Emphasis* conditions of long-term and coherent professional development (NRC 1996, p. 72).

Another key feature was collaboration between program staff and teachers at the local school, as well as among the teachers themselves. Teachers' interests and ideas guided the design of workshop sessions, during which they worked together to make changes to their teaching approaches. As Loucks-Horsley, Hewson, and Love (1998) emphasized, "Reflection by an individual on his or her own practice can be enhanced by another's observations and perceptions" (p. 127). The NSES Professional Development *More Emphasis* conditions calling for collegial collaboration and for the teacher as creator of knowledge about teaching were vital for this program.

A final key feature was the individual, on-site teaching support provided to the teachers by the program staff, who taught model lessons and gave feedback and suggestions to teachers as they tried new instructional strategies. Because members of the program staff were former elementary teachers, the participants found them to be "credible peers" (Bandura 1997) and reliable sources for collaborative professional development, particularly for the on-site classroom support. The ability to have individualized support for unique classroom challenges was invaluable to the teachers. The NSES Professional Development *More Emphasis* condition calling for a variety of professional development experiences was relevant in this regard—the workshops served as a way to discuss the new ideas and strategies, while the on-site supports aided teachers in adjusting instruction methods.

It is evident from classroom observations and teacher responses in interviews and on questionnaires that all facets of the professional development contributed to teachers' abilities to make substantive changes in their teaching. Their teaching became inquiry focused, and the teachers now explicitly teach about the nature of science to their students, which illustrates how the Content and Inquiry *More Emphasis* conditions influenced their work. They have also become more skilled in assessing what students understand about content, inquiry, and the nature of science through class charts, student journals, and teachers' observation of students, which shows how the Assessment *More Emphasis* conditions shaped their work. Finally, they have become better at identifying and responding to individual students' understandings, adapting curricula, conducting ongoing student assessment, and working together to enhance the science program, which illustrates the importance of the Teaching *More Emphasis* conditions on their work.

References

Bandura, A. 1997. *Self-efficacy: The exercise of control.* New York: W. H. Freeman.

Bogdan, R. C., and S. K. Biklen. 1998. *Qualitative research for education: An introduction to theory and methods.* 3rd ed. Boston: Allyn and Bacon.

Kielborn, T. L., and P. J. Gilmer, eds. 1999. *Meaningful science: Teachers doing inquiry + teaching science.* Tallahassee, FL: SERVE.

Lederman, N. G. 1992. Students' and teachers' conceptions of the nature of science: A review of the research. *Journal of Research in Science Teaching* 29: 331–360.

Loucks-Horsley, S., P. W. Hewson, N. Love, and K. Stiles. 1998. *Designing professional development for teachers of science and mathematics.* Thousand Oaks, CA: Corwin Press.

National Research Council (NRC). 1996. *National science education standards.* Washington, DC: National Academy Press.

National Research Council (NRC). 2000. *Inquiry and the national science education standards: A guide for teaching and learning.* Washington, DC: National Academy Press.

National Science Teachers Association (NSTA). 2000. NSTA Position Statement on the Nature of Science. Retrieved January 12, 2003 from *www.nsta.org/159&psid=22.*

Sullenger, K. 1999. How do you know science is going on? *Science and Children* 36 (7): 22–25.

Willis, J. 1991. *Earthmobiles as explained by Professor Xargle.* New York: Dutton Children's Books.

Young, E. 1992. *Seven blind mice.* New York: Scholastic.

Bringing School Science to College:

Modeling Inquiry in the Elementary Science Methods Course

Sondra Akins
William Paterson University

The William Paterson University College of Education, in Wayne, New Jersey, offers certification and master's programs in four departments: Early Childhood and Elementary Education, Secondary and Middle Education, Special Education, and Educational Leadership. Specialists teach elementary and secondary science and mathematics methods courses with emphasis on integrating the two subject areas.

As a professor of science methods for preservice elementary and secondary teachers, I have incorporated the National Science Education Standards (NRC 1996) for professional development, teaching, and content into my teaching. My students learn through investigation and inquiry. The investigations and inquiries used in the course emphasize the following: (a) use of scientific knowledge, ideas, and inquiry processes; (b) guiding students in active and extended scientific inquiry; (c) providing opportunity for scientific discussion and debate; (d) continually assessing understanding of science; and (e) sharing responsibility for learning with the learners.

Model lessons include strategies that address the following *More Emphasis* content recommendations of the Standards: (a) using process skills in context; (b) understanding scientific concepts and developing abilities in inquiry; and (c) investigating and analyzing science questions (NRC 1996, p. 113). Student engagement in ongoing assessment of their work is also emphasized.

I challenge preservice teachers to use science processes and knowledge in order to reason and think critically. They ask questions, plan and conduct scientific investigations, use science tools and scientific techniques, evaluate evidence and then use it to logically construct explanations, and finally communicate their conclusions scientifically. They experience, firsthand, how learning science is interdependent with learning other subjects and how the processes, knowledge, and attitudes associated with doing science contribute to lifelong learning. They experience and appreciate the meaning of scientific literacy, assess their own literacy in science, and consider what they can do, as elementary teachers, to contribute to the goal of scientific literacy for all students. Assessments indicate that preservice teachers' confidence and disposition toward learning and teaching science increase in ways modeled in the methods course. With such experiences, preservice teachers will be able to model the attitudes, knowledge, and skills of a scientifically literate person. With continued support, they will be better able to teach elementary science in ways recommended by the Standards.

Description of a Science Methods Learning Community

I began teaching methods in science and mathematics and principles of science for preservice elementary teachers in September 2001. I had previously taught and supervised science and mathematics in one of the urban school districts where our students acquire field experience. At William Paterson, elementary methods students attend weekly 100-minute classes in each of the subject areas—science, mathematics, social studies, language arts, and art—and spend two days per week in the field. Most are majors in fields other than science and mathematics, which require two semesters of college science and two semesters of college mathematics. Environmental science and biology, rather than physical science, are the most frequently chosen.

Unique Features of the Program

The teaching model—the Inquiry-Based Teaching and Learning Model for Science Methods—has evolved during the past three years. It includes interconnected inquiries—that is, class activities that are inquiry based and that integrate science and science teaching. Curriculum and pedagogy, based on the National Science Education Standards, have been selected and adjusted as a result of monitoring student views by means of class observations, weekly reflective writing, and other assessments that are described later. Each inquiry has a primary focus as shown in Figure 1. The following section explores each focus (A–E in the figure).

A. Inquiring Into Past Learning Experiences and Existing Beliefs

On the first day of class, it is my goal to have the preservice teachers begin confronting their personal conceptions about science, science teaching, and scientists—conceptions that can influence the teaching of science in elementary school. We also explore past experiences that may have affected present attitudes and learning in science.

Who Does Science?

This activity invites each student to draw a picture showing a scientist at work. Class members share their pictures and ideas that stimulated the images they drew. We note similarities and differences in the drawings and the ideas the drawings convey. We compare class members' views with common views that elementary children hold about scientists.

Figure 1. Inquiry-Based Teaching and Learning Model for Elementary Science Methods

A. Inquiring Into Past Learning Experiences and Existing Beliefs: What Are Common Conceptions About Science, Scientists, and Science Teaching? (1 period)

   1. Who does science?

   2. Science memories

B. Inquiring Through Science Investigations (facilitated by professor) (5–6 periods)

   1. Investigating Rocks, Shells, and Leaves (1–2 periods)

     What Are Science Process Skills? How Do Science Process Skills Facilitate Learning Science and Other Subjects?

   2. Orange Investigation: What Percentage of an Orange Is Edible? (2 periods)

   3. Investigating Sinking and Floating: Why Do Objects Sink and Float? (2 periods)

C. Inquiring Into Research and Theories of Learning: How Do Children Learn Science? (1 period)

D. Investigating Classrooms: What Are Best Practices for Teaching Science in Schools? (1–2 periods)

E. Inquiring Through Science Investigations: Standards-Based Lessons in Life, Earth/Space, and Physical Science (facilitated by preservice teachers) (4–5 periods)

Science Memories

I then ask the preservice teachers to recall their science learning experiences from early childhood, middle school, and high school. We share memories, categorize them as positive or negative, and find common features. Through these activities, students are to find implications for their own practices as elementary teachers and they begin to identify their own needs for professional preparation that can be addressed in the course.

These activities help us to personalize our discussion of the status of science education and conditions that work against the inclusion of all students. I sprinkle some of my own school memories in the discussion of historical events and initiatives in science education (pre-Sputnik through the sixties). I also highlight positive teacher characteristics and initiatives that contributed to my successful pursuit of science and mathematics during a science education era when there were few role models with whom females and minorities could identify. This leads to discussion of equity issues and the rationale for showcasing historical and contemporary contributions to science and technology by persons of diverse backgrounds.

B. Inquiring Through Science Investigations
Investigating Rocks, Shells, and Leaves

This inquiry is preceded by textbook reading, which discusses science as process, knowledge, and attitudes. Cooperative groups choose between collections of rocks, leaves, and shells and take time to manipulate the objects in order to experience processes and mathematical applications that are discussed in the textbook. I facilitate the loosely structured activity by stimulating students through questions and suggestions. Centimeter cubes and square centimeter transparencies are on hand so that the concepts of volume (rocks), capacity (shells), and area (leaves) have conceptual meaning. Balances, graduated cylinders, and water are readily available for measuring.

The preservice teachers make observations and use descriptive language and drawings to describe the objects. They state "wonder questions" that are generated from observing the objects, and they discuss how they can find the answers to their questions. They state questions about quantitative properties of the objects: "How much does it weigh? How long is it? How much water does it hold?" They answer the questions using comparisons such as "as much as a quarter" and "as long as a paper clip." After making guesses, they use laboratory equipment and materials to make measurements of length, area, mass, volume, and capacity. They recall how to find the area of a rectangle and volume of a rectangular solid and make sense of answers by comparing answers with the area of the face of the centimeter cube and the volume. To stress *meaning,* as well as *quantity,* I ask them to consider approximately how many of the centimeter cubes the rock can be divided into and about how many milliliters of water the cubes could hold. Volumes of solids are measured by water displacement, and shell capacity is determined with graduated cylinders and eyedroppers.

Each group plays hosts to other groups so that all class members hear an explanation of the processes and measurements involving the solid objects (rocks), the hollow objects (shells), and the flat objects (leaves). In this way concepts of mass, length, area, capacity, and volume, as well as the measuring of the quantities, are stressed. Each student has an opportunity to share with visiting groups all of the qualitative and quantitative descriptions of a "pet" object, and the visitors try to pick out an object on the basis of descriptions. This activity elicits the importance of observation skills and communication skills. The preservice teachers sort the objects in the collection according to physical attributes and find ratios, fractions, and percentages that describe the subsets in relation to the entire collection.

Orange Investigation: What Percentage of an Orange Is Edible?

The concepts and process skills featured in the previous investigation are extended and applied through an investigation of oranges. Concepts of mass and volume are essential in clarifying the question that will drive the investigation. In the *first stage,* a very large, thick-skinned orange and an ordinary orange are distributed to each group. By handling the oranges and being asked, "Which do you think is the better buy?," students usually think of the fact that a larger proportion of the large, thick-skinned orange is waste. The *second stage* focuses the groups on the question under investigation: "What percent of the orange is edible?" After the groups have had a chance to discuss their challenge and how they will proceed, I visit with questions to check for understanding: "What have you agreed on as the meaning of *edible?*" "Are you thinking of comparing masses or volumes?" (Most groups initially focus on mass and require questions and suggestions before realizing that the problem can be interpreted in different ways.) While they consider one or the other, a number of students have been successful in focusing on both mass and volume of the orange in the same experiment. Students write their own procedures for the investigation.

In the *third stage,* groups carry out the investigation. They must locate and choose equipment from the apparatus available in the laboratory. In the *fourth stage,* groups report to the class their procedures and results. They note difficulties and unexpected events, concerns about their procedures, and questions for further investigations. They also evaluate the activity and discuss how an investigation dealing with fractional compositions of an orange (or other objects of interest) could be adapted for different grade levels and integration of subjects.

Investigating Sinking and Floating: Why Do Objects Sink and Float?

This inquiry is suggested by a discrepant event encountered in the orange investigation. Nearly all students are surprised that the whole orange floated and the peeled orange sank in the course of determining volumes by water displacement. Much student discussion results from sharing detailed observations about the orange in water. Some students suggest that the orange sank because removing the peel allows water to penetrate. Others have noticed that orange peels inadvertently dropped in the water floated on top of the water. They reason that the peel tends to float, while the orange without the peel tends to sink so that the behavior of the whole orange is something in between (floats with a portion above the surface).

During the *first stage* of the sinking and floating inquiry, class members "play" with solid objects made out of different materials, first guessing whether they will sink or float in water before testing their predictions. The plastic centimeter cube (with a mass of one gram and a volume of one cm³) is among the tested objects. It is observed to float with its top even with the surface of the water. Class members observe that blocks, cylinders, and spheres made of wood float partially out of the water and objects made of other materials sink. Student statements such as "heavier objects sink and lighter objects float" and "larger objects sink and smaller objects float" are challenged when a penny sinks, whereas a larger, and more massive, block of wood floats.

The *second stage* depends heavily on active student participation and discussion with more teacher instruction. It varies according to needs of students. My goal is to help students acquire a deeper understanding of volume, which has been encountered in previous investigations, and develop a conceptual understanding of density that will make sense of the equation, $d = mass/volume$, which students often memorize without having conceptual meaning.

This is a time-consuming stage that pays off in many ways. It integrates the philosophy and content of our science and mathematics methods courses. It demonstrates how a deeper understanding of science concepts can result from an inquiry approach. It emphasizes the use of manipulatives, which are effective in developing conceptual understanding of measurement in science and mathematics. It is also an opportunity to model the dispositions of teachers who hold high expectations for all learners and take time to help learners make sense of experiences.

Every preservice teacher handles centimeter cubes, which are described in different ways with careful attention to language and measuring units: "The cube is 1 cm in length, 1 cm in width, and 1 cm in height." "Each face is 1 cm by 1 cm and has an area of 1 cm²." Containers of various sizes and shapes (cubes, cylinders, spheres) are available so that students can visualize the number of centimeter cubes that will fit into the larger containers and also transfer water between containers for comparison.

I pose questions such as the following: "Think of the centimeter cube as hollowed out so it holds water. If the water is poured into a graduated cylinder, what would it measure? What would be the mass of the water that the cube can hold? How do you know? How can we find out?" We take the time to measure different volumes of water and their corresponding masses (or share predetermined measurements). Then we distribute the total mass of the water over the total volume, by dividing, to demonstrate that one gram of water is packed into each cubic centimeter of space it occupies, regardless of the total amount of water or the shape of the container. Hence, the density of water is one gram per cubic centimeter or one gram per milliliter.

Similarly, we confirm the density of the plastic material that constitutes the centimeter cubes that float with the tops just even with the water surface. The interlocking cubes allow us to do this in two different ways: (1) weighing 20, or more, cubes and distributing the mass over the total number of cubes to get the mass of one cubic centimeter of the material; and (2) making large rectangular solids and finding the mass and volume, then using the formula. This allows us to confirm that the number of cubes, or total volume, is always length × width × height. We reason that the total mass divided by the total volume of the plastic object is one gram per cubic centimeter and, if the plastic were reduced to a fraction of a cubic centimeter, the density would still be one gram per cubic centimeter. No matter the size or shape, the density of an object made out of the plastic is one gram per cubic centimeter.

Densities are determined for a wooden object and a sinking object using mass and volume data from an earlier investigation. We summarize the values of the density of water, the density of an object that floats partially above the surface of the water, the density of the special centimeter cube, and the density of the pet rock, and emphasize the behavior of each in water. At this point I ask class members to use clear language to state a hypothesis about the relationship between the density of an object and whether it will sink or float.

When pressed for time, I have confirmed students' stated hypotheses that objects less dense than water float with a portion partially above the water surface; objects with the same density float with the top even with the surface; and objects that are denser than water sink. Then we turn our attention to getting the density of the orange, using data from the orange investigation and dividing the mass by the volume. However, feedback from class members indicates that by omitting the testing of the hypothesis, which gives student a chance to handle objects and feel a variation in densities of the objects, the idea is not well solidified or retained. Therefore, I have inserted an activity previously used in the science principles class at the beginning of the third stage and delayed the determination of the density of the orange until after this step.

The *third stage* begins with confirming the hypothesis stated in the *second stage* through a hands-on activity. Students determine the mass, volume, and density of standard materials; observe whether they sink or float; and record information in columns under the following headings: mass, volume, density, observations of sink or float. They also make entries under the columns for density and sink/float for unknowns whose masses and volumes are given in the table, by using the formula to calculate the density and using reasoning to predict sink or float. Afterward, students focus on a whole orange and the question arising from the discrepant event is restated: "Why does the whole orange float and the peeled orange sink in water?"

According to the concept that has been learned, the whole orange must be less dense than water and the peeled orange denser than water. I have asked additional questions to reinforce the concept of volume and density before the students use the equation to emphasize that the peel and edible orange do not necessarily have the same density and we are getting an average density: "Into how many chunks can the orange be divided that have the size of the centimeter cube?" "Would all the little chunks of orange weigh the same?" "Do you think a cubic centimeter of peel would weigh more or less than a cubic centimeter of 'edible' orange?" Questions are raised by students about seeds within the edible portion, as well as air between the peel of the thick-skinned orange and the edible part that may have different densities as well, and the way these factors might affect the sinking and floating. Students also inquire about changes in the orange over time and how the properties might change.

Students share and discuss data from the orange investigation and find logical answers to these questions. They find a theoretical answer for the density of the "edible orange" and the density of the peeled orange by dividing the mass of each by volume. Using data from the investigation of the groups who used very thick-skinned oranges is advisable because there is opportunity for errors and inconclusive results when using data taken by students with limited hands-on experience. Students who measured the circumference of their orange, or improvised to find the diameter, have successfully found and shared the volume of the orange using the formula for the volume of a sphere in the orange investigation. Like those who used water displacement, they use the density formula to find the density of the orange. As a follow-up of the hands-on investigation, students read and discuss a textbook chapter about buoyancy, Archimedes' principle, and density.

As a *fourth stage* of the sinking and floating inquiry—and an overall look at our science investigations—we discuss experimental findings, "thought experiments" (investigations that we do not actually carry out, but contemplate or visualize—e.g., what if we put the orange in salt water or cooking oil instead of water), real-life examples, and applications of what has been learned in the orange and density investigations. We make connections to the nature of science and scientific attitudes by reflecting on our experiences. We have noted that playing around with and observing natural objects can lead to "wonder questions" that can drive an investigation. A discrepant event in one investigation can generate a question for the focus of a new investigation. Accidents, such as peels inadvertently dropped in water, may lead to insight and discovery. We discuss ways in which the available equipment and technology in our lab limited the quality of data gathered in the investigation and how compromises were made in order to carry out an investigation in a timely fashion.

C. Inquiring Into Research and Theories of Learning: How Do Children Learn Science?

Using the methods textbook, class members learn about cognitive and biological theories and brain research as well as characteristics and needs of learners. They then consider this information in light of their recent science investigation experiences. Implications for constructivist teaching approaches are discussed. A rationale for multistage learning cycles is given and students are formally introduced to the 4E learning cycle (Martin, Sexton, and Gerlovich 2001).

D. Investigating Classrooms: What Are Best Practices for Teaching Science in Schools?

In their end-of-course reflections, most science methods students indicate that they did not observe—during their concurrent practicum experience—science teaching that reflected what is stressed in the science standards and in the methods course. Some report that they did not encounter science instruction at all in the schools where they had their practicum experiences. By inquiring into best practices in schools, I try to help the class members make a connection between their methods experiences and what goes on in real classrooms where science education recommendations are being implemented. The class views a videotape of a multicultural classroom in which a first-grade teacher and her students are engaged in an interdisciplinary unit about the diversity of leaves. The preservice teachers identify the teacher's strategies, process skills the students use, connections to New Jersey Science Content Standards, and ways in which the teacher supports scientific literacy.

As a review of the inquiries, an overhead presentation, "Bringing School Science to College," shows images of school science with children in multicultural classrooms engaged in activities like our investigations. Images of younger children completing tasks (such as testing sinking-and-floating investigations) connect to our investigations. In this way the preservice teachers can see how development of a science concept, such as density, builds on experiences acquired in the earliest years of school and must be supported by teachers across the grades.

E. Inquiring Through Science Investigations: Standards-Based Lessons Taught by Preservice Teachers

In the final weeks, preservice teachers present their own lessons in life, Earth/space, and physical science, using a constructivist learning cycle. Most adapt a lesson from the collection in the methods textbook, which uses the 4E learning cycle. I encourage this because the textbook lessons emphasize concept development (invention), process skills, and connections to the history of science and technology as well as inquiry. Preservice teachers also use the internet to acquire resources to support their lessons and to collect a file of lessons in physical science, Earth/space science, and life science, which they correlate with the state science content standards.

Evaluation (Assessments and Outcomes)

Multiple assessments are used to determine student learning outcomes. Since the inquiry topics are interconnected, it is possible to see the growth of some ideas over time. By observing and questioning preservice teachers in class, examining their weekly writing and special written assignments, and observing their performance, it is possible to view the same outcome in different ways. It is also possible to acquire comprehensive information for evaluating students.

Scientific literacy, for example, is actually stressed and assessed, in different ways, throughout the semester, by course activities and self-evaluation by the student. To some extent, science ideas have also been focused on and, hopefully, have taken on a deeper meaning for the student in the course of the inquiries. Volume, for example, was introduced and related to capacity during the first science investigation, "Rocks, Shells, and Leaves." This inquiry stressed process skills while giving the preservice teachers the opportunity to work with natural objects. During the second science investigation, which was the inquiry about the orange, the concept of volume was reinforced and extended. In the third science investigation, the inquiry on sinking and floating, the concept of volume was re-emphasized before a mathematical formula was used to determine density. These concepts were also revisited by the midterm examination assessment, which is seen as a means of confirming that the preservice teachers have accomplished the outcomes or as a method to raise their awareness of the importance of the concepts and further facilitate their understanding.

In this section, I draw some conclusions based on feedback from the preservice teachers in response to a variety of assessments, the most prominent of which is reflective writing. I have also included excerpts from the reflective writings of one student, Ann Marie (a pseudonym) who was adept at describing instruction, class interactions, and, most important, her own thinking processes.

Inquiry Into Past Learning Experiences and Existing Beliefs: Analysis of Student Reflections

As a result of this inquiry, preservice teachers become aware of practices and conceptions that work against the inclusion of some students in science, from early education throughout high school, and they find implications for their own practices. They become conscious of the infrequency with which science is taught in the early grades, of the meaning of passive as opposed to active learning, and of stereotypes that they and their classmates hold with respect to participation in science. They recall characteristics and effects of past teachers and science instruction, and they indicate what professional needs they would like the course to address.

Ann Marie's Memories of Early Childhood Science

As far as I can recall, we never did science in the classroom. Obviously, if we did, it was never a memorable experience.

By middle school I switched to public school and we had science in seventh and eighth grades. I cannot recall the teacher's name, but he had a skeleton in his classroom, which he incorporated into our lessons. The skeleton became an integral part of our class, and his/her outfits changed with the seasons and with the topic of study. Although the specifics of the curriculum escape me (this is many years ago!), I do remember that my teacher made science enjoyable and that it was one of my favorite classes.

Ann Marie's Picture of a Scientist

My picture of a scientist was a female. This is not because I am free of sexual stereotypes, but because I became conscious of them before I began to draw. If I had not stopped to panic about having to draw a picture, I most likely would have composed the same Mr. Nerd–type that most of the other students drew. But I decided in that moment to make my scientist a female, with long hair, and no glasses! If I were an artist, I would have even tried to make her attractive.

My best friend, and one of the most intelligent people I know, majored in biology in college and spent most of her free time hanging out in the laboratory. She was always swimming in paperwork, so I made sure to give my scientist a clipboard. Also, that tough biology teacher I referred to earlier was a woman and very serious about science.

Ann Marie's Implications for Teaching

When I teach, I hope to convey to my students that gender is not a factor when it comes to competency in a particular subject. During my experiences substituting, I've noticed that textbook pictures have changed since my time in school in an effort to break these stereotypes. Based on my own personal experiences, although limited, I hope to teach science in a positive way—through hands-on lessons which are educational, fun, and, hopefully, memorable. I want to arouse the curiosity of my students by relating science to their world whenever possible.

Inquiring Through Science Investigations: Analysis of Student Reflections
Investigating Rocks, Shells, and Leaves

Preservice teachers' writing, across semesters, indicates that they recognize that playing with natural objects elicits wonder questions that can inform the teacher's curriculum and lead to inquiry and investigation. When process skills are experienced in context, preservice teachers appreciate these skills as tools for learning across subject areas and see connections between science and mathematics. Virtually all preservice teachers convey, in their class behavior and writing, genuine enjoyment and curiosity when viewing objects found in the natural world, and they display a positive disposition toward doing observation activities with children. In addition, they successfully identify process skills and explain the benefits to children on the midterm examination.

Ann Marie's writing conveys enjoyment of the inquiry on process skills ("Investigating Rocks, Shells, and Leaves") and an awareness of the role and benefits of process skills in learning science and other subjects. From the experience she finds implications for her teaching practices.

Ann Marie's Reflection on Investigating Rocks, Shells, and Leaves

This science activity was hands-on and fun. Because of these two critical elements, I believe I learned far more about process skills than I would have by reading a chapter in a book! My group chose to analyze the rocks. It was great to touch them, compare them with each other, and I especially liked that we were able to choose a "pet." I felt as if I was in grammar school again, and my choice became very important to me. I began my observation by describing my rock in the most obvious ways: how it looked and how it felt. The three of us in the group exchanged descriptions of our pet with each other to confirm they were satisfactory. Later, when I looked at the "Processes" sheet, I realized we were "communicating orally" and, therefore, using a valuable science skill. My rock was a combination of two different materials—crystal and stone. As a result, my wonder questions were directly related to this situation: "How did this specimen get this way?" "Did it happen in nature?" "If so, how?" "What would cause something like this to happen?" "If it did not happen naturally, what man-made incident could have caused it?"

The next step was to measure our specimens, and we recorded the information in centimeters and named a well-known object of similar size for comparison (a quarter in the case of my "pet"). Following the linear measurement, we weighed our object using balanced scales and recorded the mass in grams. Moving on to [volume], Professor Akins led us in a discussion to figure out how to accomplish this particular measuring technique. Rather than give us the answer outright, I think she modeled good teacher behavior by guiding us with appropriate responses to lead us to the conclusion on our own—which we did get to eventually!

During this capacity section of our analysis, I learned a valuable lesson. I understood exactly what needed to be done and it made sense to me (put the water in the graduated cylinder, etc.). However, when the professor asked me to explain it to another student who didn't understand it as well, I felt as if the words wouldn't come out right! I knew it, but not clear enough to explain it to someone else. Hopefully, as the semester moves on, my oral science skills will improve! Certainly, in just this one lesson, my science vocabulary increased.

After our diligent "data gathering," we had the opportunity to "play detective" and try to pick out the "pets" of the other preservice teachers. I did several and, thanks to their good work, was able to discover the specimen each time. I really enjoyed this part of the lesson—it seemed like a reward for a job well done. In our next activity, my group began sorting and classifying our rocks into three types and counted the number of rocks in each type. Under Professor Akins's guidance, we figured out the percentage each type was of the whole (data which could easily be put into a pie graph). We then calculated the mass of each type and found the percentage of the total mass. Interestingly enough, the two percentages, quantity and mass, were closely related. Therefore, we concluded that the composition of all three types must be similar. This exercise used higher-level process skills ....

I learned a lot during this exercise. Within just a few minutes, and a fairly brief description, we used a good portion of the process skills on our sheet, some without even realizing it (communication, for example). I learned that it is important to make careful, detailed observations and to look beyond the obvious descriptions. I think this will be a useful science skill in all aspects of science. I also learned that teaching science is a verbal skill on its own and one that I need to work on! In addition, I was reminded of how integrated science is with the study of math. This particular lesson used measuring skills, graphing skills, basic addition and subtraction, as well as percentages. Finally, I learned that science can be taught in an enjoyable way. This one small lesson has made a big impact on my attitude toward science.

Orange Investigation

Preservice teachers' observed behavior during the investigation, together with their reflective writing, indicates that they enjoyed the activity and collaborated in planning and carrying out the investigation. Student reflections, as well as a midterm assessment (discussed on pp. 28–30), provide feedback about the degree to which the preservice teachers process the orange investigation experiences.

In her reflection, Ann Marie describes conceptual and procedural aspects of the investigation, the interaction among group members, and her own thoughts and feelings. She suggests that carrying out the investigation to determine the composition of the orange according to mass and volume deepened her understanding of basic concepts, and she credits the use of manipulatives for facilitating her understanding. She describes how her group used formulas and calculations to determine the volume and composition of the orange and how she and the group considered factors that might affect the accuracy of their determination.

Ann Marie's Reflection on the Orange Investigation

We used all of our observing skills as we came up with our wonder questions: We saw the oranges, we felt them, and we certainly could smell them. I came up with three wonder questions: "Why is the big orange rougher?" "Why is there a hole in the bottom of the big orange and not the small orange?" "Why does the small orange have brown spots?" However, when I heard some of the questions from the other preservice teachers, I was disappointed in my list.

After being given our challenge—"What percentage of the orange is edible by mass and by volume"—we were instructed to write out a plan for our experiment. I was anxious to dive right into work and, at first, I thought this writing exercise was a waste of time. Well, once again, I was proven wrong (at least I'm learning from these errors). My two partners and I communicated about what we needed to figure out and the order in which we needed to proceed. Obviously, once the peel was off, there was no getting it back on, and we needed to take that into account as we organized the sequence of events of our experiment. It didn't take too long for me to realize that taking the time to write this all down could save errors in the long run.

The mass portion of the experiment was simple enough and went exactly according to plan. We measured the weight of the peeled orange, then measured the unpeeled orange later on, after we had taken the necessary measurements for volume. We made our comparison and came up with the percentage of the mass of edible orange (71%). However, the volume portion hit a few snags. First, we used the water displacement method, but the unpeeled orange floated. We couldn't push down the orange because the graduated container we were using wasn't large enough to hold the water necessary. Michele, my partner, had predicted this would happen, so we had planned for an alternate method. Once again, communication paid off! We had measured the circumference just in case this happened. So, after peeling, we measured the circumference of the peeled orange and began our calculations. However, we soon discovered, as we were following our numbered steps, that we neglected to include a step for figuring out the radius. We needed the radius in order to use the formula for volume. With all the data gathered, we made our calculations and had our result—61% of the volume of the orange was edible.

When it came to the water displacement test, I know Michele and I were both more anxious about doing it because we each had a different prediction about what would happen. I think it was a good learning experience to think through the steps before we actually took them. And, as careful and thorough as we thought we were in organizing and writing down the steps we were going to take, we still did miss one! It's amazing how many processes we used in this short experiment—communicating, comparing, measuring (linear, weight, and capacity), and especially, organizing—both sequencing and data gathering. Once again, having a partner to share this experience with made it more meaningful and made me feel more secure when it was time to take the next step.

The orange experiment was multifaceted and progressed step-by-step as we all learned along the way. We began with one question, "What is the percent of edible orange in mass and volume?" As I've discussed in previous reflections, we all used many processes to achieve our results: observing, communication, comparing, measuring, and more. In addition, this one experiment clearly shows how science is integrated with mathematics. With all of the measuring, comparing, and calculations and formulas necessary, sometimes this experiment felt like a math lesson! As we attacked this question, we also learned about the concept of mass and volume. Addressing the various learning styles, Professor Akins often explained ideas in different ways, always using manipulatives to make her point. This even helps those who "get it" the first time because it reinforces the concept and allows them to see it from another perspective.

Investigating Sinking and Floating

Observation of preservice teachers in class and analysis of reflective writing of students who work in the same group indicate that preservice teachers interact with instructors and each other in an effort to understand science concepts and explain science phenomena related to both the orange and density investigations. (In a class of 12 students, whom I taught both science and mathematics methods, the level of interest and success in understanding concepts and applying mathematical equations was high in comparison to other classes.)

Ann Marie was able to identify her strengths and knowledge gaps and ways in which she self-corrected ideas, with assistance from others. She reports that she understood the formula for calculating the density of the orange and that she assisted the group in making the calculation (consistent with my observations of her group).

To get the density of the orange, Ann Marie's group used the mass and volume of the orange and the density formula. To get the volume of the orange they had also used a formula because of problems with the equipment they had chosen. They questioned the effect of the imperfect shape of the orange on the accuracy of their determination, in comparison with others who had used the liquid displacement method, and they considered factors that might have affected the accuracy of determinations based on liquid displacement.

Ann Marie connected the investigation experiences to real-life science phenomena (oil floating on water and people floating in the ocean) and theories about learning (constructivism). She considered that the way she learned from the investigation was instrumental in helping her to comprehend the textbook reading and to retain what she had learned.

After going through the calculation of the density of the whole and peeled orange, Ann Marie reflected on the method in which she and her group had determined the volume using an approximate radius and a mathematical formula for volume. She shows awareness of how using the method affects accuracy and also realizes that the limited precision of the volumetric equipment that another group had chosen might have also contributed to errors in their determination by the preferred method.

Ann Marie's Reflection on Investigating Sinking and Floating

The next step of our lesson led us to experiment with other materials to see if they would float or sink in water. Before placing an object in water, Professor Akins had us predict the result.

After making comparisons, we were ready to make our generalizations: "Items will float if their density is less than water," "Items will sink if their density is greater than water," and "Items will rest at the water line if their density is equal to water."

I found our density/floating discussion to be very interesting. Although I understood the formula right away, and assisted in figuring out the density, the lightbulb really went off when Dr. Akins mentioned comparing the density of an object to water (1 g/ml). I must admit it took a minute or two to get it, but it really brought it all together. I suppose I never considered why things float before (shame on me!).

When we discussed what would be more dense than water, my first thought was oil since it appears thick. However, as soon as someone mentioned how oil sits on top of water, I realized I had it backwards and it was indeed less dense. When we were asked what would add density to water, I never thought of salt. But I did know that people float better in the ocean. I just never put the two together in a scientific way. So, in this relatively brief discussion, I learned a lot of things that now make a lot of sense. I feel as if I have grasped the concept much more than if I had read about it in a science textbook. That is the point our own textbook is trying to make, but experiencing it has a much more profound effect.

After we all understood the concepts presented, Professor Akins introduced a new word, buoyancy, *and distributed an article for us to read. As I read it, I realized that without this orange experiment experience, I most likely would not have comprehended the information in this article or I would have "zoned out" while reading. Even if we had read it after one of the first steps in the experiment, I might not have "got it." But, the step-by-step experience of this lesson made me ready to learn about the force of buoyancy.*

The important aspect of all this is that we as students came to our own conclusions—we constructed the knowledge on our own. Professor Akins guided us along the way, but, ultimately, we were able to make the conclusions ourselves. This is the constructivist approach to learning science. By making the connections on our own, we construct our own learning. This type of knowledge is more likely to "stick" than knowledge acquired by reading about concepts in a textbook.

Finally, I thought it was interesting that Donna's group used the volume figure obtained from the water displacement method, and it was not as accurate as the circumference/radius/ formula method my group used. I felt as if our group was dealing with a large margin of error due to the imperfect shape of our orange. Yet, Professor Akins said our results (71% mass/61% volume of edible orange) were consistent with many others. I would have thought that water displacement would have been more accurate. Maybe their container did not have close calibrations. Maybe our orange wasn't as far from a sphere as I thought.

Assessment on Goals of Science Education and Scientific Literacy

Early in the course, after the discussion of the goals of modern science education and the investigation on process skills, preservice teachers write an essay addressing scientific literacy: What is scientific literacy? What can you do to enhance your own scientific literacy? What can you do as an elementary teacher to contribute toward the goal of scientific literacy for all? Throughout the semester, I encourage the class members to continue to think about the meaning of scientific literacy and to make self-assessments. (Ann Marie assessed her growth in relation to the investigations.) Assessment related to scientific literacy is also addressed in other activities and on the midterm examination.

Ann Marie's Essay on Scientific Literacy

Scientific literacy means that science is an integral part of a person's life. A scientifically literate person can understand scientific issues and underlying concepts and ideas, be knowledgeable, and see the science in everyday life. It means that person is able to communicate effectively about science, capable of explaining theories and conclusions. Scientific literacy is an ongoing process in an individual that continually develops and expands over the course of one's lifetime. One should always strive to improve his/her own level of scientific literacy. Personally, I think an interesting way I could improve my own scientific literacy would be to ask more questions about the world around me and take the time to look for the answers. Also, reading articles or other materials related to science would expand my own knowledge, concepts, and ideas and, therefore, improve my scientific literacy.

As a teacher, I hope to continually expand my student's scientific literacy through interesting, hands-on science lessons which give the students an opportunity to construct meaning on their own or in group activities, while I serve as their guide. Also, integrating scientific ideas throughout the day, and taking advantage of teachable moments when they occur, would help them grasp the importance of science, as well as realize that it is a part of their daily lives. In addition, I hope to encourage communication among my students while they are in the process of acquiring scientific skills and by having them explain orally the conclusions and concepts they've learned to understand. However, probably the most important thing I can do to promote scientific literacy in my students would be to project a positive attitude about science itself.

Assessment Related to Theories and Research: How Do Children Learn Science?

Ann Marie noted similarities between children's misconceptions , her own misconceptions, and those of her classmates, as did other class members. She indicated that she and her group mates found connections between what she learned from science investigations and constructivist approaches.

It is significant that this inquiry stimulated Ann Marie to reflect on previous activities and topics, including scientific literacy, and on her confidence in teaching science.

Ann Marie's Reflection on "How Do Children Learn Science?"

One of the areas that Chapter 4 addresses is the fact that many students come to class with misconceptions. Well, adults are no exception. Several of the students in our class were under the impressions that heavier items sink and lighter items float. If they had read in a book that its density made the determination, they may not remember it....

The lesson truly followed the constructivist theory. We, as learners, were always active. Even though we spent a lot of time working on these concepts, it never got boring because we were always busy. If we were done ahead of the others, there [were] always additional ideas and questions to consider, discuss, and make predictions about.

It was especially amusing, talking about our misconceptions and seeing how easily they can occur. Cathleen had the most technical section about the function of the brain, but she made us all study guides to help us out (very thoughtful!). We spent quite a bit of time on this, as it was the least familiar to many of us. In my section, "What Do Children Need to Help Them Learn?," I connected each aspect to the orange experiment. My group mates responded to this and were even making the connections themselves before I mentioned them.

Another area addressed by Chapter 4 is "What Do Children Need to Help Them Learn." We covered all of the areas in this [orange] experiment: Thinking (making our plan, making our generalizations), Physical Activity (the actual procedures that we carried out to find our results), Language (discussing our procedure and our conclusions with our partner, and relating them to the group), Social (feeling secure in having someone else to work it out with, as well as developing relationships with our classmates), and Time (we spent considerable time learning in a step-by-step fashion).

Although our text recommends this type of learning for teaching children science, I would expand that statement to include adults as well. As for myself, I can't wait for one of my students to ask me why things float, or why people float better in the ocean. In addition, my scientific literacy has certainly come a long way in a relatively short time. But, probably the most important thing I have learned is that science is not frightening— it is something I can do. I believe it will be easier to motivate my students to "do" than to just "listen."

Comprehensive Written Examinations

There were similarities and differences in the fall and spring midterms during the year 2002–2003. Both were comprehensive, testing content on all inquires. This section will focus only on the performance of students on the examination sections related to the understanding of scientific literacy and the understanding of concepts and processes related to the inquiries dealing with the orange investigation and the sinking and floating investigation.

Midterm, Fall 2002

On the fall examination, students were given a table with mass and volume data for mercury, copper, and three unknowns. They were asked to complete the table by making entries under the columns headed *density* and *sink/float,* thus using the formula for density and the ability to predict sinking and floating properties based on density. The allotted credit for the table was 10 points. Only 9 points were given if the units for density were not specified. In addition, 5 points were given for an explanation of their reasoning for classifying the object in the table as sinkers or floaters.

Out of 31 students (three classes), most performed satisfactorily on the task of determining the value for the density using the equation. Students received an average of 76% of maximum credit for the density table, with 65% of the students receiving 90% or more of the credit on the table. Of those students receiving less than 70% of the credit for the table, 33% correctly calculated the densities of at least four of the five objects. However, they performed poorly in classifying the objects as sinkers or floaters.

Students received an average of 54% of the maximum credit on an explanation of their reasoning for classifying the objects in the table as sinkers or floaters. Only 29% of the students received 90% or more of the credit allotted for the explanation. An average of 66% of the total credit (15 points) was received for the overall performance of calculating density, identifying objects as sinkers or floaters, and explaining the reasoning.

Students also responded to the following question on the 2002 fall midterm:

What is scientific literacy? (You may answer this question by describing what a scientifically literate person knows and is able to do.) Describe ways in which you may enhance your scientific literacy. What are some specific strategies and topics you would use in the classroom with elementary children to support the goal of scientific literacy?

Students received an average of 91% of the credit allowed for this question.

Midterm, Spring 2003 (Integrated Assessment)

A section of the spring 2003 midterm was an integrated assessment focused on concepts and processes related to the science investigations, scientific literacy, learning theories, and equity. The heart of the assessment was a vignette, based entirely on our methods experiences, with characters who were upper elementary students and their teacher. In the vignette, students and teacher face the same types of challenges, pose the same questions, and make statements similar (sometimes verbatim) to those made in the methods class. But the students are children with diverse backgrounds. The integrated tasks require preservice teachers to read, comprehend, and analyze the vignette, which they are able to do having participated in and gained knowledge from the course investigations.

On a section of the assessment, preservice teachers must define scientific literacy and identify specific strategies and content in the lesson that support the goal of scientific literacy for all children. They must identify the New Jersey Science Content Standards reflected by the lesson. They must also give an explanation for the discrepant event encountered by the children and propose an activity to help the children find an answer to their question "Why did the whole orange float and why did the peeled orange sink?" The preservice teachers must also define the term *constructivism* and identify specific strategies and behaviors of the teacher and behaviors of the children that reflect a constructivist philosophy in the classroom.

Twenty students (two classes) who took the spring midterm received an average of 80% on the question addressing scientific literacy; they received 93% on the question addressing the New Jersey Science Content Standards, which are geared toward scientific literacy. Students in the spring semester received an average of 88% on the question requiring an explanation of sinking and floating.

One of my science methods classes also took mathematics methods from me. In addition to the regular midterm, they had the option of taking a separate section that required more mathematics calculations. On that optional section, preservice teachers were asked to use the data collected by the vignette students to find the percentage of the orange (according to mass and volume) that is edible. They were asked to find the volume of the orange in two different ways (water displacement data and use of the measured circumference). They were also asked to give a scientific explanation for the difference in behavior of the whole orange and the peeled orange.

Three out of 10 students in the class were interested in taking the optional section (Ann Marie and members of the group in which she worked). Each achieved a score of 100%.

Reflecting on Teaching (Self-Assessment)

Ann Marie's reflection on her lesson tells of her preparation and presentation of a lesson adapted from a collection of model lessons in the science methods textbook. She demonstrates the qualities of an inquiring and reflective teacher. She uses the internet and the university's curriculum library to enhance her conceptual background on the subject and resolves a discrepancy about science content among her sources.

Ann Marie's Reflection on the Lesson She Prepared

This science lesson on "taste" turned out to be a lesson on "process" for me. I originally chose it because the text recommended it for grades K–4, and I hoped I would be able to use it in my third-grade classroom, in addition to learning something new. I felt quite a sense of relief when Professor Akins recommended we use the lessons in the text. After all, they are well-written, current, hands-on, and educational. I firmly believe that teachers should use whatever quality resources are available. To be original is fun at times and very rewarding, but expecting that of yourself for every lesson could definitely lead to early burnout.

I suppose because the lesson was written so well, I did my research in a calm, methodical way, since there was no pressure to make changes. I did some digging in the WPU curriculum library and found some other things on taste, but, in the end, they weren't as good as the procedure in our text. I also located some lessons on the internet, and one in particular was remarkably similar. I did extract the taste/smell portion of the lesson with the apple and the vanilla from one of these internet sources. All of the picture books I found were centered on all five senses, so I chose not to use one in the lesson.

There was one dilemma I came across. Most of the information I found stated that specific tastes were detected on certain areas of the tongue, whereas our text said that some people could taste all four basic tastes on all areas of the tongue. This discrepancy bothered me since I was to be the "expert" on the subject. Well, in the end, the experiment I did at home and at WPU proved that the text was correct, and I was very excited about that. People with a large amount of taste buds on their tongue (supertasters!) are able to do this. So much for Encarta!

When I subjected my family to the lesson, we discovered two important things: the cocoa powder the book recommended for taste did not mix effectively with water in order to produce the desired taste of "bitter," and the wax paper needed to remain on the tongue, when counting fungiform papillae, because the blue dye spreads if it is removed. I turned to the internet lesson for help....

I was pleased with how the lesson turned out. As I've said in the past, it is difficult to do these lessons with adults, and yet my fellow preservice teachers did seem engaged and were certainly game to play around with their tongues (including dying them blue). But, I think I taught it in an understandable way. I was lucky to find such a good illustration of the tongue on the Scientific American *website and I think it enhanced my handouts. As far as doing this particular lesson with my [practicum] third grade, I'm still not sure.... One of my goals during my two weeks in the field is to do a 4Es lesson on science. I think if I'm careful about which one I [choose], they will get a lot out of it.*

After all I have experienced in this class, I firmly believe in the constructivist approach to teaching science. However, I also realize that to teach science this way may be a goal that I will have to work toward if I have a class such as my current third grade. I feel that even if we only cover a portion of the material, a more in-depth look at a few concepts would be more meaningful and educational than the read-and-regurgitate method....

Final Reflections and Comments

According to science education standards, school science should reflect the characteristics of science in the real world and include inquiries across the science disciplines. These standards challenge most elementary teachers who have limited science backgrounds, particularly in physical science, and few models for teaching and learning science through inquiry from their own learning experiences. Hence, I arrived at the mission expressed in the title of this chapter and the focus of my efforts and those of my students, the preservice teachers, in the methods course.

Teaching preservice teachers all the science concepts they need to know is an unrealistic and inappropriate goal for the science methods course. But providing opportunities for preservice teachers to have experiences that foster positive attitudes toward science and an appreciation for conceptual understanding as a goal of scientific inquiry—these have been important goals. For me, these goals have gone hand in hand because advocating for conceptual understanding and doing science in the methods course can be very intimidating and upsetting for persons who have different expectations from the course.

Many preservice teachers have indicated that they acquired a better understanding of science concepts and explanations as they participated in the methods lessons and prepared for lessons presentations. A substantial number have indicated that the few formulas, which they previously memorized, had more meaning as a result of the lessons. Students with more science and mathematics background have indicated that the hands-on, 4E approach was new and that they found it interesting and beneficial in getting them ready to teach elementary science.

Virtually all students indicate in their final reflections that observing and participating in a variety of peer lessons is beneficial and satisfying and that they feel better prepared to teach elementary science as a result. During the past two years, an increasing number actually taught a science lesson to children in the field, although they were not pressured to do so by supervisors or cooperating teachers. I feel confident that more and more will be taking their college science methods course to school and that they will contribute to the goal of scientific literacy for all.

Excerpts from Ann Marie's Final Reflections

This methods course has taken the excitement that I felt in the biology lab and spread it over all the different disciplines of science. I can't express how much I enjoyed working with those oranges, manipulating those numbers, and trying to keep up with Michele, who was always half a step ahead of me! Each lesson the [others] presented made me feel like I was discovering the concept for the first time. Cutting that clay ball in half to "reveal" the layers of the earth was a thrill, even though I knew what I would find. Whether we were taking core samples of Mars, experimenting with magnets, or predicting whether an object would sink or float—it has all been fascinating. I am totally "sold" on the concept of students constructing their own knowledge through exploration and discovery. It just makes sense and, after these last few months, I can't imagine doing it any other way (for my own sake, as well as my students).

Another important idea that never occurred to me prior to this class is that science goes beyond understanding concepts such as density, earth layers, life cycles, etc. Without the knowledge I now have about the processes of science, and an appreciation of their importance, I would have likely rushed through my own science lessons to get my students to the "punch line." Instead, my experiences in this class have shown me that the incremental steps the students are taking as part of their discovery are all individual skills. These skills are being developed and learned by the students, along with the main objective or concept of the lesson. In addition, I can now see how easy it will be to incorporate the study of science with other subjects in the curriculum. Math is an obvious connection, but even language arts can be integrated into almost any science lesson.

I think students need to be exposed to this type of learning early on. The one thing I'm certain of, they will enjoy it, and they will learn something, if I can just maintain control!

Today, in mid-April, I can tell you that whether an object will sink or float depends on how its density compares to that of water. We did that lesson in early March. I can say with conviction that I would not have remembered that if I read it in our textbook, read it in an article, or heard it in a lecture. Obviously, I was taught it prior to this class, and forgot about it. And now, oddly enough, it seems so reasonable that I can't imagine not knowing it. It just makes sense. Well, if I hadn't learned it the way I did, the result would not have been the same. Learning by doing, learning by exploration followed by explanation—that makes sense, too. I hope I can make it work in the real world.

References

Martin, R., C. Sexton, and J. Gerlovich. 2001. *Teaching science for all children.* Boston: Allyn and Bacon.

National Research Council (NRC). 1996. *National science education standards.* Washington, DC: National Academy Press.

Suggested Readings

Abdi, W. 2001. Multicultural teaching tips. In *Science learning for all: Celebrating cultural diversity,* pp. 38–41. Arlington, VA: NSTA Press.

Abruscato, J. 2000. *Teaching children science.* Boston: Allyn and Bacon.

Akins, S. 1993. Restructuring the science and mathematics curriculum: Elementary leadership teachers' perspectives. Doctoral diss., Columbia University.

Akins, S. 2001. It's apeeling: Diversity and constructivism in the classroom. Unpublished classroom vignette as an assessment tool for science methods. (Available on request from the author.)

Bryant, N. 2001. Make the curriculum multicultural. In *Science learning for all: Celebrating cultural diversity,* pp. 12–15. Arlington, VA: NSTA Press.

Buffington, K., L. Ecklund, S. Mercier, and A. Wiebe, eds. 1987. *Fun with foods.* Fresno, CA: AIMS Education Foundation.

Champagne, A., and L. Hornig, eds. 1987. *Students and science learning.* Washington, DC: American Association for the Advancement of Science.

Fosnot, C. 1989. *Enquiring teachers, enquiring learners.* New York: Teachers College Press.

Fosnot, C., ed. 1996. *Constructivism: Theory, perspectives, and practices.* New York: Teachers College Press.

Fulp, S. 2001. The status of elementary science. In *2000 National Survey of Science and Mathematics Education.* Chapel Hill, NC: Horizon Research.

Harlan, W., ed. 1988. *Primary science: Taking the plunge.* London: Heinemann Educational Books.

Jakobsen, A. M. 2003. Selected class reflections from science education and mathematics education journals. *Celebrating student writing across the curriculum.* 4th annual ed. Wayne, NJ: William Paterson University.

New Jersey Department of Education. 1998. *New Jersey science content standards. www.state.nj.us/njded/cccs/s5_science.htm*

Osborne, R., and P. Freyberg, eds. 1985. *Learning in science.* Portsmouth, NH: Heinemann.

Samples, B., B. Hammond, and B. McCarthy. 1985. *4-MAT and science.* Barrington, IL: Excel.

TEAMS:
Working Together to
Improve Teacher Education

Dale Baker, Michael Piburn, and Douglas Clark
Arizona State University

TEAMS (Teacher Education in Arizona for Mathematics and Science) is a fast-track, post-baccalaureate program at Arizona State University (ASU). It was created with support from the National Science Foundation, through a Collaboratives for Excellence in Teacher Preparation (CETP) grant designed to implement standards-based reforms in teacher education. The purpose of TEAMS is to increase the number of well-qualified middle and secondary science and mathematics teachers and to meet the needs of career-changing adults. It provides middle/secondary certification and a master's degree. Each course is structured to meet specific National Science Education Standards (NRC 1996) and to address the Standards' call for changes in emphasis in science education.

Setting

Teacher education at ASU takes place in Tempe, Arizona, a metropolitan area of 3.5 million people. The community is a mix of Native American, Latino, and European-American peoples. TEAMS preservice teachers were originally (in 1995) placed in urban schools where many students are poor and monolingual Spanish or bilingual English/Spanish speakers. There were also substantial numbers of Native American and Southeast Asian students in the schools. Since 1999, TEAMS preservice teachers have been placed in the Chandler School District, where 50% of the students are minorities with characteristics similar to students in the urban core. The other 50% are children of engineers or scientists working in the computer industry.

The Faculty

The university faculty who teach in the TEAMS program have expertise in mathematics, technology, science education, the history and philosophy of mathematics and science, teacher research, and middle-level education. Three Chandler district personnel also teach in the program; they are middle and high school specialists in staff development, mathematics, science, technology, curriculum, and special education. They are also involved in the supervision, evaluation, and hiring of TEAMS students.

The Students

TEAMS students are mature adults who have had science, mathematics, and engineering careers and who now want to be teachers. They enter the program with bachelor's, master's, and PhD degrees. A small number enter the program immediately after graduating from the university. The modal age is between 26 and 35. The program has drawn students from 20 states, as well as Mexico, Canada, India, and Africa.

Meeting the *More Emphasis* Conditions of the National Science Education Standards

TEAMS was designed (by the authors of this chapter) with the National Science Education Standards (NRC 1996) in mind, in collaboration with 10 school districts. Its purpose was to prepare teachers to help students *experience* the natural world, *use* science to make personal decisions, *engage* in public discourse about scientific and technological matters, and *increase* the number of individuals entering scientific careers. The program models what we expect to happen in classrooms. To these ends, we used the Professional Development and Program Standards *More Emphasis* conditions to create a school-based program that would educate new teachers, who in turn would be change agents in their schools. We included action research on teaching and learning in the program, in addition to reflective journals, collaborative work, and professional development at the district and university levels.

The Science Teaching Standards *More Emphasis* conditions led us to include multiple ways to

- ◆ assess student understanding and explore alternative conceptions and conceptual change teaching;
- ◆ examine equity issues and the needs of special education students;
- ◆ examine adolescent development issues and evaluate curriculum to meet student interests, strengths, experiences, and needs; and
- ◆ provide a student teaching program that is student centered and standards based.

Following the Assessment Standards *More Emphasis* conditions, we involved preservice teachers in the creation of assessments to measure understanding, reasoning, and conceptual knowledge. Moreover, we explored the strengths and weaknesses of formative and summative assessments in a variety of formats with the preservice teachers (oral, written, projects, standardized, teacher made).

To meet the Science Content Standards *More Emphasis* conditions, we selected activities that exemplified topics such as

- ◆ inquiry and models;
- ◆ integrated technology, mathematics, and science;
- ◆ history and philosophy of science; and
- ◆ analysis or synthesis of data with tools.

We also provided opportunities to communicate through PowerPoint presentations, debates (e.g., the trial of Galileo), and written documents.

Unique Features of the Program
Structure
TEAMS is an intensive, post-baccalaureate, cohort program in which graduates receive a secondary teaching certificate with a middle school endorsement and a master's degree in education. Students enter once a year, in July, and graduate the following summer. Course work and field placements are accelerated in comparison to traditional teacher education programs. The program integrates science, mathematics, and technology through innovative teaching in a tools- and computer-infused environment.

Twenty-five to thirty students are admitted per cohort. Students must have a bachelor's degree and the required number of courses to qualify for a content certificate in biology, physics, Earth science, chemistry, or mathematics. They must also submit three letters of recommendation and be interviewed by ASU faculty. In addition, they must have an undergraduate GPA that qualifies them for admission to the graduate school.

School District Collaboration
For the first three years of the program (1995–1998), fieldwork and student teaching in the TEAMS program took place in the Phoenix Urban Systemic Initiative (USI) schools. TEAMS faculty developed workshops with district leaders to familiarize cooperating teachers with TEAMS's philosophy, methodology, and instructional strategies using technology. These workshops became part of districtwide staff development.

In 1998, TEAMS was redesigned to be a school-based program while keeping the basic philosophy of the program. An agreement was crafted between ASU and the Chandler District to allow both ASU and district personnel to teach courses and supervise students. Almost all TEAMS course work, internships, and student teaching placements take place in six schools in the Chandler District.

Courses and Internships

Table 1 lists the specific courses, connections to the National Science Education Standards, and the hours of the program. In addition to ensuring that the courses reflect the changing emphases described in the Standards, the program addresses three additional criteria:

1. a middle school endorsement;
2. courses that meet state certification requirements for secondary certification; and
3. courses and experiences that meet the hours and categories of knowledge necessary to qualify for a master's degree in education at ASU.

Table 1. TEAMS (Teacher Education in Arizona for Mathematics and Science): Courses, National Science Education Standards Addressed by Courses, and Hours

Courses	National Science Education Standards	Hours
Technology Tools for Middle School	Science and Technology Standards	2
Field Experiences	Professional Development Standards	1
Middle School Curriculum, Philosophy, and Organization	All Content Standards	4
Creating Positive Classroom Climates	Teaching Standards	2
Literacy in Science	Science Education Program Standards	2
Psychology of the Adolescent	Science Teaching Standards	3
Research Methods in Science and Mathematics Education–Part I	Professional Development Standards; Science Teaching Standards	2
Technology in Middle School Science and Math	Science and Technology Standards	3
Field Experiences	Professional Development Standards	1
Science or Math Methods for Early Adolescents	Unifying Concepts and Processes Standards; Science as Inquiry Standards	3
Inclusion Practices in Science and Mathematics Classrooms	Science Education Program Standards	2
Student Teaching		8
Field Experiences	Professional Development Standards	1
Equity in Science and Mathematics Education	Assessment Standards; Science Education Program Standards	2
History and Philosophy of Science and Mathematics	History and Nature of Science Standards; Science in Personal and Social Perspectives Standards	2
Research Methods in Science and Mathematics Education–Part II	Professional Development Standards; Science Teaching Standards	1
Final Project		2

The program starts with team-building activities and a three-day orientation. Students do a ropes course and visit science-related sites such as the Lowell Observatory in Flagstaff, archaeological ruins, and a meteor crater. They get to know each other and the faculty in a relaxed environment and begin their induction into what it means to be a teacher.

Since TEAMS was designed to model the middle school philosophy, team teaching and multidisciplinary thematic instruction are emphasized. This approach also prepares teachers to work in junior high and secondary schools through exposure to a variety of instructional techniques and through the study of the cognitive development of students learning science in K–12.

Internships start immediately after the three-day orientation. The internships are designed to give students firsthand knowledge of middle and secondary school students, to provide opportunities to observe good teaching, and to do pre–student teaching. The internships also allow students in the program to participate in activities associated with their course work, such as interviewing students or conducting action research for the master's degree. Students do internships in summer, fall, and spring with different teachers. One internship must be in a middle school classroom, another in a secondary classroom, and a third in a setting of the student's choice.

Courses are scheduled in the summer and fall semesters and resume in spring after student teaching has been completed at week 11 of the semester. This arrangement provides an opportunity, following student teaching, to examine equity issues as well as the history and philosophy of science and mathematics. The students are able to step back and explore these complex topics in the context of their classroom experiences. We also place the Research Methods in Science and Mathematics Education–Part II segment after student teaching, allowing students to finish their master's projects and their culminating presentations free of the demands of student teaching. TEAMS students can also serve as substitutes, with pay, prior to student teaching.

Internship teachers are paid a stipend to evaluate the students working in their classrooms, using criteria agreed on by the district and university. The criteria reflect the Standards and include professionalism, interactions with students, interactions with school faculty and administration, student-centered teaching, classroom management, and mastery of content. Internship teachers are selected collaboratively by the district and university.

Student Teaching

Student teaching is a 10-week, all-day activity and includes attending district meetings, attending or conducting parent-teacher conferences, and attending district professional development activities. Student teaching takes place in one of the internship classrooms, and a teacher can request that a specific student return to his or her classroom for student teaching. This arrangement provides a head start for the student teachers because they already know the cooperating teachers (who were formerly the internship teachers), classroom rules, students' names, curriculum, and district policies. Consequently, student teachers are able to take full-time control of the classroom at an accelerated rate.

Cooperating teachers evaluate student teachers at the end of 5 and 10 weeks, meeting with the university supervisor after he or she has observed the student teacher. The cooperating teacher also writes a recommendation as to whether the district should hire the student teacher. These evaluations play a major part in whether an individual is hired. The evaluation criteria for student teaching were developed in cooperation with the Chandler District to reflect the National Science Education Standards and address the knowledge, skills, and dispositions that both the district and university considered as representing excellence in teaching mathematics and science. The cooperating teachers are paid a stipend by the university and are also evaluated for the quality of their supervision. Former TEAMS students have gained enough experience as classroom teachers to allow them to serve as internship and cooperating teacher supervisors. This ensures continuity of expectations and a familiarity with the program that is difficult to achieve unless one has been a TEAMS student.

The Master's Degree

Central to the master's degree is a two-semester course that introduces the concept of action research, teacher as researcher, research design, and research methodologies. Students prepare a proposal that is reviewed by an ASU faculty member whose expertise matches the focus of the proposal. The student works closely with that person as the research is conducted, data are analyzed, and conclusions are written. The culminating activity (final project) is a presentation to ASU faculty, district teachers, and fellow students.

TEAMS and Technology

Classes were initially taught in a room at the university equipped for technological applications. Networked computers, connected to the internet, were available for group work. The room also had a server, Proxima projector, scanner, printer, VCR, laserdisc player, graphing calculators, and a "smart" blackboard. There were also computer-based laboratories. The same technology is now provided on-site in the Chandler District schools.

TEAMS students are expected to learn and use the tools, in teaching, on a Windows application, in Word, Excel, and PowerPoint. Students also create home pages, which are on a dedicated server. Electronic communication is facilitated by a Listserv.

Research on the Effectiveness of TEAMS

To determine the effectiveness of TEAMS, we investigated (1) the acquisition of content addressed in the Standards and courses; (2) the effect of the Standards addressed in the program on attitude toward science and science teaching and on classroom teaching; and (3) the effect of teachers prepared in a Standards-based program on students' knowledge. We discuss each of these three topics below.

Acquisition of Content Addressed in the Standards and Courses

The impact of the content standards on the TEAMS students was determined by an alternative conceptions test called the Test of Scientific Frameworks (Piburn, Mills, and Villanueva 1998a) and a standards-based Scientific Knowledge Survey (Piburn, Mills, and Villanueva 1998b). The Test of Scientific Frameworks asked respondents to choose the best answer, to reason, and to write an explanation of their answer. The content was taken from the middle school National

Science Education Standards and reflected the content and standards in the TEAMS courses, together with the content the TEAMS students were expected to teach. The Test of Scientific Frameworks poses problems such as the following: Imagine there is a cup of hot coffee on a table. You leave the room, and when you return its temperature is lower than before. How can you explain what happened?

The Standards-based Scientific Knowledge Survey was developed to assess understanding of the content that students encountered in their course work (and which they were expected to teach). Items were chosen from the National Assessment of Educational Progress (NAEP) (Jones et al. 1992), the Trends in International Mathematics and Science Study (TIMSS) (Beaton et al. 1996), and standardized tests. Analysis yielded 10 items for the five areas identified by the National Science Education Standards.

The Frameworks data revealed that there were no serious deficiencies in TEAMS students' knowledge about gas laws or the relationships between temperature and pressure. They lacked some information concerning the densities of a variety of substances but understood the concept of density well. A comparison of TEAMS students with university students in their junior and senior years indicates that despite instruction, TEAMS students still retained some alternative conceptions commonly found among both scientists and nonscientists regarding heat and temperature (Lewis and Linn 1994), a finding borne out by the current research on alternative conceptions.

The Scientific Knowledge Survey (Piburn, Mills, and Villanueva 1998a, 1998b) indicated that TEAMS students learned about Earth science (77% correct), life science (78% correct), and physical science (82% correct) concepts addressed in the courses, but the greatest impact was on understanding the nature of science (93% correct) and science and society (86% correct). Since the TEAMS students had strong science backgrounds, we did not expect the program to have a large impact on content knowledge. However, we attribute the strong showing in the areas of the nature of science and of science and society to our emphasis on these Standards areas. Current literature indicates that most preparation programs have little impact on teachers' understanding of the nature of science or science and society (Abd-El-Khalick and Lederman 2000).

Attitude Toward Science and Science Teaching

Attitude toward science and science teaching was assessed using the What Is Your Attitude Toward Science and Science Teaching? instrument (Moore 1973). The Attitude Toward Science scale measures the nature of theories, processes and products of science, and public understanding of science. The Attitude Toward Science Teaching scale measures confidence as a teacher, attitude toward children, and role of the teacher.

There were no significant differences between the pre- and post-program scores on the Attitude Toward Science scale. TEAMS students had very positive scores at the beginning of the program. They tended to see science as a process whereby knowledge is sought, rather than a static body of knowledge. They felt that the public needs to understand science, both for its own good and because science requires public support. They disagreed with the idea that science is something that only scientists can do.

There was a significant increase in scores ($p < 0.05$) on the Attitude Toward Science Teaching scale, from the pre- to posttest, reflecting an improvement in attitude toward teaching science. Post hoc analysis indicated that there was improvement across all subtests, but the only significant change ($p < 0.01$) was in the Role of the Teacher.

Students saw the teacher as a resource person rather than an information provider, expected the teacher to spend more time listening to children than talking, and expected the teacher to arrange the classroom so that children spent more time experimenting than listening to lectures. They were less inclined to see the teacher as one who conducts demonstrations, tells students why their experiments didn't work, or tells students what they should know. They became less teacher centered and more student centered and viewed themselves as facilitators of student learning. These changes are closely aligned with the *Less Emphasis/More Emphasis* conditions found in the National Science Education Standards, and we believe they are due to the Standards-based nature of the TEAMS program.

Effects of Standards-Based Program on Students' Knowledge

The effect of a program—built on the National Science Education Standards—on classroom teaching was measured by the Reformed Teaching Observation Protocol (RTOP) (Piburn et al. 2000). This 25-item instrument was specifically designed to assesses the degree to which a classroom meets Standards-based teaching. Scores on each item range from 0 (*never observed*) to 4 (*very descriptive*), with a maximum possible total of 100. The RTOP measures the impact of the program in promoting standards-based teaching with an emphasis on the Science Teaching and Inquiry Standards. It measures how well students have learned to put more emphasis on

- considering the prior knowledge of students;
- engaging students with concrete manipulation of data and materials before introducing abstractions;
- promoting scientific reasoning;
- selecting and adapting curriculum;
- creating a community of learners; and
- promoting engagement and group work to solve complex problems with a high degree of student-to-student interaction.

Comparisons in the first, second, or third years of teaching were made between TEAMS teachers and teachers from other programs. A statistical t-test of the RTOP scores of TEAMS and non-TEAMS teachers indicated that there was no difference for first-year teachers. Significant differences were found ($p < 0.05$) when comparing second- and third-year TEAMS and non-TEAMS teachers. The scores from year one of teaching to years two and three indicated that TEAMS teachers grew professionally in the areas of lesson design and implementation, procedural knowledge, communicative interactions, and student teacher interactions, becoming more student centered and constructivist. No gains were found for non-TEAMS teachers on any of the sections, indicating that the non-TEAMS teachers had not grown professionally between their first year of teaching and their second or third. Non-TEAMS teachers were still employing instructional strategies that the Standards recommend placing less emphasis on. The data indicate that TEAMS teachers could apply Standards-based philosophy and skills to teaching and that the program accelerated professional growth.

It is difficult to determine the effects of a teacher preparation program, even one designed to address national standards, by linking specific teacher practices to student outcomes, due to the fact that there many variables that cannot be controlled. To date, we have determined the effects of TEAMS by using RTOP scores and student achievement. We compared our biology teachers and their students to students of teachers who graduated from other programs. Teachers were observed using the RTOP, and the high school students were given a Biology Attitudes, Skills and Knowledge Survey (Adamson et al., Forthcoming) to assess attitude, understanding of the nature of science, reasoning, and biological concepts.

The results indicated that students instructed by teachers from the Standards-based TEAMS program (who were also the teachers with higher RTOP scores) had higher concept and reasoning scores than students taught by teachers from other programs. The differences in scores of students was statistically significant ($p < 0.01$) (Adamson et al., Forthcoming).

Summary

TEAMS is a Standards-based program that has prepared teachers with the knowledge and skills to teach in a way that reflects the National Science Education Standards. TEAMS teachers understand the nature of science and have positive attitudes toward science and science teaching and good content knowledge. Their ability to use student-centered, constructivist teaching has had an impact on the academic achievement of their students and their own professional growth.

References

Abd-El-Khalick, F., and N. Lederman. 2000. Improving science teachers' conceptions of the nature of science: A critical review of the literature. *International Journal of Science Education* 22: 665–701.

Adamson, S., D. Banks, M. Burtch, F. Cox, E. Judson, J. Turley, R. Benford, and A. Lawson. Forthcoming. Reformed undergraduate instruction and its subsequent impact on secondary school teaching practice and achievement. *Journal of Research in Science Teaching* 40(10): 939–957.

Beaton, A., I. Mullis, M. Martin, E. Gonzales, D. Kelly, and T. Smith. 1996. *Science achievement in the middle school years: IEA's Third International Mathematics and Science Study (TIMSS)*. Chestnut Hill, MA: Boston College.

Jones, L., I. Mullis, S. Raizen, I. Weiss, and E. Weston. 1992. *The 1990 science report card: NAEP's assessment of fourth, eighth, and twelfth graders*. Washington, DC: U. S. Department of Education.

Lewis, E., and M. Linn. 1994. Heat energy and temperature concepts of adolescents, adults, and experts: Implications for curricular improvements. *Journal of Research in Science Teaching* 31: 657–678.

Moore, R. W. 1973. The development, field test, and validation of scales to assess teachers' attitudes toward teaching elementary school science. *Science Education* 57(3): 271–278.

National Research Council (NRC). 1996. *National science education standards*. Washington, DC: National Academy Press.

Piburn, M., E. Mills, and T. Villanueva. 1998a. Coming to grips with content: The knowledge base of prospective teachers. Paper presented at the annual meeting of the National Association of Research in Science Teaching, San Diego, CA.

Piburn, M., E. Mills, and T. Villanueva. 1998b. Assessing the national standards in science: The Scientific Knowledge Survey. Paper presented at the annual meeting of the National Middle School Association, Denver, CO.

Piburn, M., D. Sawada, J. Turley, K. Falconer, R. Benford, I. Bloom, and E. Judson. 2000. *Reformed Teaching Observation Protocol: Reference manual* (Technical Report No. INOO-3). Tempe, AZ: Arizona Collaborative for Excellence in the Preparation of Teachers.

Exemplary Science: Best Practice in Science Teaching Today

Timothy Cooney and Cherin Lee
University of Northern Iowa

Setting

The University of Northern Iowa (UNI), located in Cedar Falls, is a medium-size, comprehensive Midwestern university, long known for excellence in teacher preparation and other programs. Fall 2003 enrollment was about 13,600 students, including about 1,600 graduate students. UNI was founded in 1876 and evolved from a mainstream school into a state teachers college, and then to a state college, becoming the University of Northern Iowa in 1967. Currently, UNI has 860 faculty members in the following colleges: Business Administration, Education, Humanities and Fine Arts, Natural Sciences, Social and Behavioral Sciences, and the Graduate College.

Basic Science Minor

The purpose of UNI science education programs is to prepare students to become outstanding teachers of science in elementary, middle, and high schools and to become leaders in science education. With respect to the Basic Science Minor, which will be discussed in this chapter, we address reform suggested by the *More Emphasis* vision of the National Science Education Standards (NSES) (NRC 1996) that is pertinent to teachers, teaching, and content.

One of the methods courses in the Basic Science Minor emphasizes selecting science curricula based on the needs of elementary students and adapting curriculum materials to fit local district benchmarks. Likewise, the Basic Science Minor courses reflect the NSES Content Standards that future teachers need to know and use in their teaching. All courses use an inquiry approach that models effective teaching strategies and focuses on conceptual understanding as well as science processes. The current ideas on how students learn science are incorporated into teaching styles (Bybee 2002). These are not lecture courses, and thus they lend themselves to student discussion of ideas and a shared learning environment. Students are encouraged to reflect on the evidence that leads them to their current understandings and conclusions.

Assessment

Professors continuously assess undergraduate students' understanding via formative and summative assessment. The Basic Science Minor courses model assessment processes and strategies advocated for elementary science classrooms. Conceptual understanding (in contrast to rote memorization) is assessed through various strategies, including performance assessment. Students also self-assess their work, as well as their overall gains in content and teaching knowledge, both individually and in groups, throughout individual courses.

Content

The content of science courses is based on the NSES recommendations regarding concepts for elementary and middle school science. Emphasis is on the conceptual and on inquiry. The amount of subject matter is reduced in comparison to other introductory college science courses so that students can acquire depth of understanding and have opportunities to investigate, use a wide range of science process skills, and be involved in higher-order thinking. Two pedagogical courses integrate the different content areas of science. These courses also give students the opportunity to reflect on how they have been taught so they realize that they have been taught with strategies that they should use themselves as teachers.

Professional Development

Basic Science Minor graduates have an accelerated start on the NSES Professional Development Standards. They have learned science content through inquiry and investigation. They know how pedagogy applies specifically to science teaching and thus have already begun to integrate theory and practice. They form very close collegial and collaborative relations during their Minor courses that carry them through their first teaching positions. They also view themselves with confidence and are capable of assuming leadership responsibilities in their school districts very quickly in comparison to other beginning teachers.

Faculty, Students, School Climate

The University of Northern Iowa prides itself on being a school where "Great teaching makes a difference." Within this context, science education exists as a quasi-interdisciplinary department made up of biology, chemistry, Earth science, and physics faculty within the College of Natural Sciences. They are joined by College of Education specialists in elementary science methods who are faculty in the Department of Curriculum and Instruction and by science teachers from the university's Malcolm Price Laboratory School. This arrangement means that many science education faculty members teach courses in both secondary science teaching methods and in discipline content for the liberal arts core (nonmajors) and/or introductory majors courses, thus strengthening the content background of those who teach future teachers. Science education faculties teach all content courses in the Basic Science Minor. This type of relationship is responsible for the historic sense of connection between the science departments and science education, fostering a better understanding and dissemination of current science education practices. Having science educators in the content departments gives science education faculty legitimacy with our teaching majors and our colleagues. We teach science, not just how to teach science.

Description of the Program:
Alignment with *More Emphasis* Conditions
History of the Basic Science Minor

The program started in 1988 as a "total program effort at altering the way elementary science is taught by modeling advocated teaching approaches while enhancing content knowledge, facilitating positive attitude, and providing a cohesive experience in teaching science" (Lee and Krapfl 2002, p. 248). The Basic Science Minor requires 29 credit hours; it consists of six content courses equaling 24 hours of science and two teaching courses. The program produced its first graduates in 1991. However, it has its roots in an increased concern, dating from the late 1970s, about the poor science preparation received by elementary education majors. In 1977, a three-year National Science Foundation (NSF) grant was received and work was carried out by a team of faculty members from biology, Earth science, physics, and curriculum and instruction. In 1982 this collaboration resulted in two new courses, Activity Based Introductory Science I and II. These courses were redesigned in 1988 into Activity Based Physical Science and Activity Based Life Science, which served as cornerstones for the newly conceived Basic Science Minor. Further modification of these courses took place in 2000–2001 to ensure alignment with the NSES. The College of Education Student Advising Center recommends these courses for all elementary education majors. About 200 students per year take each course.

From 1988 to 1994, a grant from NSF provided support to develop a minor program in both mathematics and science for elementary education majors. Within the science program, three new content courses were developed and two other courses were significantly revised. These courses were combined with Activity Based Physical Science and Activity Based Life Science to form a minor program of 24 credit hours (more recently increased to 29 credit hours). In addition, a cadre of teachers was prepared to serve as cooperating teachers for the student teaching experience of the science minors.

The Basic Science Minor fits within the university's elementary education program, in which majors are encouraged to take either a subject emphasis or a minor. Thus, the Basic Science Minor is one of several options open to elementary education majors. The Basic Science Minor is a unique program for elementary education majors: Students receive 24 hours of science content and 5 hours of pedagogical content knowledge, in additional to the university-wide capstone course on science, technology, and society. The content courses taken by Basic Science Minors are inquiry courses that model teaching content and methodology. This approach exemplifies the belief that "teachers [must] do inquiry to learn its meaning, its value, and how to use it to help students learn" (NRC 2000 p. 91). While the courses in the minor reflect depth of content over breadth, they are no less rigorous than standard courses offered in the science content departments. The objectives of the program require participating students to

◆ become knowledgeable about the concepts and principles of the physical and biological sciences;
◆ understand young people and the processes of learning;
◆ be able to use methods, materials, and instructional technology appropriately to contribute to learning in science;
◆ demonstrate the ability to teach groups and individuals effectively;
◆ understand the nature of reform movements in science education; and
◆ continue to develop as teachers and leaders throughout their careers.

Courses in the Basic Science Minor

The Basic Science Minor requires two introductory courses, Inquiry Into Life Science and Inquiry Into Physical Science, taken during the freshman or sophomore year. The introductory courses are followed by a trio of "investigations" courses: Investigations in Life Science, Investigations in Physical Science, and Investigations in Earth Science. Students take the investigations courses during their sophomore and junior years. The area of physical science is strengthened further by the students' choice of Principles of Chemistry, Applied General Chemistry, or Conceptual Physics. The investigations courses model teaching strategies drawn from results in the cognitive sciences, including the inquiry-embedded, learning cycles, and/or the popular 5E approaches. Teaching the concepts learned in content courses is emphasized during the senior year, in Experiences in Elementary School Science and Integrated Activities in Elementary School Science and Mathematics. (For descriptions of the Basic Science Minor courses, see Figure 1.)

Description of Life Science Courses

What began as Activity Based Life Science has evolved into Inquiry Into Life Science (IiLS). Both titles indicate the active experience of science. The slight change in title emphasizes a more pronounced inquiry teaching orientation. IiLS and its counterpart, Inquiry Into Physical Science (IiPS), are liberal arts core courses restricted to elementary education majors, thus allowing faculty to target concepts from the NSES and to do so in depth. IiLS operates within the context of teaching four to seven important ideas in biology, such as ecosystem interactions, homeostasis, diversity, and life cycles. The framework of IiLS involves student inquiry, the nature of science, science process skills, and inquiry teaching strategies, such as collaborative and cooperative groups, questioning (teacher and student), graphic organizers, and rubrics, to foster conceptual understanding.

Though IiLS serves elementary education majors who choose to take it as their life science liberal arts course, Basic Science Minors are required to take it as a prelude to a second-level life science course, Investigations in Life Science (ILS). This course comprises four units that build on the knowledge and process skills learned in IiLS. The organizational structure of ILS is one of "systems," from the individual cell system to whole organism. Units include

Figure 1. University of Northern Iowa Catalog Description of Courses in Basic Science Minor

820:031. Inquiry Into Physical Science—4 hrs. Inquiry-oriented introduction to concepts and processes drawn from chemistry, earth science, and physics using active investigation for those considering elementary education major. Integrated lecture/lab for 4 periods; plus 1 hour arranged.
For elementary education majors only.

820:032. Inquiry Into Life Science—4 hrs. Exploration of fundamental concepts of modern biology through active investigation. Content includes ecology, energy, diversity, and life cycles using
a standards-based teaching approach. Integrated lecture/lab for 4 periods; plus 1 hour arranged.
For elementary education majors only.

820:181. Investigations in Physical Science—4 hrs. Introduction to concepts and theories of physical science and modeling of effective teaching strategies related to elementary school level. Topics include electricity, magnetism, light, solutions, acids and bases, and states of matter. Discussion and/or lab, 5 periods.

860:010. Principles of Chemistry—3–4 hrs. Basic concepts of chemistry, the periodic table and its
relation to atomic structure and chemical properties. How the understanding of changes in matter and energy is important in both living and non-living systems. Work of the chemist and the
interactions of chemistry with other activities of humankind. Discussion, 3 periods; lab, 2 periods.
May be taken without laboratory for 3 hours.

860:061. Applied General Chemistry —4 hrs. Basic concepts of chemistry, with particular attention
to allied health and nutrition applications. Discussion, 3 periods; lab, 3 periods.

880:011. Conceptual Physics—4 hrs. Energy; temperature and heat; waves and sound; electricity
and magnetism; light and color; and atomic and nuclear structure of matter. Emphasis on observation, interpretation, and conceptual understanding of physical phenomena. Discussion, 3 periods; lab, 2 periods.

840:181. Investigations in Life Science—4 hrs. Introduction to significant concepts and theories of
life science and a model of effective teaching strategies related to elementary school level. Topics
include diversity and classification, structure, and function from cellular to organism level, human biology, and plant systems. Discussion and/or lab, 5 periods.

870:181. Investigations in Earth Science—4 hrs. Introduction to significant concepts and theories
of Earth science and a model of effective teaching strategies related to elementary school level.
Topics include geologic materials and processes acting on them and fundamentals of Earth history, weather, and astronomy. Discussion and/or lab, 5 periods plus arranged.

820:130(g). Experiences in Elementary School Science—2 hrs. Development of understanding science as an investigative process and how this relates to elementary science teaching. Seminar
discussions and field experiences in applying knowledge of science content and pedagogy to
working with elementary-level students.

210:141(g). Integrated Activities in Elementary School Science and Mathematics—3 hrs. Activity-
based on pedagogical investigation of manipulative materials and activities used in elementary
science and mathematics followed by critical analysis using task analysis and research investigations.

cell structure, function and mechanisms, cellular and organismal reproduction and inheritance, plant systems, and animal systems. The latter two units use organisms that are readily
available to future elementary teachers—Wisconsin Fast Plants and humans—as sample organisms. Several times during the semester, students design their own investigations—sometimes as a class, as in the plant nutrition experiment (Lee 2003), and sometimes in pairs. Investigations in Life Science incorporates learning cycles, mostly at the descriptive
empirical-abductive levels (Lawson, Abraham, and Renner 1989) and ranges from structured

to guided inquiry, with some open inquiry or hypothetical-deductive cycles included (Colburn 2000; Martin-Hanson 2002). While it is initially difficult for IiLS students to adjust to an inquiry approach, the effects of the course sequence and pedagogical approach are obvious by the time the students reach ILS. Students in the second life science course are self-directed in doing lab work. They have positive attitudes, are enthusiastic, and are even risk takers with regard to thinking about scientific ideas.

Description of the Basic Physical Science Courses

Inquiry Into Physical Science (IiPS) comprises four units of study: energy, astronomy, rocks and minerals, and chemical interactions. Each unit takes about four weeks to complete. Students work individually and in small groups. Course materials present concepts through active learning and guided inquiry. Students extend their learning in each unit by designing activities to investigate questions that arise during class activities and discussions. This course is taught regularly by physics educators from the Physics Department, but it has also been taught by faculty from the Chemistry and Earth Science Departments.

Investigations in Physical Science is a second-level physical science course taught by either physics educators or chemistry educators. The course content includes concepts from electricity, magnetism, light, solutions, acids and bases, and states of matter. The content is aligned with the NSES Content Standards. In addition to using typical laboratory equipment and materials from commonly available kit-based science curricula, students get training in using sensing instruments by doing calculator-based laboratory investigations.

Investigations in Earth Science is taught by faculty in the Earth Science Department. The course covers three major units in geology, meteorology, and astronomy. Earth materials, Earth processes, and Earth history are the main topics in geology. Meteorology covers the basic aspects of the atmosphere, the water cycle, and severe weather, incorporating the use of real-time weather data into the curriculum. The astronomy unit focuses on daytime and observational astronomy. As with all other courses in the Basic Science Minor, an inquiry approach is used. Easy-to-obtain, inexpensive materials are used throughout the course, with suggestions on how to modify the investigations for elementary classrooms.

Description of Culminating Methods Courses

The culminating course work merges content and teaching. One course, Integrated Activities in Elementary School Science and Mathematics, applies students' science knowledge and process skills as well as their mathematical knowledge in the selection, design, and teaching of integrated lessons. The other course is a pedagogical content knowledge course that specifically applies educational theories and pedagogy to science concepts (e.g., how students learn about density in relation to their cognitive thinking capabilities). The covert constructivist framework of the entire Basic Science Minor becomes overt in this course. This course also includes experiences with teaching elementary students both on campus and in area schools and visits to community resources such as museums and nature centers.

Course Scheduling

All science courses in the program have double periods (110 minutes) that allow integration of discussion and lab. This facilitates inquiry and learning cycle teaching. The Inquiry Into Life Science and Inquiry Into Physical Science courses have an additional hour of arranged work outside of the regular course schedule, which allows for students to return to the lab to complete investigations on their own.

Research on Program Effectiveness

The Basic Science Minor is an example of a program whose framework is based on inquiry and understanding. It is essential that educators have research-based evidence on the effectiveness of inquiry-based teaching and learning (NRC 2000). While the true evidence comes from the learning that ultimately happens in the classrooms of program graduates, program evaluations provide evidence of the success of the program in producing highly qualified elementary science teachers.

End-of-program and postgraduate evaluations from the 1992–1995 graduates included content and attitude assessment instruments given one month prior to graduation along with student teaching exit interviews. Additionally, teacher survey questionnaires were administered one, two, and three years following graduation. A summary of the results shows the following:

◆ An increase in science content knowledge and use of process skills
◆ An increase in knowledge and use of hands-on science
◆ Large gains in knowledge about and use of a learning cycle teaching approach
◆ Large gains in positive attitudes toward teaching experiential science

Follow-up research in 1996–1997 on program graduates from 1991 through 1995 (Lee and Krapfl 2002) provides information on the long-term effects of the preparation program:

◆ Graduates are well prepared and positive about their preparation in science content and in pedagogy.
◆ The teaching approach used in the Basic Science Minor was very important to graduates as they started to teach.
◆ Graduates were well prepared in the use of an inquiry approach to science.
◆ The inquiry teaching approach was an effective approach to learning college science content—students learned content in the context of the advocated teaching approach.
◆ Graduates were comfortable about teaching science and were well prepared to do so.

Strengths of the minor included (1) modeling of methods by faculty teaching courses in the minor, and (2) consistent and shared philosophy of the importance of inquiry-based teaching and learning by science education faculty teaching courses in the minor.

While the Basic Science Minors were well prepared to teach science, they encountered obstacles similar to those experienced by other teachers in teaching inquiry and learning cycles:

meeting the variety of student needs; time, money, and materials management; and the reality of "wanna-dos" and "gotta-dos" within curricular frameworks and school systems.

Also, former students have not been hesitant to make suggestions for improving the Basic Science Minor. Recent course changes reflect their comments on the need to

- ◆ provide specific classroom management strategies for inquiry science teaching;
- ◆ specifically address various diverse learner needs within the context of experiential science teaching; and
- ◆ incorporate more specifics on the use of technology in teaching elementary science.

Graduates of this program notice the difference between themselves and others who teach elementary science. Many program graduates say that they have a more positive attitude toward teaching science, strength and confidence in their content knowledge, dedication to making time to teach science, and differences in their teaching styles and approaches. The bonus for the Basic Science Minor program is that it produces teachers who are confident as science educators, who continue to be involved in professional development, and who quickly assume leadership positions in their school districts. Some proceed to professional involvement on the state level, and many pursue graduate work.

Summary

The preparation of well-qualified teachers for elementary school science has never been more important. This program provides meaningful undergraduate science education within a constructivist environment, teaching in-depth science through understanding and inquiry-based instruction (Leonard 2000). Teachers are well-rounded with regard to their science backgrounds in life, Earth, and physical science and easily meet the state of Iowa requirements for elementary science specialist endorsement. Experience has shown that Basic Science Minors have no difficulty in acquiring teaching positions.

References

Bybee, R. W, ed. 2002. *Learning science and the science of learning*. Washington, DC: NSTA Press.

Colburn, A. 2000. An inquiry primer. *Science Scope* 23(6): 42–44.

Lawson, A., M. Abraham, and J. Renner. 1989. *A theory of instruction*. Monograph of the National Association of Research in Science Teaching, Number One.

Lee, C. 2003. A learning cycle inquiry into plant nutrition. *American Biology Teacher* 65(2): 136–141.

Lee, C., and L. Krapfl. 2002. Teaching as you would have them teach: An effective elementary science teacher preparation program. *Journal of Science Teacher Education* 13(3): 247–265.

Leonard, W. H. 2000. How do college students best learn science? *Journal of College Science Teaching* 29(6): 385–388.

Martin-Hanson, L. 2002. Defining inquiry. *The Science Teacher* 69(2): 34–37.

National Research Council (NRC). 1996. *National science education standards*. Washington, DC: National Academy Press.

National Research Council (NRC). 2000. *Inquiry and the national science education standards: A guide for teaching and learning*. Washington, DC: National Academy Press.

Facilitating Improvement Through Professional Development:
Teachers Rising to the Occasion

Pradeep M. Dass
Appalachian State University

Emulating the Iowa Chautauqua Model in Collier County, Florida

Promoting the teaching and learning of science in the context of real-life experiences, the Iowa Chautauqua Model serves to enhance K–12 science teaching. Having emerged as an exemplary model of professional development, it was disseminated nationally through the National Diffusion Network (NDN) of the U. S. Department of Education from 1994 through 1997. The dissemination gave rise to several new professional development programs for science teachers. One of these was the Collier Chautauqua Program (CCP) developed in Collier County, Florida. The University of Iowa Science Education Center was instrumental in getting the program going in Collier County, but the key role in organizing the entire professional development program there was played by the Collier County science supervisor.

The Iowa Chautauqua Model (Blunck and Yager 1996) (Figure 1) is substantially different from traditional forms of professional development. It involves teachers in a summer workshop and supports them throughout an entire academic year, expecting from them a commitment to practice in their classrooms the instructional approaches promoted by the program while also evaluating their own effectiveness. These evaluations become the focus of discussions during the academic year, when workshops are held for the purposes of refining and improving instructional approaches, and to match individual teaching situations.

The model promotes constructivist approaches to the teaching and learning of science within the context of real-life experiences, engaging students in science through issues, con-

Figure 1. The Iowa Chautauqua Model

I Chautauqua Leadership Institute
Lead teachers meet to
- Plan summer and academic year workshops
- Enhance instructional strategies and leadership skills
- Refine assessment strategies

II Three-Week Summer Institutes
Three to four lead teachers + university staff + scientists work with teachers in local/regional workshop settings. Teachers are introduced to constructivist instruction in a science-technology-society (STS) context. Teachers
- Participate in activities and field experiences that integrate concepts and principles from all major disciplines of school science
- Make connections between science, technology, and society in the context of real-life experiences
- Use local questions, problems, and issues to provide an organizing context for science instruction
- Create a five-day teaching module

III Five-Day Classroom Teaching Trial
Teachers who were involved in summer institutes teach and assess a five-day module using constructivist principles in an STS context

IV Academic Year Workshop Series
Three to four lead teachers + university staff + scientists work with summer teachers + new teachers

Fall Short Course: 20-Hour Instructional Block
Defining techniques for developing teaching modules and assessing their effectiveness; selecting a tentative topic; practicing specific assessment tools in multiple domains of science.

Interim Project: Three- to Six-Month Interim Project
Developing a constructivist instructional module for a minimum of 20 days of instruction; developing a variety of authentic assessment strategies; administering pretests in multiple domains of science; teaching the module; communicating with regional staff, lead teachers, and central program staff.

Spring Short Course: 20-Hour Instructional Block
Discussing assessment results; analyzing experiences related to teaching the module; planning next steps for expanding constructivist and STS approaches; planning for professional leadership in local reform efforts.

cerns, questions, and problems of current local or personal relevance. This promotes a science-technology-society (STS) approach to the teaching and learning of science, which in turn makes science relevant to the lives of students—the main goal of the Iowa Chautauqua Model. In other words, the central focus of this model is to equip teachers with instructional approaches and strategies that enable them to accomplish the four essential goals of science education presented in the National Science Education Standards (NSES) (NRC 1996, p. 13). In the process, teachers have opportunities to grow professionally in a variety of domains deemed important in the NSES but generally not accomplished through traditional "one-shot" professional development activities.

The Collier County School District: Participants in the Collier Chautauqua Program (CCP)

Collier County Public Schools constitute a large, countywide school district, with 32 schools serving approximately 28,500 students. The district was growing at the rate of one new school every year when the CCP was implemented in 1995. Several schools served large proportions of immigrant students from low economic backgrounds and with limited English proficiency. Schools were involved in site-based management, and each school had been developing its own "school improvement plan."

Teacher contracts in Collier County ran August–June for a total of 196 working days, including four inservice days. Teachers were expected to put in 7.5 hours of work each day. Elementary school teachers worked with one class all day, with approximately 25 students in a class. Middle school teachers had an average of five teaching periods a day, interacting with approximately 140 students during the day. The contract salary for teachers ranged between $27,730 and $44,630 when the CCP was implemented. Many teachers in Collier County took other part-time jobs to make ends meet in this touristy, expensive part of southwest Florida. Many also offered to teach the summer school to supplement their income.

The CCP, directed by the district science coordinator, was the first nonmandatory program of professional development implemented in Collier County. Thus, teachers participated in the program on a voluntary basis. It was also the first comprehensive program in the county involving teachers during the summer as well as an entire academic year. Grades preK–8 were represented by teachers participating in the program during the two academic years of program implementation reported here (1995–1996 and 1996–1997). The names of schools, number of teachers, grade levels, and approximate number of students ultimately impacted through CCP are indicated in Tables 1 and 2.

Table 1. Participant Demography, Year 1

Name of School	# Participating Teachers	Grade Levels Represented	# Students Impacted
Avalon Elementary	6	K–5	120
Big Cypress Elementary	1	Kindergarten	25
Lake Park Elementary	1	5	17
Laurel Oaks Elementary	5	K–5	100
Pine Crest Elementary	1	2	26
Village Oaks Elementary	1	3	40
Vineyard Elementary	1	5	32
Gulf View Middle	1	6–8	100
Manatee Middle	1	7	90
Oak Ridge Middle	4	7–8	400
Pine Ridge Middle	2	6–8	393

Table 2. Participant Demography, Year 2

Name of School	# Participating Teachers	Grade Levels Represented	# Students Impacted
Avalon Elementary	2	PreK–3	50
Big Cypress Elementary	2	4–5	65
Everglades Elementary	1	1	19
Golden Gate Elementary	1	5	35
Golden Terrace Elementary	1	4–5	100
Laurel Oaks Elementary	5	1–5	300
Lely Elementary	1	School Nurse	–
Naples Park Elementary	1	ESOL/LEP	–
Pelican Marsh Elementary	4	PreK–5	75
Pine Crest Elementary	1	1	22
Village Oaks Elementary	3	1–5	150
East Naples Middle	1	7–8	130
Gulf View Middle	2	6–8	200
Immokalee Middle	6	6–8	375
Manatee Middle	7	5–8	425

CCP: Promoting National Science Education Standards *More Emphasis* Conditions

The CCP was born as a result of the dissemination efforts of the Iowa Chautauqua Model by the NDN. The district science supervisor of Collier County Public Schools provided initial planning and primary leadership for the program. Emulating the Iowa Chautauqua Model, the CCP evolved into a districtwide professional development program. Though initially designed for science teachers, it also involved teachers of mathematics, social studies, and language arts. During the first two years of implementation, the program focused only on professional development of elementary and middle grades teachers.

Because of this focus and the involvement of teachers from several disciplines, the CCP fostered an integrative approach to teaching and learning, using the content of science as the primary organizer. Specific activities of the CCP can be summarized as follows:

- ◆ Summer Leadership Institute: A four-day institute for lead teachers and scientists, designed to prepare them for leadership roles for the summer and academic year workshops.
- ◆ Summer Training Institute: A three-week institute for participating teachers to experience new instructional strategies as students.
- ◆ Academic Year Activities:
  - Fall: A three-day workshop during the fall semester to evaluate teaching trials of the modules designed during the summer institute; make further plans and refinements for a 4–8 week instructional module; and develop appropriate assessment schemes.

- Spring: A three-day workshop during the spring semester to look at results of instructional modules, individual teacher actions, and plans for integrating modules into year-long curricula.
- Interim communication: Monthly meetings, electronic communications, and site-based meetings to share information, assess progress, and provide support and encouragement to peers on a continual basis.
- Interim teaching projects: Teaching trials for modules developed during the summer institute and incorporation of new teaching strategies into the entire curriculum.

These activities span one summer and a full academic year, engaging teachers in a series of professional learning experiences. Thus, the program as a whole embodies the "long-term coherent plans" and "variety of professional development activities" listed among the *More Emphasis* conditions of the NSES Professional Development Standards (NRC 1996, p. 72). Specific characteristics of the program exemplify several other *More Emphasis* conditions, as described below.

Nature and Variety of Learning Experiences

During the three-week summer institute, teachers engage in learning experiences that enable them to identify or generate specific issues that could be explored in their science classes. The learning experiences include field trips and audiovisual (or other media) reports of relevant current events. Issues potentially related to students' lives are gleaned from these experiences. After identifying the issues, teachers study the literature and other information and then gather materials needed for treating the issues in their science classes in a science-technology-society (STS) context. The first product of this exploration is a small, issue-based instructional module developed by each participant. In developing these modules, teachers are designing instruction compatible with research on effective teaching, their own teaching goals, and the real-life issues involved.

Throughout the summer institute and all follow-up meetings in the fall and spring semesters, teachers are actively involved in their own learning as they identify current issues, create instructional modules based on the STS approach, develop assessment plans to match their modules, and assess their current teaching practices in light of these approaches. Collectively, the active participation of teachers in these learning experiences exemplifies the following *More Emphasis* conditions: "inquiry into teaching and learning," "learning science through investigation and inquiry," and "integration of science and teaching knowledge" (NRC 1996, p. 72).

From Learning to Teaching: Expectation to Practice

During the early part of the fall semester, the summer institute participants implement the modules in their classes. Since the STS approach to science teaching and learning is presented in a concrete fashion during the institute and teachers personally design each module within the context of their own teaching situations, the use of these modules does not appear to be an extra, add-on activity. Rather, it fits within the context of what they would normally be doing. This increases the chances of their actually practicing what they learned at the institute. The modules and the instructional strategies belong to the teachers, not to a long-gone, phantom consultant.

If the goal is to bring about a change in teacher actions, it is important that teachers practice and apply in their classrooms the lessons they learn during professional development activities (Sparks 1983). When teachers create their own instructional modules, they are empowered to become instructional leaders and facilitators of change. Thus, the *More Emphasis* conditions of "teacher as leader" and "teacher as source and facilitator of change" (NRC 1996, p. 72) are met as a result of participation in the CCP. As teachers use the modules, evaluate their effectiveness, and modify instructional practices in the light of these evaluations, they are acting as "intellectual, reflective practitioners" (rather than mere technicians) and "integrat[ors of] theory and practice in school settings" (NRC 1996, p. 72).

Support of Teacher Learning and Practice

CCP teachers are not left on their own following the summer institute. Mentored by lead teachers from local teams, teachers receive feedback, encouragement, and constructive criticism as they try their first modules. In addition to that ongoing support, teachers participate in a follow-up workshop in the fall and spring, where they are pushed a bit further to take risks in their classrooms. These workshops give teachers the opportunity to share, assess, and reflect on the results of trying the first module. Teachers learn from their peers and are encouraged to continue the effort by refining the first module and designing a second, relatively larger, module whose trial results are discussed during the spring follow-up workshop. Thus, the workshop series not only provides feedback on the first teaching trial; it also encourages participants to continue to practice what they have learned by designing and teaching new modules. Moreover, teachers learn from each other as they share the experiences and results of their practices. This form of feedback and follow-up support contributes to the development of a community of learners. Teachers engage in "collegial and collaborative learning" and participate in this learning as "member[s] of a collegial professional community" (NRC 1996, p. 72).

A Collaborative Approach

To bring about real change, teachers must be involved in long-term learning activities and should have the support of professional learning communities, which include colleagues, administrators, parents, and other community members (Darling-Hammond and McLaughlin 1995; Guskey 1995; Lieberman 1995). As noted above, the CCP recognizes the need for long-term learning and ongoing support by offering a full academic year program. It also promotes regular communication among participants and central staff (the Collier County science supervisor and his administrative assistants) through telephone conferences, meetings, e-mail, and a newsletter. Participants are encouraged to contribute articles for the newsletter highlighting their experiences and accomplishments. Each issue of the newsletter has several first-person accounts of participants' successes and limitations.

By their very nature, the development and implementation of STS instructional modules call for collaboration among teachers, administrators, parents, scientists, business and industry leaders, and other community members. One of the key features of the program is the development of a network of professional learning communities. This is achieved by involving scientists and other community resources in the workshops, inviting administrators and parents to participate in the workshops, and encouraging teachers to develop partnerships with other teachers and community members as they design and teach issue-oriented modules. Such extensive collaboration exemplifies the following *More Emphasis* conditions: "mix of internal and external expertise," "staff developers as facilitators, consultants, and planners," and "teacher as producer of knowledge about teaching" (NRC 1996, p. 72).

Studying the Impact of the CCP

The impact of the CCP on participating teachers and their students was studied by the author of this report during the first two years of program implementation. Data were collected from all participating teachers during both years. During the first year, there were 24 teachers, representing seven elementary and four middle schools (Table 1). During the second year, there were 38 teachers, representing eleven elementary and four middle schools (Table 2). Four of the elementary schools and two of the middle schools represented during the second year were also represented during the first year. All schools involved were public schools. No high schools were involved during the period of this study. Both quantitative and qualitative data were collected. Quantitative data were collected via self-reported responses by teachers on Likert-type scales and triangulated with qualitative data obtained via observations of teachers' presentations during workshops, classroom observations, preformatted teacher journals, and in-depth interviews of the participants.

Instruments and Data Collection
Quantitative Data Collection

Quantitative data were collected by administering the Teacher Enhancement Assessment Instrument (TEAI), which contains items with Likert-type response scales. It was administered as a pretest at the beginning of the summer institute and as a posttest at the end of the spring workshop each year. The TEAI was developed at the University of Iowa Science Education Center for use in evaluating the Iowa Chautauqua Program (ICP). It has been extensively used by Iowa teachers since 1985 to document teacher enhancement as a result of participation in the ICP. The validity of the TEAI was established through review and judgment of (1) 6 teacher panels from each of the schools participating in the ICP, (2) a 12-member panel from the University of Iowa Science Education Center, and (3) a total of 30 Iowa lead teachers participating in the ICP leadership training institutes. For checking the reliability of the TEAI, a test/retest procedure, with a one-week interval between tests, was employed with 30 participating teachers each year from 1985 to 1990. Reliability ranges of 0.88 to 0.92 were attained during this five-year period (Blunck 1993; Liu 1992).

Qualitative Data Collection

Qualitative data was collected through the following means:

- In-depth interviews in focus groups, organized as school teams during the fall workshops. All interviews were recorded on audiotape.
- Observations made during the summer institute and academic year workshops, as well as within the classrooms of participating teachers. The majority of classroom observations were conducted by the district science coordinator. Data from all interviews and observations was transcribed soon after the events, on the same day in most cases.
- Preformatted teacher journals, collected at the end of the fall and spring workshops. The journals focused on the following three questions: (1) In what ways has your teaching changed as a result of your participation in the Chautauqua program? (2) How have these changes in your teaching affected your students? (3) What value has this workshop (fall/spring) had in your growth as a teacher?

Data Analyses

Quantitative Data Analysis

Selected items from the TEAI were grouped to document teacher enhancement in the following six domains of professional development.

1. Leadership Qualities
2. Use of Constructivist Instructional Approaches
3. Attitudes Toward Teaching
4. Confidence to Teach Science
5. Collaboration Efforts
6. Integration of Technology in Science Instruction

The items representing these domains represent a desirable state of affairs. Therefore, responses to all items were scored according to the following scale: *never* = 0.00; *rarely* = 1.00; *sometimes* = 2.00; *frequently* = 3.00; *almost always* = 4.00. Pre- and posttest scores were then analyzed in aggregated data sets, each set representing one of the domains of professional development identified above. Analysis of variance (ANOVA) with repeated measures was used to determine significant changes between pretest and posttest scores, thus documenting teacher enhancement in specific domains.

Scores from Year 1 and Year 2 were analyzed separately, using the statistical procedures mentioned above, to document teacher enhancement during each of the two years separately. The results of Year 1 and Year 2 were then compared with each other to check similarities and differences in areas of enhancement between Year 1 and Year 2. One-way ANOVA, using grade-level groups (preK–2, 3–5, and 6–8) as factors, was conducted on Year 2 data to examine the effect of grade level on teacher enhancement. This was done in order to investigate whether or not program activities were equally effective in enhancing teachers at all grade levels (preK–8) represented by the participants. Similar analysis was not conducted for Year 1 data due to relatively small N.

Qualitative Data Analysis

Qualitative data were collected in order to provide triangulation with the quantitative data. The validity and reliability of qualitative data were examined using a cross-checking procedure employed by Reuss-Ianni (1983). Validity was examined through cross-checks of data from different sources. For instance, data from teacher interviews were cross-checked with data from workshop observations and classroom observation. Reliability checks regarding the accuracy of data were made by cross-checking different forms of data from the same participant (e.g., his or her interview and journal).

Preliminary analyses of all data were conducted during the period of data collection using the constant comparative method in order to refine interview protocols and observation foci continually, so that relevant information might be gathered. This examination during the early part of data collection helped revise interview questions, resulting in questions that were better suited to elicit information directly related to program effectiveness.

Formal data analysis was conducted after all data had been collected. The six teacher-enhancement domains used in quantitative data analysis were used as category codes to sort qualitative data contained in the transcripts. Information resulting from this analysis was used for triangulation with the quantitative data.

The findings reported below incorporate information generated from both quantitative and qualitative data analyses. The data provided information concerning a majority of the participants but not the entire group. There was less than 100% attendance during the first year's fall and spring workshops, resulting in some missing posttest quantitative data, interview data, and journal data for those who were absent during one or both workshops. In statistical analyses of quantitative data, only those cases that included data for both pretest and posttest were used. The N in quantitative data results, therefore, is always less than the actual number of teachers enrolled in the program for each of the two years. Further, in the ANOVA tables, different items indicate different Ns because in some cases participants did not respond to particular items, or they mentioned that the item was not applicable to their specific situations; therefore, no response was chosen. Nonapplicability of test items was more common in the case of individuals whose academic responsibilities changed between pretest and posttest. The computer software SYSTAT 5.2, used for statistical analyses of quantitative data, uses only those cases for ANOVA that have a response score for a particular item in both pretest and posttest. The ANOVA results are considered significant at $p \leq 0.10$ in this study. This relatively higher p-value is used in order to decrease ß, which in turn increases the "power of the test" (Hinkle, Wiersma, and Jurs 1994).

The analyses of quantitative and qualitative data collectively revealed that participants in the CCP achieved significant enhancement in the following six domains of professional practice: leadership qualities; use of constructivist instructional approaches; attitudes toward teaching; confidence in teaching science; collaboration efforts; and integration of technology in science instruction. These results illustrate how the visions for instructional change advocated by the National Science Education Standards (NRC 1996) can be, and are being, attained through the professional development of teachers.

Teacher Enhancement and Instructional Change: Accomplishments of CCP Participants

The following sections present descriptions of teacher enhancement in each of the six domains of professional practice identified in the preceding paragraph.

Leadership Qualities

Ten items on the Teacher Enhancement Assessment Instrument (TEAI) relate to leadership qualities within the context of instructional strategies in evidence, particularly in science teaching. There are other aspects of leadership in the teaching profession, however, that were reflected in some of the qualitative data.

The ANOVA indicated significant increases during both years in areas such as participation in professional workshops, keeping up with professional literature, and the ability to design one's own instructional activities. Participants designed teaching modules during the summer institute and then expanded them or created new ones during the fall semester. These efforts helped teachers become more confident in creating their own teaching activities. The increases indicate that participation in the CCP helped teachers become more professional in their work. Regarding the effect of grade level on enhancement of leadership qualities, significant differences were noted in items related to the use of more authentic assessment techniques and the use of controversial subjects in science classes. Qualitative data indicate that authentic assessment techniques were used more by teachers of the elementary grade levels than by teachers of the middle grade levels. This is perhaps because elementary teachers are less constrained by the obligation of preparing students for standardized external exams. In dealing with controversial subjects in science classes, greater enhancement was observed in middle school teachers than in elementary school teachers. The ANOVA results are summarized in Table 3.

Qualitative data provided other examples of growth in leadership qualities. These include the ability of participating teachers to present their work at professional conferences, such as the Florida Association of Science Teachers convention, and to serve as mentors in their own schools, sharing with their colleagues the new ideas and techniques they have learned and are applying in their classrooms. As reflected in their journal entries, participants have recognized specific ways in which their leadership skills have improved, such as the ability to coordinate teams working on specific tasks. This ability led participants to develop new assessment instruments, write grants, and plan future workshops and school-improvement action plans. The most obvious development of leadership was demonstrated by the formation of an assessment team and grade-level coordinator teams to plan, design, and assess future implementation of the CCP. The progress made by members of these two teams toward achieving their goals between the fall and spring workshops during Year 1 provided clear evidence of their growth as leaders. Many started taking on leadership roles in special projects such as science fairs and field trips.

Table 3. Leadership Qualities, Repeated Measures ANOVA Results[a]

Item	N	Mean Score		Variance Within All Subjects		Variance Between Grade-Level Groups	
		Pre	Post	F	p	F	p
I feel comfortable involving students with an issue about which I feel a lack of knowledge.	17	2.65	3.00	01.55	0.23	0.44	0.65
	28	2.64	3.14	05.11	0.03*		
I allow my students to investigate problems and questions that arise unexpectedly.	18	3.11	3.33	01.15	0.29	0.43	0.66
	28	2.82	3.50	14.44	0.00*		
I use self-evaluation to improve my teaching (videotaping, audiotaping, and peer evaluations).	18	1.72	1.67	00.06	0.81	2.39	0.11
	28	2.11	2.43	01.69	0.20		
I find myself using more authentic assessment techniques.	18	2.61	2.83	02.13	0.16	5.53	0.01*
	25	2.68	3.12	03.85	0.06*		
I deal with controversial subjects in science class.	17	1.71	1.94	00.65	0.43	4.90	0.02*
	26	1.77	2.69	19.89	0.00*		
I read professional journals.	18	1.94	2.44	04.64	0.05*	0.71	0.50
	28	2.43	2.93	09.00	0.01*		
I investigate questions or answers that arise unexpectedly.	18	2.83	3.06	01.36	0.26	1.14	0.34
	28	2.50	3.29	20.55	0.00*		
I am comfortable when students ask questions that I cannot answer.	18	3.22	3.28	00.11	0.75	0.29	0.75
	28	3.07	3.46	05.64	0.03*		
I take part in workshops that will help me teach science better.	18	2.78	3.28	06.12	0.02*	2.14	0.14
	27	2.85	3.37	12.80	0.00*		
I am comfortable having to create my own teaching activities.	18	3.06	3.61	14.66	0.00*	0.19	0.83
	28	3.18	3.57	05.15	0.03*		

[a]The upper data line for each item represents Year 1 and the lower line Year 2.

* significant at $p \leq 0.10$

Thus, the "teacher as leader" condition of the *More Emphasis* Professional Development Standards (NRC 1996, p. 72) was directly accomplished through the CCP.

Use of Constructivist Instructional Approaches
The TEAI contains 16 items that relate to constructivist principles of teaching and learning. The ANOVA indicated highest increases in the mean score on the Year 1 posttest for items pertaining to active involvement of students in the learning process—through determining which activities or investigations to undertake, applying concepts to new situations, and having the opportunity to explain their thinking and ideas. Significant increases were also noted for items related to students generating their own questions, designing their own experiments, studying real-life problems and issues, and working in cooperative groups. For Year 2, all items indicated significant increase in mean scores on the posttest, except for one item related to the use of re-

Table 4. Use of Constructivist Approaches, Repeated Measures ANOVA Results[a]

Item	N	Mean Score		Variance Within All Subjects		Variance Between Grade-Level Groups	
		Pre	Post	F	p	F	p
My students design experiments to test their own questions.	17	1.82	2.29	09.66	0.01*	2.86	0.08
	26	1.42	2.65	40.00	0.00*		
Students are allowed or expected to express their own ideas and opinions.	18	3.67	3.67	00.00	1.00	0.30	0.74
	28	3.43	3.82	13.44	0.00*		
I encourage students to collect and judge information.	18	2.94	3.11	01.00	0.33	0.75	0.49
	26	2.58	3.39	26.44	0.00*		
Students generate the questions in my classroom.	18	2.67	3.17	11.77	0.00*	0.26	0.78
	28	2.64	3.36	16.27	0.00*		
Cooperative work on problems and issues is part of my science class.	17	3.06	3.53	05.89	0.03*	0.83	0.45
	26	2.77	3.54	17.01	0.00*		
My students identify and use resources other than the textbook.	17	3.17	3.59	02.86	0.11	1.07	0.36
	28	3.50	3.64	00.44	0.52		
My students determine which activities or investigations will be part of their science.	17	1.77	2.71	22.02	0.00*	2.34	0.12
	27	1.78	2.70	21.61	0.00*		
My students are challenged to apply concepts to new situations.	18	2.61	3.28	17.00	0.00*	2.61	0.09*
	27	2.63	3.22	14.92	0.00*		
Process skills are naturally incorporated into the student's investigations.	18	3.28	3.28	00.00	1.00	11.72	0.00*
	26	2.92	3.42	09.85	0.00*		
A variety of teaching styles/strategies are utilized in my science teaching.	17	3.35	3.53	01.90	0.19	1.84	0.18
	27	3.22	3.67	09.46	0.01*		
My students are given the opportunity to explain their thinking and ideas.	18	3.22	3.67	13.60	0.00*	0.76	0.48
	28	3.18	3.75	10.80	0.00*		
I expect my students to have their own ideas and opinions.	18	3.39	3.72	04.25	0.06*	0.59	0.56
	28	3.39	3.82	10.80	0.00*		
I expect students to plan solutions to problems.	18	2.78	2.94	01.00	0.33	0.63	0.54
	28	2.86	3.32	07.77	0.01*		
I help students test their own ideas.	18	2.61	3.06	07.16	0.02*	2.13	0.14
	27	2.63	3.15	06.14	0.02*		
My students compare ideas with one another.	18	2.83	3.11	02.46	0.14	0.57	0.57
	28	2.86	3.43	14.64	0.00*		
I help students find problems and issues in real life to study.	17	2.29	2.71	03.81	0.07*	4.05	0.03*
	28	2.39	3.18	18.88	0.00*		

[a] The upper data line for each item represents Year 1 and the lower line Year 2.
* significant at $p \leq 0.10$

sources other than the textbook. Highest increases for Year 2 were also noted for items directly related to more active involvement of students in the learning process.

Regarding the effect of grade levels on increase in the use of various constructivist approaches, significant differences were found only for certain items related to student initiative and active involvement in the learning process, such as designing their own experiments. Grade-level differences in these items may be attributed to a difference in the degree to which students are able to take such initiative at various age levels. These results indicate that most participants improved in their ability to use certain constructivist teaching approaches, which in turn are shown to improve student learning. The ANOVA results are summarized in Table 4.

In the reports on teaching the second module, during the spring workshop, participants demonstrated a much improved understanding of constructivist principles. Compared to their first modules, the second modules showed increased use of several constructivist strategies. For instance, the second modules focused more on topics drawn from real-life situations rather than on the traditional curricular topics. This, in turn, led to more student-generated questions and student-designed investigations. In helping teachers to learn to use constructivist approaches more efficiently in science instruction, the program accomplished the following *More Emphasis* conditions: "integration of science and teaching knowledge," "learning science through investigation and inquiry," and "integration of theory and practice in school settings" (NRC 1996, p. 72).

Attitudes Toward Teaching

A total of 14 items on the TEAI may reflect teacher attitudes about teaching in general and about teaching science in particular. The results of ANOVA indicate significant increases in mean scores for the Year 1 posttest on 9 of the 14 items. Highest increases were noted for items that indicate teacher attitudes about the real-life relevance of the science they teach. Year 2 scores indicate significant increases on the posttest for 10 of the 14 items, with highest increases noted for items related to attitudes regarding the creative aspect in science processes and to relevance of science outside the school. Thus, for the most part, it can be concluded that participation in the CCP had a positive effect on teacher attitudes toward teaching in general and toward teaching science in particular. Significant grade-level differences were noted for several items related to encouraging students to use science concepts and principles in taking actions and developing career awareness. This was certainly accomplished more by the upper elementary and middle grade teachers than the lower elementary teachers. ANOVA results are summarized in Table 5.

The general tone in the interview and journal data indicates a definite improvement in participants' attitude toward teaching and learning as a result of participation in the CCP and subsequent use of the STS approaches. Indeed, of the six domains described here, greatest improvement was noted in the attitude domain. The elementary teachers particularly demonstrated renewed enthusiasm for teaching in general and science teaching in particular. They expressed excitement as they shared the results of their teaching trials using the STS approach. Their renewed enthusiasm and excitement is best captured in one teacher's comment: "I know I will never go back to my old way of doing things."

Table 5. Attitudes Toward Teaching, Repeated Measures ANOVA Results[a]

Item	N	Mean Score Pre	Mean Score Post	Variance Within All Subjects F	Variance Within All Subjects p	Variance Between Grade-Level Groups F	Variance Between Grade-Level Groups p
I enjoy teaching science.	18	3.33	3.50	00.81	0.38	0.60	0.56
	27	3.44	3.78	05.57	0.03*		
I use self-evaluation to improve my teaching (videotaping, audio-taping, and peer evaluations).	18	1.67	1.67	00.00	1.00	3.06	0.07*
	27	2.11	2.48	02.28	0.14		
As a teacher, I learn along with my students.	18	3.56	3.83	06.54	0.02*	1.12	0.34
	27	3.52	3.89	09.35	0.01*		
Career awareness and exploration are integral parts of student learning.	17	2.82	3.00	00.46	0.51	10.86	0.00*
	27	2.74	3.26	04.22	0.05*		
As a science teacher, I want my students to take action on the issues they investigate.	17	2.71	3.24	12.23	0.00*	2.80	0.08*
	25	2.80	3.36	11.64	0.00*		
I value creativity as part of the science process.	18	3.28	3.78	17.00	0.00*	1.28	0.30
	27	3.30	3.78	12.77	0.00*		
I connect science to other areas of the curriculum (e.g., math, social studies).	17	3.35	3.82	05.89	0.03*	0.58	0.57
	27	3.41	3.67	03.58	0.07*		
Relevance is a prime concern for me in my science teaching.	18	3.17	3.72	07.59	0.01*	2.18	0.14
	27	3.30	3.56	01.34	0.26		
The application of science concepts and principles is of ultimate importance to me.	18	2.89	3.11	00.72	0.41	7.14	0.00*
	26	2.73	3.39	09.97	0.00*		
I see a need to affect change in others and myself.	17	3.06	3.41	03.43	0.08*	0.75	0.49
	28	3.14	3.25	00.52	0.48		
I prefer to teach science over any other subject.	16	2.69	3.00	06.82	0.02*	0.14	0.87
	27	2.26	2.78	04.87	0.04*		
I am comfortable focusing on activities without necessarily reaching an answer.	18	2.72	2.83	00.27	0.61	0.41	0.67
	28	2.14	2.93	24.94	0.00*		
I like it when students disagree.	18	2.94	3.28	03.40	0.08*	1.88	0.17
	28	2.79	2.75	00.06	0.80		
I expect students to use what they learn in science class outside of school.	17	3.18	3.53	03.43	0.08*	0.83	0.45
	27	3.04	3.67	15.21	0.00*		

[a] The upper data line for each item represents Year 1 and the lower line Year 2.
* significant at $p \leq 0.10$

By improving the attitude of participants, the CCP contributed toward making these teachers more "intellectual, reflective practitioners" and a "source and facilitator of change" (NRC 1969, p. 72).

Confidence in Teaching Science

The TEAI contains 10 items that relate to teacher confidence in teaching science. The ANOVA results for Year 1 indicate significant increases in mean posttest scores for only two items, which relate to teacher confidence about science content and the ability to design one's own teaching activities. Year 2 results indicate significant increases in mean posttest scores for all but two items. These two items relate to the adequacy of teachers' background in science and to teachers' confidence in coming up with explanations for a phenomenon without having done so before. Highest increases were noted for items related to integration of science disciplines, dealing with controversial subjects in science class, and helping students find real-life problems and issues to study. In terms of grade-level effect, two items showed significant differences. Both of them indicated lower scores for elementary school teachers than for middle school teachers. These items relate to adequacy of teachers' background in science and in dealing with controversial subjects in science class. ANOVA results are summarized in Table 6.

Table 6. Teaching Confidence, Repeated Measures ANOVA Results[a]

		Mean Score		Variance Within All Subjects		Variance Between Grade-Level Groups	
Item	N	Pre	Post	F	p	F	p
I am comfortable not using the textbook.	18	3.44	3.39	00.06	0.81	0.70	0.51
	28	3.21	3.71	11.12	0.00*		
I feel my background in science is adequate.	17	2.47	2.71	01.66	0.22	4.96	0.02*
	26	2.35	2.62	01.74	0.20		
I am comfortable dealing with several expert opinions that conflict with each other.	18	2.89	3.00	00.32	0.58	0.51	0.61
	27	2.37	2.85	09.72	0.00*		
In my teaching, science concepts and principles are evident.	18	2.89	3.39	09.00	0.01*		
	26	2.92	3.39	08.41	0.01*		
I try to integrate chemistry, physics, biology, and Earth science whenever it is possible.	18	2.78	2.72	00.04	0.84	2.39	0.12
	24	2.04	2.88	25.00	0.00*		
I deal with controversial subjects in science class.	18	1.72	1.83	00.14	0.72	5.43	0.01*
	27	1.82	2.63	23.22	0.00*		
I try to have my students visualize science as occuring everywhere.	17	3.24	3.47	00.79	0.39	1.69	0.21
	28	3.07	3.57	09.95	0.00*		
I help students find problems and issues in real life to study.	18	2.22	2.56	01.70	0.21	2.17	0.14
	28	2.39	3.29	26.58	0.00*		
I am comfortable having to create my own teaching activities.	18	3.06	3.61	14.66	0.00*	0.30	0.74
	28	3.18	3.57	06.25	0.02*		
I am comfortable having to come up with explanations for a phenomenon without having done so before.	17	2.47	2.71	01.36	0.26	0.29	0.75
	27	2.30	2.67	02.65	0.12*		

[a] The upper data line for each item represents Year 1 and the lower line Year 2.

* significant at $p \leq 0.10$

Increased confidence was also reflected by several elementary teachers who mentioned that they spent more time doing science in their classes than they did before participating in the CCP. Many of these teachers have been instrumental in including specific science-related goals in their school improvement plans. This increased confidence has also further enhanced their leadership potential, in addition to making them more capable of producing knowledge about teaching—both *More Emphasis* conditions (NRC 1996, p. 72).

Collaboration Efforts

Nine items on the TEAI relate to teachers' efforts to collaborate. These items cover areas of collaboration among teachers, between teachers and administrators, between teachers and parents, and between teachers and other community members used as resources in classrooms.

The ANOVA results for Year 1 indicate significant increases in mean scores on posttest for two items. These pertain to teachers communicating with each other about their science teaching, and teachers seeking the support of their administrators for trying out new things in their classes. Significant increases on these two items indicate that the CCP has fostered greater communication among teachers and between teachers and administrators. Year 2 results indicate a significant increase in mean posttest scores for all but two items. These two items relate to collaboration among teachers for improving science programs and the involvement of parents in school science programs. The fact that CCP teachers did not indicate a significant increase in parental involvement may be due to the fact that a majority of the parents in Collier County are immigrant, blue-collar workers or laborers who, much as they might want to, do not have time to participate in their children's education. In addition, many have had little education themselves, particularly in the sciences.

Highest increases were noted for items related to collaboration with administrators, scientists, and other teachers. Grade-level effects in the domain of collaboration indicate significant differences for items related to the involvement of scientists, communication with other teachers, and involvement of administrators. Higher increases in these aspects of collaboration were noted for elementary teachers. ANOVA results are presented in Table 7.

Specific examples of collaborative efforts by participants were found in their journal data and in reports of the teaching trials of their instructional modules. For instance, many teachers from the same grade-level teams within the same school commented positively about working together in planning instructional modules, as well as in working together on school improvement plans.

However, the interview data revealed problems with both communication and collaboration between CCP teachers and non-CCP teachers within the same schools. This may explain why the first item in Table 7 did not show significant increase during either Year 1 or Year 2. Program participants reported involving more community resources in their teaching activities than they had done formerly. For example, students in one teacher's class made phone calls to resource people and contacted local area physicians during the module; another class developed a partnership with the Nature Conservancy to grow a garden of native medicinal plants. Overall, the CCP fostered a spirit of collaboration in participants. Their efforts to enhance instructional activities through collaboration increased as a result of participation in the program. The

Table 7. Efforts to Collaborate, Repeated Measures ANOVA Results[a]

Item	N	Mean Score		Variance Within All Subjects		Variance Between Grade-Level Groups	
		Pre	Post	F	p	F	p
I feel comfortable working with other teachers to improve my science program.	18	3.50	3.61	00.49	0.50	1.14	0.34
	27	3.48	3.63	02.08	0.16		
Parents are actively involved in my science program.	16	1.69	1.94	01.36	0.26	1.64	0.21
	27	1.78	1.96	00.60	0.45		
I work with other teachers on classroom projects.	18	2.33	2.39	00.06	0.82	1.06	0.36
	28	2.21	2.71	04.20	0.05*		
I involve administrators in my science program.	17	1.65	2.06	02.86	0.11	0.55	0.59
	27	1.44	2.11	12.00	0.00*		
Resource people are a valuable asset to my science program.	17	2.35	2.65	02.04	0.17	1.55	0.23
	27	2.00	2.82	13.68	0.00*		
I use scientists from colleges/ universities and/or business/ community as resources in my science teaching.	17	1.65	1.82	00.35	0.57	3.00	0.07*
	27	1.30	2.04	15.29	0.00*		
I am comfortable involving community leaders/members in my science teaching.	17	2.59	2.59	00.00	1.00	1.90	0.17
	27	2.44	3.04	09.30	0.01*		
I enjoy discussing science topics and science teaching with other teachers.	18	3.00	3.33	04.25	0.06*	3.76	0.04*
	28	2.79	3.57	31.72	0.00*		
I involve administrators when I need support for trying something new in my classroom.	18	2.11	2.67	03.86	0.07*	5.22	0.01*
	28	2.21	2.75	09.45	0.01*		

[a] The upper data line for each item represents Year 1 and the lower line Year 2.

* significant at $p \leq 0.10$

increase in efforts and in the ability to collaborate enabled these teachers to start working "as a member of a collegial professional community" rather than "an individual based in a classroom"(NRC 1996, p. 72).

Integration of Technology in Science Instruction

Nine items on the TEAI relate to the integration of technology in instructional activities. Of these, two are concerned with technological issues such as organizing topics for science teaching units, and the other seven relate to direct use of technology as an aid in instructional activities. The ANOVA results for Year 1 indicate significant increases in mean scores on posttests for four items, with highest increases noted for items pertaining to the use of computers by students in gathering and reporting information and to the use of technologies other than those listed in the survey instrument. Year 2 results indicate significant increases in mean posttest scores for all but two items, with highest increase noted for items related to the use of computers and CD-ROMs. Thus, the CCP helped teachers become more comfortable in integrating computer technology in instruction. However, increase in the use of specific technologies, as indicated by scores on individual items, depends on the availability of or access to the particular technology in the school building. Grade-level effects showed significant differences for two items. One of these pertains to the use of computers for gathering, manipulating, and reporting data. This was incorporated more in the upper elementary and middle-level grades than in lower elementary grades. The other item relates to the use of current technological issues as a focus for science instruction. In this case, a higher increase was noted for middle school teachers. The ANOVA results are summarized in Table 8.

Data from teacher journals and presentations about the teaching trials of their instructional modules revealed more specific examples of the integration of technology by participating teachers. These examples include use of the video camera, use of "still" video shots, use of e-mail lists

Table 8. Integration of Technology, Repeated Measures ANOVA Results[a]

Item	N	Mean Score		Variance Within All Subjects		Variance Between Grade-Level Groups	
		Pre	Post	F	p	F	p
My students use the computer to gather, manipulate, and report data/information.	16	2.06	2.69	05.95	0.03*	4.39	0.02*
	27	1.89	2.82	37.97	0.00*		
My students use computer networks.	14	1.79	2.29	01.05	0.33	2.20	0.13
	28	1.68	2.71	07.73	0.01*		
My students use a variety of commercial computer programs.	15	2.80	3.20	01.22	0.29	2.35	0.12
	28	2.50	3.14	08.58	0.01*		
My students use the video camera in scientific investigations.	16	1.25	1.25	00.00	1.00	1.93	0.17
	27	0.56	1.04	07.16	0.01*		
My students use the CD-ROM.	16	1.63	2.69	08.76	0.01*	0.34	0.71
	27	2.11	2.82	10.99	0.00*		
My students use the laserdisc in their investigations.	16	0.88	1.19	00.85	0.37	0.04	0.96
	26	0.77	1.19	02.75	0.11		
My students experiment with technologies beyond those listed above.	17	1.06	1.82	10.56	0.01*	1.12	0.35
	24	0.96	1.75	06.18	0.02*		
My students are encouraged to see connections between technology and its role in the future.	17	2.88	3.35	04.23	0.06*	1.37	0.27
	27	2.89	3.07	00.80	0.38		
I identify current technological issues and use them as a focus for my science teaching.	17	1.88	1.94	00.19	0.67	5.70	0.01*
	27	1.78	2.41	07.67	0.01*		

[a] The upper data line for each item represents Year 1 and the lower line Year 2.

* significant at $p \leq 0.10$

such as Listserv, use of a variety of software such as Hyperstudio and PowerPoint, use of interactive laserdiscs, and development of multimedia presentations. In many of these cases, technology was actually used by students as part of their academic work, which is certainly more desirable than if only the teacher uses or demonstrates the technology. For instance, in one upper elementary class, students created a video journal of their work rather than the usual book-type journal. This video journal was shown weekly on the school video network. In general, the CCP participants started integrating technological resources in their instruction more than they had done formerly.

The NSES at Work in CCP Classrooms

The six domains of professional development identified in this study were derived from the directions provided by the National Science Education Standards. The specific features of the CCP, as described earlier, and teacher enhancement resulting from participation in this program, collectively indicate that all of the *More Emphasis* conditions of the Professional Development Standards were fulfilled in Collier County Public Schools. It follows that the fulfillment of these conditions ought to result in fulfillment of the *More Emphasis* conditions of the Science Teaching Standards. In other words, professional development based on the NSES should result in change in teaching practices that are themselves congruent with the NSES.

Both quantitative and qualitative data gathered over the two-year period of CCP implementation collectively provide evidence that instructional practices of participating teachers have changed. As they developed instructional leadership skills, the teachers became more comfortable and confident in the use of constructivist approaches, in the integration of technology, and in collaboration with their colleagues and resource persons in the local community. The use of the STS approach to science teaching and learning, through participation in the CCP, has enabled these teachers to improve science learning experiences for their students in specific ways that match the *More Emphasis* conditions of the National Science Education Standards.

Acknowledgments

The author expresses sincere gratitude to the participants of the Collier Chautauqua Program (CCP) for cooperating in the data collection process and providing all the data reported here; to Mr. John Egana, Collier County science supervisor during the period of CCP implementation, for allowing access to the teachers and their classrooms; and to Dr. R. E. Yager for guidance in the implementation of the Iowa Chautauqua Model in Collier County and in the analyses of the data reported here.

References

Blunck, S. M. 1993. Evaluating the effectiveness of the Iowa Chautauqua Inservice Program: Changing the reculturing practices of teachers. Doctoral diss., University of Iowa.

Blunck, S. M., and R. E. Yager. 1996. The Iowa Chautauqua Program: A proven in-service model for introducing STS in K-12 classrooms. In *Science/Technology/Society as reform in science education,* ed. R. E. Yager, pp. 298–305. Albany, NY: State University of New York Press.

Darling-Hammond, L., and M. W. Laughlin. 1995. Policies that support professional development in an era of reform. *Phi Delta Kappan* 76: 597–604.

Guskey, T. R. 1995. Professional development in education: In search of the optimal mix. In *Professional development in education: New paradigms and practices*, eds. T. R. Guskey and H. Huberman, pp. 114–131. New York: Teachers College Press.

Hinkle, D. E., W. Wiersma, and S. G. Jurs. 1994. *Applied statistics for the behavioral sciences*. 3rd ed. Boston, Toronto: Houghton Mifflin.

Lieberman, A. 1995. Practices that support teacher development: Transforming conceptions of professional learning. *Phi Delta Kappan* 76: 591–596.

Liu, C. 1992. Evaluating the effectiveness of an inservice teacher education program: The Iowa Chautauqua Program. Doctoral diss., University of Iowa.

National Research Council (NRC). 1996. *National science education standards*. Washington, DC: National Academy Press.

National Science Teachers Association (NSTA). 1999. The NSTA position statement on science/technology/ society (STS). In *National Science Teachers Association Handbook, 2004–2005* (pp. 238–240). Washington, DC: National Science Teachers Association.

Reuss-Ianni, E. 1983. *Two cultures of policing*. London, UK: Transaction Publishing.

Sparks, G. M. 1983. Synthesis of research on staff development for effective teaching. *Educational Leadership* 41: 65–72.

The Contextual Teaching and Learning Instructional Approach

Shawn M. Glynn and Thomas R. Koballa, Jr.
University of Georgia

Setting

At the University of Georgia (UGA), we are making significant, innovative changes in preparing science teachers for the classroom. For almost 10 years now, the National Science Education Standards (NRC 1996) have provided us with a vision for science education reform in the areas of teaching, professional development, assessment, and content. The Standards have helped us to prepare professionals who can plan lessons, teach effectively, assess validity, and refine knowledge and skills continually. In particular, the *Changing Emphases* conditions of the Standards have provided guidance in how we can foster real learning and a spirit of inquiry in our preservice teachers. We have implemented these conditions by placing less emphasis on what teachers and programs have traditionally done and more emphasis on what should be done to promote excellence. Our practices, which are easily adaptable to other teacher preparation programs, are based on a contextual teaching and learning (CTL) approach (Johnson 2002; Sears and Hersh 2000). This approach emphasizes using concepts and process skills in real-world contexts that are relevant to students from diverse backgrounds.

Public school populations in Georgia are, for the most part, quite diverse. African Americans, Hispanics, Native Americans, and other minorities constitute almost 40% of the state's student population. A language other than English is spoken in about 10% of the students' homes, and about 43% of the students come from homes with incomes low enough to qualify them for federal programs.

Within the state, a major responsibility for teacher education is assumed by UGA. More teachers graduate from UGA than from any other institution in the state. At UGA, the science education faculty prepares undergraduates to teach science at the elementary, middle, and secondary school levels in urban, suburban, and rural settings throughout the state. Guided by the Standards, the faculty endeavors to provide future science teachers with the knowledge and skills they will need to foster real learning in diverse and challenging school environments. By "real" learning, we mean learning in authentic contexts that are relevant to future careers in which science knowledge and skills will be employed.

Meeting the *More Emphasis* Conditions of the National Science Education Standards

At UGA, the Standards play a fundamentally important role in teacher preparation because they serve as a guide for our preservice teachers throughout their careers. Our preservice teachers internalize the Standards and use them to engage their students in inquiries that are relevant to a scientifically literate society. Specifically, our program prepares science teachers who will help their own students achieve the following goals (NRC 1996, p. 13):

Experience the richness and excitement of knowing about and understanding the natural world. This goal is particularly relevant to the *More Emphasis* conditions our program has met, such as helping students to understand scientific concepts and guiding them in extended scientific inquiries.

Use appropriate scientific processes and principles in making personal decisions. This goal is relevant to the *More Emphasis* conditions our program has met, such as responding to individual students' interests, abilities, and experiences—while also considering the personal, social, and historical aspects of science.

Engage intelligently in public discourse and debate about matters of scientific and technological concern. This goal pertains to the *More Emphasis* conditions we have met, such as providing students with opportunities to discuss and debate issues that bear directly on quality of life.

Increase their economic productivity through the use of the knowledge, understanding, and skills of the scientifically literate person in their careers. This goal corresponds to the *More Emphasis* conditions we have met, such as helping students to integrate fundamental science concepts and use them for inquiry.

Teacher Educators, Preservice Teachers, and the Science Teacher Education Program

As professors, we have each been preparing science teachers at all levels for more than 20 years. We recognize that society is constantly changing and, consequently, so is the nature of teaching and learning. We must change too, if we wish to prepare teachers successfully. Accordingly, in 2000, we adopted new goals for teacher preparation, together with strategies for achieving these goals. We welcomed the vision of science education reform that the Standards offered us, we made the Standards' goals our own, and we have relied heavily upon the *More Emphasis* conditions for personal guidance in our work with preservice teachers.

Our preservice teachers are, for the most part, recent high school graduates who are earning a bachelor of science degree for the elementary (K–4), middle (5–8), or secondary school (7–12) levels. Our preservice teachers also include older students who already have an undergraduate degree in a science area and who wish to qualify for science teacher certification; some of these students are in an alternative certification program, teaching full-time on a provisional certificate.

How the Science Teacher Education Program Supports the *More Emphasis* Conditions

UGA, with the support of the U. S. Department of Education, began in 1998 to design a model program for the preparation of science teachers. In its present form, the Science Teacher Education Program reflects the significant influences of the Standards, the book *College Pathways to the Science Education Standards* (Siebert and McIntosh 2001), and the CTL approach (Johnston 2002). CTL is based on situated cognition research (Cobb and Bowers 1999), which has found that constructivist processes such as critical thinking, inquiry learning, and problem solving should be situated in relevant physical, intellectual, and social contexts (Driver et al. 1994; Glynn and Duit 1995).

CTL helps prepare students for learning in the complex environments they will encounter in their future careers. The CTL approach is fully consistent with guidelines for the professional development of science teachers (Chiappetta and Koballa 2002; Loucks-Horsley et al. 2003). What is new about CTL is that it is a grassroots initiative that has emerged from exemplary teachers' efforts to build on situated cognition research. It integrates into one approach a number of time-tested strategies that are too often employed independently of one another.

As implemented at UGA, these CTL strategies are inquiry learning, problem-based learning, cooperative learning, project-based learning, and authentic assessment (see descriptions of each strategy in Figure 1). The unique integration of these five strategies in our CTL program has enabled us to respond effectively to the *More Emphasis* conditions that conclude each section of the Standards, particularly those related to science teaching, professional development, assessment, and science content. In the following sections, we provide specific examples of how CTL has done this.

Science Teaching Standards

CTL has made it possible for our program to put more emphasis on fostering an active, adaptive, and cooperative learning community that values the unique qualities of its members. In this community, the members—preservice teachers, mentor teachers, and university faculty—

Figure 1. Contextual Teaching and Learning (CTL) Strategies of the Science Teacher Education Program at the University of Georgia

Contextual teaching and learning (CTL) (Johnson 2002; Sears and Hersh 2000), like any approach to instruction, is characterized by the use of some learning strategies more than others. In the University of Georgia's CTL program for the preparation of science teachers, the following research-based strategies are used in an integrated fashion:

1. **Inquiry learning.** Students learn science in much the same way that science itself is carried out. Inquiry refers to those processes and skills used by scientists when they investigate natural phenomena. Inquiry involves an understanding of "how and why scientific knowledge changes in response to new evidence, logical analysis, and modified explanations debated within a community of scientists" (NRC 2000, p. 21).

2. **Problem-based learning**. Students are given either a real or simulated problem and must use critical-thinking skills to solve it. Ideally, they will need to draw information from a variety of disciplines. Problems that have some personal relevance to the students are often good choices because they encourage strong participation, learning, and perseverance.

3. **Cooperative learning**. Students work together in small groups and focus on achieving a common goal through collaboration and with mutual respect. Each student within the group is viewed as making a significant contribution to the goal.

4. **Project-based learning**. Students work independently or collaboratively on projects of personal interest. The projects often benefit others, have social relevance, and may be described as *service learning*. There is an emphasis on constructing realistic and valuable work products.

5. **Authentic assessment**. Students are evaluated by means of their performance on tasks that are representative of activities actually done in relevant, real-life settings, often associated with future careers. An example of an authentic assessment is a portfolio that is "a purposeful and representative collection of student work that conveys a story of progress, achievement and/or effort" (NRC 2001, p. 31).

---

share responsibility for fostering inquiry and understanding through respectful discussion and debate. We have used CTL, with its inquiry learning feature, to effectively prepare our preservice teachers for controversial, important issues that will be raised in their classrooms—issues such as the origin of the universe, the theory of evolution, animal rights, and population growth, to name only a few. Rather than take a traditional "cookbook" approach to teaching science, we have modeled both guided inquiry and open inquiry.

We have used CTL to promote a social-cognitive approach to classroom management that values self-concept, self-regulation, and self-efficacy. We encourage our preservice teachers to practice shared governance whenever possible and discourage them from creating autocratic, teacher-centered classrooms. Their classrooms should be collaborative, learning oriented, and student centered—and characterized by trust, caring, and reflection. Consistent with CTL, we ask our preservice teachers to regularly and systematically engage in reflective practice, which "is characterized by opportunities to analyze, both individually and as a group, problematic situations; evaluate multiple forms of evidence; and make decisions and recommendations that lead to action" (Koballa and Tippins 2004, p. 7).

We also use case-based pedagogies as useful "tools" for promoting reflective inquiry, engaging experiential learning, and strengthening decision-making and problem-solving skills. Our cases portray dilemmas that serve as contexts for inquiry, discussion, and debate. Figure 2 presents such a case; it is based on the experience of one of our program graduates. We use cases such as this to provide a context for preservice teachers to become aware of problematic issues, recognize their own positions on these issues, and assess the theoretical, practical, and ethical implications associated with these issues.

Professional Development Standards

Our CTL program, and its cooperative learning feature in particular, has helped us emphasize collegial inquiry, reflective practice, long-term planning, and a shar-

A mentor biology teacher shows a preservice teacher how to safely handle a green iguana.

ing of mutual expertise. Cooperative learning among our preservice teachers prepares them for their roles as facilitators, consultants, and planners. Cooperatively, they become producers of knowledge and future leaders in the integration of theory and practice. CTL accomplishes this, in part, by creating strong bonds of cohort membership. Throughout the entire program, each preservice teacher learns in a cohort of about 20 peers. Even during and subsequent to student teaching, the members of the cohort interact through planned activities.

Within cohorts, there are smaller, structured study groups of three to five students. We find that membership in cohorts and study groups supports reflective practice, an important aspect of CTL. In cohorts, our preservice teachers learn to take responsibility for their own professional development and for enhancing the teaching profession.

Our CTL program also fosters professional development through our use of mentor teachers who, in collaboration with university faculty, guide the internships and student teaching of our preservice teachers. What distinguishes our mentor teachers from conventional supervising teachers is that they have all completed a mentoring skills education program that emphasizes research-validated professional development practices.

University faculty are field based, working in the schools in a genuine collaboration with the mentor teachers to achieve a mutual goal of fostering the preservice teachers' professional development. We make a special effort to make available to our preservice teachers experiences in culturally diverse schools in urban, suburban, and rural areas; many of our students have internship experiences in more than one of these school settings.

Our CTL program involves preservice teachers in the many valuable professional development opportunities offered by the Georgia Science Teachers Association and the National Science Teachers Association. Frequently, our preservice teachers participate with faculty and mentor teachers in presentations, field trips, and a variety of professional activities, such as serving as judges at school science fairs and science bowl competitions.

Assessment Standards

By implementing CTL in our program, we are able to place more emphasis on the authentic, performance-based assessment of rich, well-structured knowledge. For example, our preservice

Figure 2. Example of a Contextual Teaching and Learning (CTL) Case

New science teachers often inherit science materials and equipment left in classrooms and storage rooms. These items may have been purchased for a specific experiment that is no longer considered safe or given to a teacher by a well-meaning individual affiliated with a science-related business or industry. Sometimes these items may be dangerous or considered inappropriate for instructional purposes given today's standards.

Ms. Maria Garcia, who has been teaching ninth-grade biology for only one semester, inherited a classroom that was occupied by Ms. Sandy Davis for 26 years. Ms. Davis was a great wildlife enthusiast and collected specimens from all over the world. She and her zoologist husband, who taught at the local college, often conducted seminars for the community during which they would display their mammal skeletons, mounted fish and birds, and sundry jarred specimens. When Ms. Davis retired in the middle of the year due to complications associated with gallbladder surgery, many of the specimens were left in the classroom and storage room. Now they were Maria's responsibility.

On the day Maria moved into the classroom, two student volunteers, Steve and Gina, helped her box up the contents of the crowded storage room. An hour into their work, Maria was feeling pretty good about their progress and was thinking about how she might reward the students for their effort. Suddenly, a loud scream came from the storeroom and the two students ran out into the classroom.

Gina: Ms. Garcia, it's a baby. It's a baby in the jar. I'm gonna be sick. I can't believe it.
Steve: Yeah, Ms. Garcia, we saw a baby, at least it looks like a real human baby.
It's in one of those jars in the back of the storeroom.
Maria: Slow down. Catch your breath. Show me what you're talking about.

Maria then followed the students into the storage room. The students were right. In the back, on a bottom shelf, there was a gallon jar of alcohol with a human fetus in it.

Case Questions for Discussion:
1. What actions should Maria take next?
2. What should Maria say to the students?
3. Should Maria report finding the fetus to others? If so, to whom should she report it?
4. What should school administrators and science teachers do to guard against similar occurrences in the future?

teachers construct and update portfolios of learning products, such as model lesson plans. The contents in the portfolios allow us to conduct formative and summative evaluations of their knowledge. The portfolios also contain reflective dialogues about their own teaching and how it can be improved. Using portfolios to structure and reflect on knowledge helps to ensure that it is highly valued and understood (NRC 2001).

We emphasize portfolio products because our assessments are performance based. In addition to portfolios, we make extensive use of individual interviewing, group discussions, concept mapping, attitude surveys, investigative projects, videotaped lessons, and laboratory activities in schools, as well as analytic and holistic rubrics to ensure that assessment is authentic, reliable, and valid. By "valid," we mean that our assessments complement the instructional goals of our program.

CTL also helps us to evaluate scientific understanding, reasoning, and achievement in an ongoing fashion. We do this by helping our preservice teachers engage in reflective practice throughout the program. By writing reflective journal entries and discussing their reflections in groups, our preservice teachers analyze their strengths, weaknesses, and progress with respect to their current levels of understanding, reasoning, and achievement.

Science Content Standards

In our program, CTL has helped our preservice teachers to develop inquiry abilities and master inquiry strategies for learning subject-matter disciplines. We achieve this by routinely combining inquiry learning with problem-based and project-based learning. For example, our preservice teachers investigate "model" organisms such as *Melittobia digitata*, which are a species of parasitic wasp (Matthews 1997). These tiny, easily maintained insects are harmless to people and found all over the world. They are ideal for the classroom because they have an extremely rapid life cycle: They mature in about two to three weeks, making it easy to observe their life history—from eggs, to larvae, to pupae, to adults. Our preservice teachers also investigate plants such as *Brassica rapa* because of their five- to six-week life cycle, their size, and the ease of cultivating them. These plants, which can grow to 30 cm, are members of the crucifer family of plants, related to broccoli, cabbage, and turnips. We have found that model plants and animals such as these are ideal for inquiry learning, problem-based learning, and project-based learning. Our preservice teachers will use these model organisms in their own future classrooms.

CTL also has helped us to place more emphasis on the understanding and integration of fundamental science concepts—and on the personal, social, and historical contexts of those concepts. For example, we ask preservice teachers to investigate the energy sources of plants, relating their findings and understandings to the personal, social, and historical contexts of scientists such as Jan Baptista van Helmont who investigated this issue in the 17th century. Along similar lines, we have them study and discuss the personal, social, and historical contexts surrounding the interactions of scientists such as Francis Crick, Rosalind Franklin, Linus Pauling, James Watson, and Maurice Wilkins and how those interactions led to the discovery of the double-helical structure of DNA.

Evidence of Achieving the *More Emphasis* Conditions

The Standards, in conjunction with CTL, have helped us achieve goals consistent with the *More Emphasis* conditions. The specific details that distinguish our current program, begun in 2000, from the one that preceded it or from programs in many other institutions, are

- a greater emphasis on inquiry and problem solving;
- the encouragement of learning that is project based and self-regulated;
- the anchoring of teaching and learning in a variety of contexts, such as school, home, and community;
- the formation of student teams to help students learn from each other; and
- the extensive use of authentic assessments.

One indicator of achievement is our national ranking. The science education program at UGA is part of a larger secondary education program that was ranked seventh in the nation in 2004 by *U.S. News & World Report,* based on nominations by deans at peer institutions. A more specific indicator of achievement are scores on the Educational Testing Service's Praxis II test for prospective teachers, which is designed to measure breadth and depth of content area knowledge. In the area of biology content knowledge, UGA scored highest among the public institutions in our state, which is noteworthy since many more teachers graduate from our institution than from any other in the state.

Another indicator is the Science Education Learning Outcomes Questionnaire of our program, which was recently administered to preservice teachers in preparation for routine accreditation review by the National Council for Accreditation of Teacher Education (NCATE). In response to the question "How well did your content courses prepare you for teaching biology?" our preservice teachers, indicated, on average, "good" to "excellent." They indicated the same for chemistry and Earth science.

Yet another indicator of achievement, consistent with *More Emphasis* conditions in the Standards, was the program evaluation, *Implementing Contextual Teaching and Learning by Novice Teachers,* by Lynch and Harnish (2003) for the U. S. Department of Education, in which they drew the following conclusions regarding the science education program at UGA:

> *Our observations of the uses of CTL strategies by novice teachers in this study lead us to believe that: (a) engagement and motivation of students were increased; (b) student attitudes toward learning were improved; (c) behavior improved; and (d) resulting interactive effects will result in deeper understanding, retention, and application of knowledge and information. These are important outcomes of education that contribute to improved student achievement.* (pp. 42–43)

Taken together, the preceding indicators support the conclusion that the Standards, implemented at UGA with the help of CTL, have had a strong positive impact on the performance of our preservice and new science teachers. Our continued contact with our science education program graduates, such as the teacher highlighted in Figure 3, indicates that the effects are long lasting.

Summary

Quality teaching fosters quality learning. One of the major goals of recent reform efforts in science has been to ensure that new science teachers are well prepared for classroom practice. Beginning science teachers often have difficulty relating various theories and methods taught in courses to what actually happens in their daily teaching practice. In an effort to address this, science teacher education programs across the nation are re-examining their goals and reconceptualizing their approach to preparing teachers with the help of the National Science Education Standards.

By implementing the Standards in conjunction with a contextual teaching and learning (CTL) approach to science education, we have significantly enhanced the preparation of science teachers at our university. Our graduates have proven to be successful in diverse science classrooms in urban, suburban, and rural settings throughout our state. Our graduates help their own students understand how science knowledge and skills can benefit their lives outside of school, particularly in their future careers. CTL integrates the strategies of inquiry learning, problem-based learning, cooperative learning, project-based learning, and authentic assessment. It anchors teaching and

Figure 3. Interview With a Contextual Teaching and Learning (CTL) Science Teacher

Ms. Tasha Fields, a 2001 graduate of the University of Georgia's secondary science education program, is teaching life science to seventh graders at South Hall Middle School, Gainesville, Georgia. In a recent interview, she made the following comments about her use of contextual teaching and learning (CTL) methods and assessment. Her comments are typical of those provided by the other graduates of our program.

CTL Methods

In my opinion, CTL teaching practices are far more interesting and helpful than traditional teaching practices. Students have the opportunity to learn concepts through hands-on methods.... Also, students are more engaged in their learning when they are taught through CTL methods.... It is much easier to learn about the steps of scientific method when one can perform an actual experiment rather than learning through rote memorization.... I think one of the great things about CTL is that one may call on the strategies when appropriate and necessary. This means that all don't have to be used all the time. One can pick and choose so that the classroom is an effective learning environment.

CTL Assessment

CTL plays a vital role in implementing authentic assessment. Not only is it important that students learn and comprehend various concepts we teach in the classroom, but also it is even more important that they are able to apply [the concepts] to real-life situations. Therefore, when appropriate, I try to have my students apply various concepts to everyday life....

Aside from standardized test scores, our student's science achievement is measured in different ways. I assess a student's achievement through traditional testing, but also through lab experiments, projects, journals, daily assignments, and other ways. I think that by using a variety of assessment methods, which is recommended by CTL, it is possible to see all students' weaknesses and strengths.... Because CTL uses authentic assessment techniques, it allows me to identify different needs of students. Because I teach students at an age that they are just learning to think for themselves, they need reassurance of their abilities and capabilities.... CTL allows the students to use knowledge they have obtained and apply it to real-life situations to test themselves.... Authentic tasks motivate students to love science.

---

learning in students' diverse life contexts. CTL complements the Standards and enables science teachers to successfully implement the *More Emphasis* conditions associated with them.

Acknowledgments

We wish to thank the members of the National Advisory Board who reviewed an earlier version of this chapter for their very helpful suggestions. The work reported on here was prepared in association with the Contextual Teaching and Learning in Preservice Teacher Education project and the Studies of Novice Teachers' Implementation of CTL Approaches in the Classroom project, both at the University of Georgia, with funding support from the U.S. Department of Education, Contract No. ED-98-CO-0085, 1998–2003.

References

Chiappetta, E. L., and T. R. Koballa. 2002. *Science instruction in the middle and secondary schools*. 5th ed. Upper Saddle River, NJ: Pearson.

Cobb, P., and J. Bowers. 1999. Cognitive and situated learning: Perspectives in theory and practice. *Educational Researcher* 28(2): 4–15.

Driver R., H. Asoko, J. Leach, E. Mortimer, and P. Scott. 1994. Constructing scientific knowledge in the classroom. *Educational Researcher* 23(7): 5–12.

Glynn, S. M., and R. Duit. 1995. Learning science meaningfully: Constructing conceptual models. In *Learning science in the schools: Research reforming practice*, eds. S. M. Glynn and R. Duit, pp. 3–33. Mahwah, NJ: Erlbaum.

Johnson, E. 2002. *Contextual teaching and learning*. Thousand Oaks, CA: Corwin Press.

Koballa, T. R., and D. J. Tippins, eds. 2004. *Cases in middle and secondary science education: The promise and dilemmas*. Upper Saddle River, NJ: Merrill/Prentice Hall.

Loucks-Horsley, S., N. Love, K. E. Stiles, S. Mundry, and P. W. Hewson. 2003. *Designing professional development for teachers of science and mathematics*. 2nd ed. Thousand Oaks, CA: Corwin Press.

Lynch, R., and D. Harnish. 2003. *Implementing contextual teaching and learning by novice teachers* (Final Report, Contract # ED-98-CO-0085). Athens, GA: University of Georgia.

Matthews, R. W. 1997. Teaching ecological interactions with mud-dauber nests. *American Biology Teacher* 59: 152–158.

National Research Council (NRC). 1996. *National science education standards*. Washington, DC: National Academy Press.

National Research Council (NRC). 2000. *Inquiry and the national science education standards: A guide for teaching and learning*. Washington, DC: National Academy Press.

National Research Council (NRC). 2001. *Classroom assessment and the national science education standards*. Washington, DC: National Academy Press.

Sears, S. J., and S. Hersh. 2000. *Best practices in contextual teaching and learning: Program profiles and cross-profile analysis*. Columbus, OH: Ohio State University.

Siebert, E. D., and W. J. McIntosh, eds. 2001. *College pathways to the science education standards*. Arlington, VA: NSTA Press.

Applying the National Science Education Standards in Alaska:
Weaving Native Knowledge Into Teaching and Learning Environmental Science Through Inquiry

Leslie S. Gordon, Sidney Stephens, and Elena B. Sparrow
University of Alaska, Fairbanks

Setting

The Observing Locally, Connecting Globally (OLCG) or Global Change Education Using Western Science and Native Observations program, funded by the National Science Foundation, focuses on professional development in environmental science for K–12 teachers in Alaska. The OLCG program, begun in 2000, is based at the University of Alaska, Fairbanks (UAF) School of Natural Resources and Agricultural Sciences and is co-directed by three UAF faculty members who are also the course instructors for the program. Rather than simply delivering science content, the program weaves together localized environmental research, Native knowledge, and best teaching practices in science and math with the goals of enhancing the inquiry abilities and the cultural well-being of K–12 students. Through an intensive summer institute and ongoing program support, the program employs a number of strategies for teaching science process, bringing content alive, and making it more relevant and tailored to local conditions, both environmental and cultural.

The OLCG program was originally intended to work primarily either with teachers in small, rural Alaskan villages whose residents are predominantly of Aleut, Yupik, Inupiat, or Athabascan Indian heritage or with teachers in urban and suburban communities with predominantly Native American student populations. While this focus has shifted a bit because of teacher interest, the majority (35) of our total participants (53) in 2003 (the year reported on in this chapter) taught in rural Alaska villages that are only accessible by air or water, and are separated by hundreds of miles—as well as by different languages and cultures. Many villages now have some internet capability and adequate-to-excellent physical environments at the schools, but often lack curricula or teaching strategies that connect school to home and culture. The teachers come from classrooms representing all grades (K–12) and have a wide range of goals, skills, and experiences in teaching. About half of our participants teach at an elementary school level, while the other half teach grades 6–12. Urban grade level and course distributions look much like they do anywhere in the United States (e.g., single-grade elementary school classes, with certified secondary science teachers responsible for courses within their major). In rural Alaska, however, because student numbers are small, teachers often have a multigraded classroom (e.g., grades 2–5), or are responsible for multiple classes in multiple disciplines across grade levels (e.g., science, math, and technology classes for grades 6–12). This wide variation in demographics makes the program quite challenging, but also quite rewarding as we learn from each other.

More Emphasis Conditions and the National Science Education Standards

Table 1 shows which *More Emphasis* conditions in professional development from the National Science Education Standards (NRC 1996) have been met and how they tie in to the Goals for School Science (NRC 1996, p. 13). OLCG uses a constructivist framework and developmentally appropriate and culturally responsive teaching that includes inquiry and a learning cycle model integrated with science content. Teachers use new knowledge to teach about the local environment. OLCG supports the sharing of teacher expertise as mentors and lead teachers provide professional development opportunities. Using their new knowledge, teachers have influenced OLCG program development, other teachers, and local communities. Teachers identify and discuss important environmental issues relevant to their community.

Program Leaders

The OLCG program is led by three UAF faculty members, known as co-principal investigators, and by a program coordinator from the Fairbanks North Star Borough School District. Collectively, the four program members represent a wide range of experience and perspectives. Dr. Elena Sparrow, the principal investigator, is a microbiologist with more than 25 years of research experience. She is coordinator of the Alaska GLOBE partnership and has been involved in education outreach for many years. Sidney Stephens has a master's degree in cross-cultural education and has taught almost 30 years, including K–12 classrooms and preservice and inservice science, math, and environmental education courses, with a focus on cross-cultural education. Dr. Leslie Gordon is an education specialist and master teacher of science and math, with numerous teacher awards. She taught elementary school in Fairbanks for over 20 years and currently teaches science and math classes for preservice teachers at UAF. Martha Kopplin, program coordinator, has a master's degree in biology and coordinates grant activities. Program personnel collaborate with many exemplary teachers, scientists, and Native Elders and experts, using a range of learning environments, as described below.

Table 1. National Science Education Standards Professional Development *More Emphasis* Conditions Met in the OLCG Program and How They Tie Into the Goals for School Science

More Emphasis Conditions Met	Goals for School Science[a]	How *More Emphasis* Condition Ties Into Goals for School Science
Variety of professional development activities for lifelong learning	Meet science education goals 1, 2 and 3, given below.	OLCG provides a summer institute, face-to-face follow-up sessions, on-site visits, phone calls, and e-mails throughout the year to meet the needs of teachers with different experiences, expertise, and proficiencies. Continuous program assessment provides ongoing feedback to teachers and program.
Learning science through investigation and inquiry Integration of science and teaching knowledge	Produce students who can experience the richness and excitement of knowing about and understanding the natural world (goal 1)	Teachers investigate climate change of critical importance to Alaska and are introduced to scientific literature, media, and technological resources, learning both science content and how to teach inquiry by doing their own inquiries in the classroom, in computer labs, and in the field with scientists, Native experts, and staff.
Teacher as intellectual, reflective practitioner Teacher as source and facilitator of change	Produce students who can use appropriate scientific processes and principles in making personal decisions (goal 2) and can engage intelligently in public discourse and debate about matters of scientific and technological concern (goal 3)	OLCG provides frequent opportunities for individual and collegial examination and reflection on classroom practice through fast-writes at workshops and during the year via e-mail journals, surveys, phone calls, and face-to face meetings.
Teacher as leader and member of a collegial, collaborative professional community	Produce students who can engage intelligently in public discourse and debate about matters of scientific and technological concern (goal 3)	OLCG encourages teachers to participate as teams in OLCG and provides considerable time for collaboration, discussions, and other continuing support activities among people involved in the program (e.g., teachers, teacher educators, scientists, and Native Elders), with clear respect for the perspectives and expertise of each.

[a]The Goals for School Science also appear on page 13 of *National Science Education Standards* (NRC 1996).

Unique Features

Inquiry-based pedagogies, constructivism, localization of science, culturally responsive curriculum, and *reflective practice* are all common buzzwords in professional development programs, but the OLCG program has focused on these concepts and practices in earnest as it designs and refines its program for Alaskan teachers. OLCG strives to provide teachers and students with opportunities to engage in original global-change research using the international GLOBE investigations (Butler and MacGregor 2003) and other climate-change studies relevant to Alaska, in ways that are tailored to local environmental and cultural conditions and that support teachers from the time they join the project. This constructivist theoretical framework (Brooks and Brooks 1993) and culturally responsive theoretical framework (Alaska Native Knowledge Network 1998) underlie all of our professional development efforts as we strive to address the *More Emphasis* conditions listed in Table 1 and discussed more fully below.

Provide a Variety of Professional Development Activities for Lifelong Learning

The OLCG program recognizes the developmental nature of teachers' professional growth and the diverse needs of Alaska teachers, who have a range of teaching assignments and varying degrees of experience, education, and proficiency. We also acknowledge and learn from the fact that each teacher will make his or her own meaning and implement what is personally and professionally relevant from any staff development opportunity. Consequently, the OLCG program provides continuing relevant, research-based professional development opportunities to program participants in the often far-flung reaches of our state.

OLCG offers a two-week intensive summer institute, a two-day face-to-face workshop in December, and other occasional one-day sessions to work on specific tasks, such as developing a climate-change interview/survey to be used with Elders. Travel, lodging, and meal support are included for these activities. Program staff members are available throughout the year to consult with participants via phone or e-mail; they are also available to travel to teachers' classrooms for the purpose of modeling lessons, troubleshooting difficulties, developing appropriate strategies, or just plain collaborating. The staff also helps teachers connect with Native Elders and scientists for classroom visits, which are subsidized by the program. Included in program support are release time to visit other classrooms; science and pedagogical resources; GLOBE Teacher's Guide; scientific equipment; videotapes; Project Jukebox programs documenting local knowledge on climate change; and websites for OLCG (*www.uaf.edu/olcg*) and GLOBE (*www.globe.gov*).

Learning Science Through Investigation and Inquiry

Fundamental to the OLCG program is the goal of learning science through inquiry. According to the National Research Council (2000), inquiry has two different but related meanings: (1) it is what students need to know, and be able to do, in order to design and conduct scientific investigations, and (2) it entails the teaching and learning strategies that teachers use to help students master science concepts through hands-on investigations. We believe, and research suggests, that teachers learn best how to teach science by doing it (Darling-Hammond 1997). As a consequence, the majority of the time spent in the summer institute is dedicated to providing experiences wherein teachers learn science through modeling, guided practice, and their own inquiries. Teachers actually have an opportunity to participate in all the activities they will be using with their students when they get back to their classrooms.

Teachers regularly and actively investigate phenomena that can be studied scientifically, interpret results, and make sense of their findings consistent with currently accepted scientific understanding. On days one and two of the summer institute, teachers participate in an overnight field trip on the Tanana River with Athabascan river experts who share their observations and understanding of the environment as an interconnected Earth system. Teachers are asked to reflect on the nature of Elders' observations, collect data, make inferences, and generate questions about the changes to the river. They also do exploratory science activities and receive training in the use and adaptation of GLOBE protocols and learning activities. This process

Teachers practice using a GPS receiver to determine study site locations.

continues throughout the two-week institute with the ultimate goal of having teachers and students become comfortable with inquiry—with asking and answering their own questions about the environment and "messing with" the gray areas of science.

These learning activities are all focused on the issue of climate change and related environmental change because while global climate change is an issue of critical importance throughout the world, it takes on a particularly visible and immediate character in Alaska. Climate trends over the last three decades have already shown considerable warming and have had major impacts on the environment (Weller and Anderson 1998). To understand, monitor, and prepare for changes in their environment, K–12 students must develop a deep understanding of the place in which they live. They must also be able to compare their own observations with historic information about that same environment, and they must develop a sense of the cyclic, interrelated, and nonlinear nature of Earth system processes and human interaction. Elders and other expert observers can often provide just such knowledge because they have a very detailed and highly refined awareness of their environment gained from years of living on the land. For these reasons, Elders are a critical part of our summer institute and supporting activities. They lead our initial river exploration, share observations throughout the institute, and visit classrooms when invited. The information they share, and the way they share it, stimulates not only inquiry questions but also discussion about the similarities and differences between science and Native knowledge systems and the strengths and limitations of each system (Stephens 2000). Because it is sometimes difficult for teachers to identify or access Native experts in their communities, we have also begun to audiotape some Elder/expert discussions of the effects of climate change and have made these tapes available to teachers and students in the Project Jukebox section of our website (*www.uaf.edu/olcg*).

Beyond immersing teachers in inquiry activities and exposing them to observations and conceptions of the environment through Elder/expert sharing, we introduce teachers to a variety of climate-change resources such as research scientists, current reports, videotapes, and internet sites. We also provide training and all of the equipment necessary to do the basic GLOBE protocols that can then be used or adapted for use in local environmental-change investigations.

Integration of Science and Science Teaching Knowledge

Teachers need more than content knowledge to be good science teachers (Loucks-Horsley et al. 1998). They also need to understand the ways in which students with diverse interests, abilities, and experiences construct knowledge. In addition, they need to know how to support student inquiries, how to develop curriculum, how to manage materials, and how to assess understanding in a variety of ways. Generally these "how-to's" take many years, and a good deal of support, to master.

Hence, science and science teaching knowledge are completely interwoven during the summer institute and in implementation support throughout the year. Because the program has a constructivist theoretical perspective, we have modeled differentiation of the learning environment and curriculum for teachers from the beginning, and our teachers are supported to do the same. Some examples of these differentiations are

- ongoing discussions, in person and on the internet, on how to make GLOBE and environmental research developmentally appropriate for primary students;
- scaffolding the learning of science in Native villages by the use of Native expertise and culturally responsive teaching strategies;
- professional development on alternative assessment to help teachers understand what their students know and are able to do as a result of local environmental studies; and
- integration of research-based strategies such as using the learning cycle model in order to design lessons and applying the theory of multiple intelligences (Gardner 1983).

In addition, teachers can request staff visits to their classrooms to model or troubleshoot a lesson or lessons with which they are having difficulty. Teacher reflection also promotes learning and plays a key role in the OLCG project, as we see in the discussion that follows.

Teacher as Intellectual, Reflective Practitioner and Source and Facilitator of Change

An important part of supporting teachers as they work toward their own goals for learning consists in providing opportunities for them to ask and answer their own questions, to reflect on their practices, and to make personal decisions regarding the changes they wish to implement in their classrooms (Loucks-Horsley et al. 1998). Consequently, teachers are asked to reflect regularly on their thinking and on student reactions. They do this through fast-writes and discussions within small and large groups during workshops and through e-mail journals sent from their classrooms to course instructors during the year. These reflections have been invaluable and serve a dual purpose. They provide the teachers with an opportunity to reflect on the teachers' learning in content and pedagogy, and they provide feedback to the course instructors about additional support and staff development that might be valuable. Teachers have repeatedly told us that the opportunity to network and reflect on their teaching has greatly supported their efforts to change.

Teacher as Leader and Member of Collegial, Collaborative Professional Community

Collegial support and reflection are key components of the OLCG program and are fundamental to professional development in science teaching. When teachers apply to our program, they are encouraged to apply as a team with other educators (e.g., aides, resource teachers, environmental specialists, and Native Elders) at their site. During the summer institute and December follow-up meeting, teachers share their successes and frustrations as they network with other teachers from their site and other schools. This collaborative support continues back in the classroom through e-mail conversations (formal and informal), phone calls, and classroom visits.

The OLCG program staff relies on partnering with Native Elders, scientists, teachers, and teacher leaders to plan and implement program activities. OLCG provides funding for honoraria for teacher presenters, Native Elders, and other local experts and for release time so that teachers can visit other classrooms. Feedback from course evaluations, conversations, journals, and surveys are all used to adjust the content and timing of program plans. Feedback to teachers influences their classroom practice. OLCG also encourages teachers to take a leadership role by providing opportunities for teachers to be lead teacher presenters during the institute and follow-up sessions, or to be teacher mentors. Following these experiences, teachers have conducted their own teacher workshops funded by external sources and/or taught science courses for preservice teachers at the University of Alaska.

Evidence of Program Effectiveness

The OLCG program is conducting a long-term evaluation to try to understand its impact on teachers and students. A variety of quantitative and qualitative assessment procedures are being used.

Assessment Activities Related to the Summer Institutes

- Formative and summative evaluation by internal and external evaluators—Leslie Gordon, co-principal investigator, designed and collected assessments, analyzed and interpreted data, and wrote the annual report; Tom Hinojosa, from SRI, wrote the outside evaluator's report.
- Needs assessment (conducted at the beginning of the institute).
- Pre- and Posttest Attitude Assessment for Teachers—This Likert-scale attitude assessment contains 11 items that address comfort levels with global climate-change teaching, the integration of Native knowledge/local experts into the classroom, and best practices in science education (e.g., inquiry learning, constructivism, teaching for understanding). This instrument was administered to each teacher on the first day of the summer institute and the last day.
- Pre- and Posttest Teacher Content/Achievement Assessment—Teachers were asked to discuss their understandings of the value of using Native Elders in the classroom and various aspects of GLOBE. This instrument was administered on the first and last days of the institute.

- Daily Fast-Writes—The fast-writes included formative assessment questions to determine how much teachers were learning, what their perceptions were about the benefits of each day, and what their questions and concerns were.
- Final Teacher Survey—Program leaders used this Likert-scale instrument at the end of the institute to determine teacher perceptions about the relative benefits of each component of the summer institute.
- Inquiry Project/Multiple Intelligence Final Assessment Project—Presentations on personal inquiry projects related to teachers' local environments that were begun at the institute will be continued with students during the school year. Teachers attended an inservice workshop on the theory of multiple intelligences (Gardner 1983) and then were given the opportunity to demonstrate what they had learned from their inquiry using their preferred intelligence(s).

Research, Assessment, and Evaluation Related to Implementation in the Classroom

- Pre- and Posttest Student Achievement Assessment—This instrument, adapted from one developed by TERC and SRI, was piloted in the spring of 2000 and has been administered to students in participating classrooms each spring and fall. It provides a locally relevant color photograph to students and asks them to respond to certain questions about global climate change and Native knowledge based on what they observe in the photo of either a tundra or boreal forest environment similar to theirs.
- Pre- and Posttest Student Attitude Assessment—This Likert-scale attitude assessment, piloted also in 2000, was administered to all students in participating classrooms in the fall and again in the spring.
- Teacher Attitude Assessment—The same assessment that teachers took as a pre- and posttest during the summer institute will be repeated each spring to track any longitudinal effects.
- Student Performance Assessment—This assessment focused on the student collection and reporting of environmental data to the GLOBE website and on other student work submitted by teachers.
- Level of Implementation Analysis—This analysis examined the project's impact by focusing on the level to which each teacher implemented each strand of the program into his or her classroom. Findings will then be compared to student attitude and achievement test results to see if there is any relationship.
- Teacher journal entries—These journal entries were submitted monthly in response to prompts from the local evaluator.
- Student journal entries—These journal entries were submitted monthly in response to prompts from the local evaluator.
- Teacher-designed assessments of student learning.
- Needs assessment—This assessment was conducted after the summer institute to determine topics/areas to be covered during follow-up.
- Videotapes of students working on OLCG activities.

- Interviews with selected students and teachers.
- Classroom observations and reflections by staff.
- Student individual research projects.

OLCG and the Teacher as Intellectual, Reflective Practitioner, Collaborator, Producer of Knowledge, and Facilitator of Change

Teachers in the program have proved to be thoughtful and honest reflectors and have had a great deal of influence on the contemporary format of the project. Feedback from the teachers has supported, and even extended, our understandings in areas as diverse as student assessment and the potential for teacher change. The following excerpts are a few of many teacher reflections about how the program has affected them and their students.

I have a new realization. It is to affirm my students and their culture, and the things that they know and observe outside of school.... I think it's especially important as a white teacher in the village to make sure that I learn from them, if I expect them to learn from me. GLOBE is a great way to connect the things we learn from each other. The way that the GLOBE protocols are all hands-on student inquiry is a great way to teach things through the practice of self-discovery. (KD, 9/2002)

I think my students have gotten to be more "experimental" in their thinking; not just follow[ing] steps in an experiment. I emphasize "predictions" and the change of variables in everything we do. (JJ, 2/2001)

My students have definitely benefited positively. Expectations were higher, more work was required, and they rose to those levels—many changed their opinions of science from a negative to a positive—they feel science is fun. (AH, 12/2002)

Teachers have also taken a leadership role in solving problems and issues that arose in their classrooms as they attempted to implement the project. One example of this is the Listserv set up for the primary teachers who were trying to understand how GLOBE could successfully be adapted for use in K–3 classrooms, where many concepts and skills are not developmentally appropriate. Throughout the fall, primary teachers shared the things they tried and their results. They also designed a number of wonderful teacher assessment instruments since GLOBE did not have any. By sharing these ideas, teachers definitely helped each other ("I really enjoyed the integration part as I learned a lot from my peers. They gave a lot of good ideas for us to use in our own classrooms" [MS, 12/2002]).

The following are examples of program changes made in response to teacher feedback:

- Lengthening the river trip to two days
- Restructuring time with Native Elders to better facilitate comfortable sharing of stories and information, using the Elder knowledge as a basis for inquiry projects
- Decreasing the number of GLOBE protocols taught (many were made optional as teachers

decided which ones to use in their classrooms)
- ◆ Spending less time on pedagogy assignments (e.g., lesson writing) and more time on modeling and writing individual inquiry plans
- ◆ Moving assessment discussions to follow-up workshops
- ◆ Creating a script to help teachers administer student achievement assessments
- ◆ Brainstorming sessions on what student evaluations would be appropriate for K–2 students

Learning Science Through Investigation
Inquiry and Integration of Science and Teaching Knowledge

While inquiry is a primary goal of our program, we know that teacher implementation is highly dependent on individual teachers' needs. As a consequence, the program's implementation looks different in each of our classrooms. Some teachers complete wonderful inquiries during their first year in the program and others need a good deal of support to integrate simple hands-on investigations. Others feel that enhancing their connections to culture and local environmental studies is critical, and they focus on that. Still other teachers have become teacher leaders in the project, offering their wealth of knowledge about integrating inquiry or local knowledge into curricula and about assessing what students are understanding and able to do because of the OLCG program. All accomplishments are celebrated.

The following is an example of one successful teacher in our program who has become a teacher leader. Mary loops with her class between second and third grade. She took the OLCG summer institute two years ago and was very stressed about how to make it work with primary students. After the institute, she decided to do a year-long inquiry about wetlands and to use the GLOBE phenomenology and atmosphere protocols, as well as the OLCG supplementary unit on water. Her journal entries throughout the year indicated that she spent a great deal of time helping her students gain inquiry skills. She tried a variety of alternative assessments to understand what the students were learning. Staff members were asked to visit her class regularly to help teach important concepts and skills and to observe important milestones. Her students presented their studies during the institute and follow-up workshop.

Teacher feedback over the years definitely suggests an appreciation of both the inquiry approach to teaching and the integration of science and teaching knowledge. During the final institute evaluation each year, teachers are asked to rank 11 key elements of the institute. The best practices components (e.g., hands-on science, inquiry, collaboration, multiple intelligences) have consistently ranked in the top five. Reflections from teachers during the school year continue to support this ranking, as this quotation attests:

Working with the OLCG program has supported my goal of incorporating more hands-on curriculum in my classroom. It also is conducive for teaching using all content areas, or better said, across the curriculum. The cloud protocol (Atmosphere) has been an easy subject to involve Elders coming in and talking to the children. (MM, 12/2002)

Teachers also ranked the contributions of Native Elders in the top five elements of the institute. The following is an example of a reflection commonly expressed:

> *Interacting with and listening to Elders helped me to feel more at home with the idea of involving Elders in my classroom. It also helped me see more clearly what they have to offer and how to use their knowledge and life experience to improve the learning and enjoyment of my students.* (FH, 6/2002)

Results of the Teacher Attitude Assessment Related to Inquiry and the Achievement Assessment

To track changes in teacher attitudes and achievements, assessments were administered to all participants before and after the institute; the attitude assessment was also

Inupiat Elder Velma Brown with student Esther Brown by the weather shelter.

administered to every participant each spring. The instrument was a 5-point Likert scale, and two of the questions on the teachers' attitude assessment related to inquiry. Table 2 shows the mean gain change in attitude for all teachers and all years for items related to inquiry and significance levels of results from paired *t*-tests. The positive score change for both items was significant. Analysis of the data suggested that teachers from all three years of the program felt more comfortable using inquiry for their own learning and for supporting science learning in their classrooms.

Table 2. Pre- and Posttest Teacher Attitude Assessment: 2001–2003 Mean Change Scores and Paired *t*-Test Results

Item	Change Score	p
"I feel comfortable with inquiry learning and teaching."	+1.31	0.00*
"I feel comfortable integrating inquiry learning into my classroom."	+1.18	0.00*

* Level of significance $p < 0.05$

On the teacher achievement assessment, which addressed understandings related to Native knowledge and global climate-change education, each item had a possible score of 3 points, and a rubric was used to score each item. Content validity was established using experts in the field. Inter-rater reliability was established at 80%. Analysis using paired *t*-tests of the data from the achievement assessment suggested that there was a significant improvement for every item, at a significance level of $p < 0.05$ (Table 3). This represents a mean improvement of 0.45 out of a 3-point scale.

Results of both teacher assessments suggest that the use of inquiry in learning science has supported these teachers' understanding of key science concepts related to Earth systems and global change. The teacher comments below are typical of many that seem to support these results.

> *Best practices—I am really pushing this year to add more inquiry and performance assessments. Having OLCG has kept me on track so I don't regress or forget best practices and their benefits.* (CM, 12/2002)

> *In my plot study, individual teams developed a research project (inquiry) and I made the GLOBE equipment and protocols available to them in addition to the protocols the entire class did (green up and soils). I also have started the year with information on multiple intelligences and had the students do an MI self-evaluation. This year I've done a better job of trying to give opportunities for a variety of assessment activities using different intelligences.* (KE, 12/8/2002)

Table 3. Pre- and Posttest Teacher Content/Achievement Assessment: 2001–2003 Paired *t*-Test Results

Item	p
"List and discuss several of your ideas about the value of engaging your students in long term research in your local environment."	0.00*
"List and discuss several of your ideas about global environmental change and its impacts on your local community."	0.02*
"List and discuss several ways in which your students might benefit from integrating Native knowledge into your studies of the local environment."	0.04*
"List and discuss several ways in which you might integrate Native knowledge to support and enhance student understanding of their local environment."	0.00*

* Level of significance $p < 0.05$

Results of Student Achievement and Attitude Assessment

The Pre- and Posttest Achievement and Attitude Assessments given in the fall and spring each year to students of OLCG teachers also suggest that students are experiencing growth in their understanding of the key concepts of science covered by the program as well as changes in their attitudes about science. The Attitude Assessment is a Likert-scale instrument that asks students if they enjoy learning the different areas of science supported by the project. Every year students have shown a significant change from pre- to posttest on a majority of the attitude items. The Achievement Assessment is a color photo similar to the area in which they live; students are asked questions about Earth systems and their components (e.g., hydrologic/water cycle, nutrient cycle) as well as plants and animals. Results for this assessment over the years also consistently indicate a significant improvement from pre- to posttest for the majority of items, with an average of 12% improvement for all students on all items. Feedback from the teacher journals also suggests that students have been positively impacted by OLCG (e.g., "I believe my students are a lot more aware of their environment and are aware of how much impact we have on the land. I think it has also sparked a growing curiosity about the cause and effect of climate change" [KD, 12/2002]).

Furthermore, students of OLCG teachers have conducted their own inquiries and presented their investigations at many local science fairs, the district science fair, the Alaska State Science and Engineering Fair, and the Alaska Statewide High School Science Symposium. Two Alaska high school projects were chosen from a national competition and presented at the International GLOBE Conference in Croatia in July 2003.

With our focus on Earth systems and global change, we have been able to integrate all eight of the NSES Science Content Standards into our program, at the same time supporting teacher change in grades K–12. Table 4 lists some of the methods of inclusion for each content area.

Table 4. National Science Education Content Standards and Methods of Inclusion in the OLCG Program

Standard	Methods of Inclusion
Unifying Concepts	OLCG students and teachers study Earth as a system and global climate change.
Science as Inquiry	At the OLCG institute and in the classroom, the focus is on learning science through inquiry.
Physical Science	OLCG has developed supplementary units for GLOBE atmosphere and hydrology protocols on the physics of air and water.
Life Science	Life science is addressed in the plant inquiry unit and the GLOBE phenology and land cover strands.
Earth and Space Science	OLCG teachers and students study GLOBE Earth as a system, atmosphere, soils, hydrology, land cover, and phenology strands.
Science and Technology	OLCG teachers and students use/design tools of technology to support science inquiries and better understand local environments.
Science in Personal and Social Perspectives	OLCG students and teachers study change in their environment, its possible causes, and its observable and potential impact on community life.
History and Nature of Science	OLCG teachers and students engage in original research and contribute data to ongoing investigations supported by GLOBE and UAF. They also compare the similarities and differences between Native knowledge systems and science, and the strengths and limitations of each.

Dissemination of the OLCG professional development model has begun. Components have been used in two other Alaska science institutes for teachers and two national professional development workshops.

Summary

The OLCG professional development program for K–12 teachers intertwines Western science, Native knowledge, the National Science Education Standards, and inquiry-based pedagogies focused on the local environment and climate change in Alaska. It is constructivist in nature and provides teachers with a variety of professional development opportunities that are tailored to teacher needs and to local environmental and cultural conditions. These opportunities are planned with teacher input and actively engage teachers in doing the activities they will perform in their classrooms. Teachers are asked to reflect regularly on their own practices and on student responses to such practices. OLCG also promotes a collegial, collaborative learning community (including teachers, Native Elders, and scientists) in which teachers learn from each other as much as they do from the instructors. This entire process has not only supported teacher efforts to change but has provided the program with valuable feedback. Analysis of the data collected from a variety of evaluation tools indicates that the program is beginning to increase teacher understanding and implementation of scientifically accurate and culturally relevant best classroom practices. We have learned a great deal in the last four years about how to support teachers from diverse backgrounds and environments as they implement a culturally responsive and rigorous science inquiry curriculum in their classrooms. OLCG also has started to influence other professional development efforts in Alaska and elsewhere in the United States.

References

Alaska Native Knowledge Network. 1998. *Alaska standards for culturally responsive schools.* Fairbanks, AK: Alaska Native Knowledge Network.

Brooks, G., and M. Brooks. 1993. *The case for constructivist classrooms.* Alexandria, VA: Association of Supervision and Curriculum Development.

Butler, D., and I. D. MacGregor. 2003. GLOBE: Science and education. *Journal of Geoscience Education* 51: 1, 9–20.

Darling-Hammond, L. 1997. *The right to learn.* San Francisco: Jossey-Bass.

Gardner, H. 1983. *Frames of mind.* New York: Basic Books.

Loucks-Horsley, S., P. Hewson, N. Love, and K. Stiles. 1998. *Designing professional development for teachers of science and mathematics.* Thousand Oaks, CA: Corwin Press.

National Research Council (NRC). 1996. *National science education standards.* Washington, DC: National Academy Press.

National Research Council (NRC). 2000. *Inquiry and the national science education standards: A guide for teaching and learning.* Washington, DC: National Academy Press.

Stephens, S. 2000. *Handbook for culturally responsive science curriculum.* Fairbanks, AK: Alaska Rural Systemic Initiative.

Weller, G., and P. Anderson, eds. 1998. *Implications of global change in Alaska and the Bering Sea Region.* Proceedings of a workshop at the University of Alaska Fairbanks, June 3–6, 1997. Fairbanks, AK: Center for Global Change and Arctic System Research.

Operation Chemistry:
Where the Clocks Run by Orange Juice and the T-Shirts Are Never Bare

Paul Kelter
University of Illinois at Urbana-Champaign

Jerry Walsh
University of North Carolina–Greensboro

C. W. McLaughlin
University of Nebraska–Lincoln

Setting

Dan Sitzman teaches chemistry at North High School in Omaha, Nebraska. He has always been interested in science, and his first teaching job was general science at an Omaha middle school. But chemistry has become his passion—so much so that in 1997, he co-wrote a paper in *Science Scope* about his three-year experience in a summer program called Operation Chemistry, or Op Chem for short. The paper, "Nebraska Operation Chemistry: Summers with Polymers, Pasta, and Pedagogy" (Sitzman and Kelter 1998), describes a program that changed the way in which he taught and that inspired him to make chemistry teaching his career. Dan is not alone in his passion for the Op Chem program. Over the past 15 years, well over 1,000 teachers in at least six states have devoted two to three weeks of their summers, along with inservice days during the academic year, to Op Chem.

What is it that has made this program so popular and, we think, successful? ("We" are the authors of this chapter; lead author Kelter is the co-founder of the program.) Part of the answer lies in the training-of-trainers approach. The success can also be traced to a logical sequence of case-based, hands-on activities, most of which can be done safely in the middle school science classroom. The excitement and knowledge of the Op Chem teaching staff (whose members include former participants in the program) play a part. So does the fact that the participants keep in touch with each other and develop a sense of family. Further, the fact that we treat the teacher participants with a special sense of dignity is a hallmark of Op Chem.

In this chapter, we discuss the Op Chem program, including its pedagogical and content basis; its relationship to best teaching practices (including the *More Emphasis* conditions of the National Science Education Standards [NRC 1996]); and enough about the details so that you can plan an Op Chem workshop in your own school district. We want to spread the model of case-based science education and the training-of-trainers approach.

Reaching All Kinds of People

The Op Chem program began in 1988 with a grant from the National Science Foundation. It has since been funded in many states via a variety of state grants. The authors have led the workshops primarily in Wisconsin, Nebraska, and North Carolina. These three states are very different in the nature of their students, yet the program has been assessed by an internationally respected science education assessment firm (PS International) to be highly effective in each state. Wisconsin has a population that is about 93% white and 1% to 2% each African American, Hispanic, and American Indian. The American Indian students typically live in federal reservations in the northern half of the state. Most of the minorities in the state live in the Milwaukee metropolitan area, with African Americans making up about 25% of that city's population (FedStats). Nebraska is also fairly racially homogeneous, with whites making up just short of 90% of the population, Hispanics 5%, and African Americans about 4%, many of whom live in the Omaha metropolitan area. North Carolina has a completely different mix, with a population that is about 61% white, 30% African American, 7% Hispanic, and 2% Asian. The major cities in North Carolina are racially and ethnically diverse, and the local schools reflect the traditional segregation in housing patterns.

The demographics of a typical Operation Chemistry cohort can be represented by the 22 participants in the summer 2001 program, all of whom were inservice teachers. Fifteen taught both math and science, five taught science but not math, and two taught a broad range of courses. Eighteen were white females, two were white males, one was an African American female, and one was an Asian female. Seventeen did a majority of their teaching at the K–5 level; five taught in middle school. Five had certification or endorsement in science, and one had a background in science and science education. Assuming that the typical teacher is part of a team and teaches three classes of 24 students per day, approximately 1,500 students per year are influenced by teachers who participated in Operation Chemistry in 2001.

The Big Picture

To give the reader a sense of Op Chem workshops, let us return to former program participant Dan Sitzman. The home page for his chemistry course at North High School outlines his philosophy on the nature of science and learning science.

Science is communicating our understandings to other people, drawing in different perspectives to support a question that was asked, and inspiring new questions. Science enables humans to make decisions and to develop applications of the knowledge of our world (technology).

I believe learning is an activity. I would rather see all students involved in trying out ideas and doing "hands-on, minds-on" activities than for the teacher to stand in the front of the room and lecture or assign terms to define. Granted, we will have some lectures and notes, and some terms to define. Sometimes the content of this course seems relevant to us; other times we may be unaware how astonishing this quest for understanding is. Therefore, it is the enthusiasm of the students and the teacher that can lift us beyond the basic course content and procedures and take us to deeper understanding, expanded knowledge, new skills, and questions we previously never thought to ask. (Sitzman 2002)

That, in a nutshell, is what we—the program organizers and staff—are about. We are about active learning. We are about context and case studies. We are about taking time to learn how to think like a scientist. And we are about the power and beauty of ideas.

At the core of Op Chem is a three-year series of two-week summer workshops, with the first year introducing teacher participants to the nature of chemistry and to the role of the chemistry teacher. The second and third years of the summer workshops are devoted to developing the ideas and teaching strategies. By the end of the third (final) year of training, the participants are ready to train others in Op Chem workshops. But even after the first year, we have participants give inservice classes based on Op Chem to teachers in their own school districts. This training-of-trainers approach is successful at spreading this active learning, inquiry-based, and case-study-based model of chemistry education to middle school teachers.

The content basis of the Op Chem program consists of the series of 12 Op Chem modules that include discussions and directions about the activities. Each module is based on a central theme, such as the Space Shuttle Program (PK's personal favorite), acids and bases, and the nature of matter.

Meeting the National Science Education Standards Professional Development *More Emphasis* Conditions

The training-of-trainers approach develops self-sufficiency in our participants. We are inquiry-based. This means that the lessons are driven by our good, varied questions about the chemistry that the teachers are doing. It is typical for an Op Chem instructor to ask 60 to 100 questions for each hour of instruction. We mix internal and external expertise. In a recent North Carolina Op Chem workshop, for example, roughly one-third of the instructors were faculty members at the University of North Carolina at Greensboro, one-third were national experts flown in from throughout the country, and one-third were former participants who were previously trained at Op Chem workshops.

Master Teachers and the Relationship to the Training-of-Trainers Model

The training-of-trainers model is one of the most exciting parts of Op Chem because it is indicates that the program continues to prosper with "alumni" as teachers. Master teachers from all educational levels teach in the Op Chem program, helping the participants to develop the content and classroom skills to be teacher-trainers. Once they complete their work with the master teachers, the new teacher-trainers show their expertise in three important ways: They, along with all Op Chem participants, are better classroom teachers; many are given additional, higher-level district science responsibilities because of their newly gained expertise; and they combine their special classroom experience with the Op Chem work to run some really outstanding local programs.

You *Can* Run This Program in Your School District

This section contains the core technical information needed in order to run an Op Chem program.

The goals of the Operation Chemistry program are to

- ◆ enhance the conceptual and activity-related chemistry understanding of sixth- through eighth-grade teachers via a training-of-trainers approach;
- ◆ instill in participants a sense of confidence about their ability to learn and teach chemistry;
- ◆ foster professional growth, including presentation and grant-writing skills;
- ◆ nurture the sense of community among participants that is possible with an intensive, long-term program;
- ◆ prepare participants to present inservice workshops in their schools; and
- ◆ continue a multiyear Op Chem program that will influence science teaching throughout the service region.

First-year Op Chem participants are expected to accomplish the following objectives:

- ◆ Demonstrate knowledge of content and related activities of several nationally field-tested fundamental Op Chem modules and safety in the work area.
- ◆ Design lessons reflecting the relationship of chemistry to other sciences, math, and social concerns.
- ◆ Teach chemistry-related lessons using cooperative learning principles and new multimedia technologies.
- ◆ Plan and deliver six hours of Op Chem–related inservice.

Second-year Op Chem participants are expected to accomplish the following objectives:

- ◆ Demonstrate knowledge of content and related activities of several nationally field-tested fundamental and applied Op Chem modules.
- ◆ Demonstrate the technical and affective skills to be lead physical science teachers in their schools and resource persons in their districts.

- Design Op Chem–based workshops for presentation throughout the state.
- Develop activities using multimedia and prepare a web page for their class.
- Write grade-level-appropriate chemistry activities using the Op Chem model.
- Plan and deliver six hours of Op Chem-related inservice lessons.

Third-year Op Chem participants are expected to accomplish the following objectives:

- Demonstrate knowledge of content and related activities of several nationally field-tested applied Op Chem modules.
- Write their own grants to local, state, or national funding agencies.
- Develop activities using multimedia and prepare a web home page for their school.
- Write districtwide curricula based on their understanding of and experiences with the Op Chem model.
- Design Op Chem–based workshops for presentation throughout the state to demonstrate the content knowledge and teaching skills to be part of the teaching staff in future Op Chem summer teacher workshops.
- Plan and deliver six hours of Op Chem–related inservice.

How We Recruit Participants for the Summer Programs

We typically appropriate state-based grant funding by the middle of December for a June workshop. The Eisenhower program funding that used to be available to states to fund just this sort of program has been replaced by the funding for the No Child Left Behind law, which each state administers according to a specific set of guidelines. North Carolina's program is typical and can be found at the following website: *http://21stcenturyschools.northcarolina.edu/ESEA.html.*

The Op Chem program recruits participants through the coordinated effort of the project staff and the science and curriculum coordinators of the collaborating school systems. The coordinators assist in identifying prospective teachers at targeted public and private schools. School systems typically provide information on targeted lateral-entry teachers (i.e., teachers who do not have a state certification but because of their past experiences—typically as a subject major—are hired to teach with the expectation that they will gain certification within a specified time, typically two years). The program organizers and staff make many phone calls and send out lots of advertising. When a teacher signs on for a summer workshop, we always address him or her on a first-name basis, typically with a handwritten note to accompany any formal letters and information. This makes the participant feel as if he or she is not one of the crowd but is an individual whose participation really matters to us——and it does!

The Op Chem program has a history of inclusion of underrepresented groups. Our diversity is less a product of a forced program design than it is a reflection of who we are, a diverse group of committed science educators who attract just this kind of participant to our workshops. Roughly 80% of all past program participants were women. Well over 200 teachers (of roughly 1,000 who have participated in the program) have taught minority and/or economically disadvantaged students.

We Introduce the Op Chem Modules
With the Space Shuttle Lessons

The Space Shuttle Module (see Table 1), part of the Year 1 curriculum, is an excellent example of the interplay of content, process, and relevance beyond the chemistry fundamentals. The class begins with the core question "What are the needs for life onboard the shuttle?" Discussion topics include food, temperature control, and waste disposal. The shuttle is a materially closed system—just like Earth. Participants see the relationship between the chemistry of the shuttle and the chemistry on Earth, and the module activities reinforce this understanding. Table 1 lists the activities in the shuttle module, their chemistry focuses, and additional curricular branches. For example, in one activity, energy exchange is examined by having participants make a clock run by using orange juice as an electrolyte. The activity can be done at a variety of grade levels, from second grade through university graduate level. In the Op Chem workshop, we use it to discuss the nature of electron-exchange reactions and the ability to get useful work done from these exchanges. Such a setup is more commonly known as a battery. The discussion is extended to fuel cells (vital on the shuttle), their future use in cars, and other environmental issues.

Table 1. Sample Space Shuttle Module Activities

Activity	Chemistry Focuses	Examples of Curricular Branches
Balloon Rockets	Gas laws	Friction, travel
Flame Tests	Energy, wavelength, frequency	How we know the composition of the universe
Elephant Toothpaste	Gas laws, energy exchange	Food science, energy, and life
Chemical Cold Pack	Why reactions occur, entropy	Sports injuries, role of food in the body
Copper/Zinc Reactions	Reduction/oxidation	Nature, refining and societal uses of metals
Orange Juice Clock	Electrochemical cells	Electrolytes in the body, batteries, power sources
Electrolysis of Water	Electrochemistry	Fuel cells for powering cars, personal items, and cities
Shuttle Menu Selection	Biochemistry	Role of foods in the human body, polymers in society
Paper Chromatography	Polarity and bonding	Detection of substances in the body's blood and urine

The first part of Table 2 lists the modules that serve as the content basis of Operation Chemistry in each of the three years of the training. The related coverage areas are given in the second part of the table. As the table entries show, we place a very high priority not only on content, but also on cooperative learning, science across the curriculum, and assessment. We also recognize the importance of multimedia training, though it is our view that it should not be the dominant instructional method in any class. We value the personal interaction between teacher and student, and would not want to lose that.

Table 2. The Levels of Operation Chemistry Training

Year 1	Year 2	Year 3
Primary Coverage—Chemistry Modules		
Safety Language of Chemistry Matter and Its Changes Density, Chemical Reactions, Space Shuttle	Energy Acids and Bases Food Chemistry Space Shuttle Environmental Chemistry Bread Chemistry	Chemistry of Life Polymer Chemistry Industrial Chemistry Chemistry of Eggs
Secondary Coverage—Instructional Activities		
Integrating Chemistry Into Other Curriculum Areas Relating Curriculum to State and National Standards Cooperative Learning Strategies Planning and Delivering an Inservice Multimedia Techniques Modern Assessment Techniques	Relating Curriculum to State and National Standards Multimedia Techniques (Web Design) Modern Assessment Techniques Integrating Chemistry Into Other Curriculum Areas Cooperative Learning Strategies Planning and Delivering an Inservice	Multimedia Techniques (Web Design) Modern Assessment Techniques Integrating Chemistry Into Other Curriculum Areas Cooperative Learning Strategies Grant Writing Planning and Delivering an Inservice

Each Op Chem workshop lasts 9 to 10 days and includes about 50 hours of instruction. Participants can either earn three credits of graduate course work in the school of education at the college with which the program is affiliated or earn the state's continuing education credits, which are required for teachers. Whether commuting locally or staying at a good hotel (the personal dignity aspect again!), participants generally arrive to coffee and a light breakfast between 8:00 and 8:30 a.m. The sessions begin with a discussion of a core concept in chemistry, such as the nature of the periodic table, chemical mathematics, or atomic structure. We often take time to show how the knowledge of chemistry is used to explain important current events, such as the biochemical behavior of weapons of mass destruction or how oil is converted to plastics. We are cheerleaders for science, and we want our participants to know that while science can be used for good and bad pur-

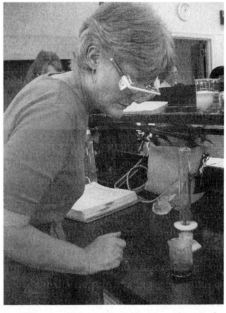

Op Chem participant investigating chemical reactions.

Op Chem instructor questioning participants about the orange juice clock.

poses, on balance it has enhanced the quality of our lives. One beauty of science is that when unintended or unfortunate things happen (such as air pollution), science generally has the remedies. Implementing those remedies is in the realm of public policy, something with which scientists, science teachers, and science students ought to be concerned.

Two long sessions are typically spent doing module-based laboratory work. Most of the activities can be done safely in the middle school classroom. A key here is that we reject the "60 activities in 60 minutes" model. We spend 15 to 30 minutes on each activity, such as those listed in Table 1 for the Space Shuttle Module, with 3 to 5 minutes doing the activity and the remainder of the time spent in all-class discussion on the chemistry, context, and experimental aspects of the activity. We want the teachers to be quite clear about each activity. As an example, we can cite the "orange juice clock" activity. Participants are shown a battery-operated clock in which the battery is replaced by a copper wire at the positive terminal and magnesium wire at the negative terminal. We dip the wires in distilled water, and nothing happens. When the wires are dipped in orange juice, as described more fully in Kelter et al. (1996), the clock begins to tick, and does so for several hours. In discussing why this arrangement works, we talk about electron exchange, the chemistry of batteries, many practical applications, and also changes that students can try in the experimental setup to answer different questions, such as, "Will using different liquids make the clock tick slower or faster?" and "Will different wires work better?" This style of in-class involvement is characteristic of the Op Chem workshops.

Figure 1 shows how Op Chem I, II, and III are blended together in a typical week. Other technical issues include giving our participants "meal cards" with enough money (often about $100 for the workshop) to enjoy lunch at our university's food court. They enjoy the flexibility of eating what they want, and with whom. We always start and end each session promptly. There is nothing that upsets participants more than having to stay late during the summer. We generally give our participants $500 to $750 as an honorarium for their time, along with $100 for small equipment purchases. The money, along with the equipment and the three graduate credits, adds to the sense that these professional teachers are valued.

During the year, we ask that our participants give three to six hours of Op Chem–based instruction in their home school districts or at regional or state workshops. We provide a support system so they can give presentations at the state science teachers' convention, which they enjoy greatly. This is yet another way that we instill in teachers the confidence they need to become trainers of other teachers.

Figure 1. Operation Chemistry Schedule Summer 2002: Activities for Op Chem I, II, and III

	Monday			Tuesday		
	I	II	III	I	II	III
8:30–9:30	Content Class	Content Class	Content Class	Content Class	Content Class	Content Class
9:30–11:30	Safety	Food	Environment	Space Shuttle	Food	Environment
12:30–3:30	Space	Food	Environment	Content and State Standards	Content and State Standards	Content and State Standards

	Wednesday			Thursday		
	I	II	III	I	II	III
8:30–9:30	Content Class	Content Class	Content Class	Content Class	Content Class	Content Class
9:30–11:30	Chemical Reactions	Life	Earth Elements	Acids/ Bases	Polymers	Industrial Soap
12:30–3:30	Chemical Reactions	Life	Earth Elements	Pancakes	Polymers	Industrial Soap

	Friday		
	I	II	III
8:30–9:30	Content Class	Content Class	Content Class
9:30–11:30	Acid/ Bases	Life	Industrial Soap
12:30–3:30	T-Shirt Chroma-tography	Web Page Design Workshop	Eggs Revisited

Program Evaluation and Assessment

Many complementary methods of assessment have shown that Operation Chemistry leads to improvements in student learning and understanding of science. PS International has done evaluations for 14 of the 15 years of Op Chem summer workshops. The evaluations include traditional methods such as questionnaires, along with more modern methods of qualitative, but no less meaningful, data acquisition, including focus groups and pictorial journals to characterize Op Chem and its role as a professional development program. Evaluations take place prior to teacher participation in the program, during the program, and one year after the program. Questionnaires probed several aspects of the Op Chem program, including the quality of the summer workshop; the value of the activities; the attitudes of the participants; the perceived importance of, and preparation of the participant for, various aspects of classroom experiences; and the frequency of use of various forms of classroom activities.

In evaluating the specific Op Chem modules, teacher responses have been consistently favorable. The responses reflected in Figures 2 and 3 from the summer 2002 workshops are typical. They are representative of 14 years of assessments.

After the 2002 workshop, teachers responded to a survey that asked them to rate different aspects of the program. Data presented here focus on the outcome—Is the material appropriate for the classroom, and is it likely to produce a change? In responses rated from *Strongly Disagree*

Figure 2. Number of Teacher Responses in Each Category for the "Classroom Practice" Activities (Summer 2002)

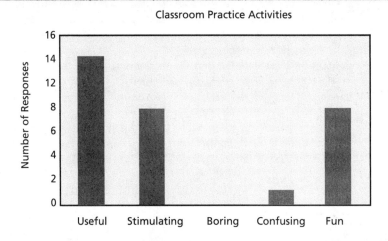

Figure 3. Number of Teacher Responses in Each Category for the "Matter" Module (Summer 2002)

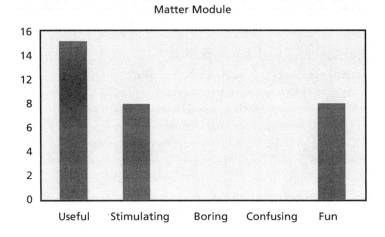

Table 3. Rating of Desirable Characteristics of the Operation Chemistry Program (Summer 2002) (*N* = 40)	
Statement	**Score (5 = best)**
This activity addressed the most pressing needs I have as a teacher.	4.4
Materials presented at appropriate level of difficulty for my background.	4.1
Instructional techniques appropriate for reaching the intended outcome.	4.6
Useful methods for transferring new knowledge and skills.	4.7
I plan to use information from this activity in my classroom.	4.7

(scored as a 1) to *Strongly Agree* (scored as a 5), the findings shown in Table 3 were obtained. The data, which include responses from all participants to all questions, show that Op Chem is producing significant changes in the participants' classrooms.

Summary of Indications of the Success of the Program

The Operation Chemistry program has had a significant impact in the classrooms of teacher participants. In one case, a private school teacher (who may have had more flexibility than other teachers!) threw out her textbook and used the Operation Chemistry modules as the basis for her lesson plans. In another case, a participant stated, "I am redoing the way science will be taught in my middle school classes." We have 15 years of such anecdotes, where the approach to classroom science teaching has been revolutionized as a result of participation in the Operation Chemistry program.

A significant number of teachers return for multiple years of Operation Chemistry training. They leave the workshop having focused on the National Science Education Standards *More Emphasis* goals of

- understanding scientific concepts and developing abilities of inquiry;
- integrating all aspects of science content;
- implementing inquiry as strategies, abilities, and ideas to be learned;
- investigating and analyzing science questions;
- doing more investigations in order to develop understanding, ability, values of inquiry, and knowledge of science content;
- teachers as members of a collegial professional community;
- teachers as leaders (training-of-trainers);
- teachers as producers of knowledge about teaching; and
- learning science through investigation and inquiry.

We hope that, having read this essay, you have the sense that you can run an Op Chem program in your school district or state. We want you to know that we will support you via e-mail discussions, help with writing grant proposals, and, if at all possible, in person to teach a session or two for you. Please remember Dan Sitzman's words from his home page: "Science is communicating our understandings to other people." How right he is.

References

FedStats. *www.fedstats.gov/qf/*. FedStats is a compendium of information from many federal government agencies.

Kelter, P. B., J. D. Carr, T. Johnson, and C. M. Castro-Acuña. 1996. The chemical and educational appeal of the orange juice clock. *Journal of Chemical Education* 73: 1123–1127.

National Research Council (NRC). 1996. *National science education standards.* Washington, DC: National Academy Press.

North Carolina Quest Website. *http://21stcenturyschools.northcarolina.edu/ESEA.html.*

Sitzman, D. 2002. Omaha North High School Home Page/Chemistry Course: *http://teachers.ops.org/dsitzman/stories/*

Sitzman, D., and P. B. Kelter. 1998. Nebraska Operation Chemistry: Summers with polymers, pasta, and pedagogy. *Science Scope* 21 (6): 68–70.

Community of Excellence: More Emphasis on Teacher Quality

Susan B. Koba
Omaha Public Schools

Carol T. Taylor Mitchell
University of Nebraska-Omaha

Setting

The Omaha Public Schools (OPS) is the largest urban district in Nebraska. The 45,000-plus students in our district are ethnically diverse compared to other regions in the state. Over 80% of the state's African American student population is in the OPS, making up approximately 31.2% of the student enrollment. Caucasian students make up 49.1% of the student population, Hispanics make up 16.6%, and all other ethnic groups (primarily Asian and American Indian) combined represent the remaining 3.1% of the student population. There are a total of 83 schools: 62 elementary schools, 9 middle schools, 7 high schools and 5 ungraded schools. District teachers of mathematics and science total 2,257.

The OPS has successfully completed a five-year Comprehensive Partnerships for Mathematics and Science Achievement (CPMSA) award, funded by the National Science Foundation (NSF). At the time of this writing we are in our fourth year of another NSF award, the Urban Systemic Program (USP). The USP is named Banneker 2000: CEMS (Community of Excellence in Mathematics and Science). As a systemic initiative site, our district addresses all areas of the National Science Education Standards (NSES) (NRC 1996). This chapter details one aspect—that is, implementation of the NSES Professional Development Standards—of our broader systemic work and shares the story of our district's strong model of professional development, designed to enhance teacher learning so that we can provide rigorous, quality science experiences for all of our preK–12 students.

National Science Education Standards *More Emphasis* Conditions in the Omaha Public Schools

CEMS professional development, designed around the NSES, results in more emphasis being placed on Standards-based practices. (In this essay, the *More Emphasis* conditions of the NSES appear in italics.)

We know that simply distributing the NSES, defining congruent district standards, and putting in place assessments does not ensure their implementation. Implementation requires teacher change—a complex process given that it targets teachers' beliefs and philosophies (Koba and Clarke 2002; Lortie 1975; Fullan and Stiegelbauer 1991; Hargreaves and Fullan 1998). In CEMS, participants commit to work-embedded learning and demonstrate their learning through a portfolio with four segments: (1) beliefs and philosophy, (2) content, (3) curriculum and instruction, and (4) action research. Although beliefs are the focus of Part I of the portfolio, they are also explicit in the teachers' reflective action research (Part IV), requiring teachers to be *intellectual, reflective practitioners*. The portfolios also require demonstration of content learning (Part II) and enhanced pedagogy (curriculum and instruction) (Part III) calling for teachers to *integrate theory and practice in the school setting*. Teachers demonstrate their learning in units of study they develop, implement, videotape, and reflect upon. Data are collected between rounds of implementation, analyzed, and used to facilitate changed instruction, *integrating theory and practice in the school setting*. Finally, the participants' research results are included in a database of resources available to teachers, honoring participants as *producers of knowledge about teaching*.

Our flexible but carefully designed program demonstrates all NSES Professional Development *More Emphasis* conditions, with the heart of the experience an *inquiry into teaching and learning*. Teachers implement their learning in the classroom and also research its impact on student learning. The vignettes in this essay share participants' stories and illustrate how CEMS helps teachers put more emphasis on Standards-based practices, creating environments more likely to result in student success in, and love of, science. To quantify the learning portrayed in the vignettes, data are presented that demonstrate teacher change and student achievement.

An Introduction to the Program and Participants

To ensure flexibility in the program, three approaches—called "paths"—are available. In each path, the participant develops and implements a learning plan, resulting in *a variety of professional development activities*. These plans are based on personal learning needs, school improvement goals, and student achievement needs. In the University Path, individual teachers choose to complete their learning through 18 hours of graduate work at the University of Nebraska-Omaha or they can opt to work with the support of a CEMS professional development specialist (PDS), a math and science specialist from the OPS. In the Team Path, member teams of two to four participants collaborate to learn and compile their portfolio; their learning plan is based on composite team needs. Finally, in the Schoolwide Path, teachers produce portfolios that are based on school needs, but incorporate the teachers' needs as well. In all cases, participation is voluntary. However, for teachers to participate the principal must commit to involve 70% of a school's fourth- to ninth-grade teachers at some point in a three-year period. The school is then a Developing School, with teachers and leaders choosing the options best suited to them.

To determine the participants' learning needs, we worked with McREL (Mid-continent Research for Education and Learning) to develop a unique online Profiler, a set of Likert-scale statements to which participants respond. This online instrument clusters teachers' responses around broad categories (e.g., inquiry, equity, motivation) and compares the results to those of exemplars. Areas of discrepancy are identified and used by participants to develop learning goals and databases of linked standards; research-based practices help participants find resources for learning. Participants complete an online plan to which their PDS responds. As these *long-term coherent plans* are implemented, participants complete an online portfolio, supported electronically by the PDS in an interactive manner. The electronic environment, coupled with face-to-face interactions, requires that the PDSs serve in the capacity of *staff developers as facilitators, consultants, and planners* and that participants work as *members of a collegial professional community*.

The following vignettes demonstrate how each of the three paths works. The stories focus on the unique, flexible aspects of the CEMS program; changes that participants experienced; and evidence of the NSES *More Emphasis* conditions in practice. The vignettes depict educators in urban schools with diverse classrooms, often composed of students very different from the teachers themselves. Some of the elementary teachers had previously ignored science instruction or had taught science only through mandate and with fear. The vignettes follow the teachers' journeys as they become more engaged in quality science teaching and learning. (All names are pseudonyms.)

Vignette 1—The University Path

Sandra is an enthusiastic teacher who is dedicated to the students in her grade 1/2 class at Elementary School A. Her students represent a subset of the 370 students at this preK–6 school. Sandra plans very carefully for her classes and has student achievement at the top of her priorities. However, as a former business worker with a limited background in biology, she admits that she needs more science content and that her university degree in education did not really prepare her to teach science and mathematics.

When her school implemented an improvement plan with an emphasis on science and mathematics, Sandra wanted to participate to increase her understanding of and confidence in science. The CEMS portfolio opportunity proved to be the answer for her. She chose the University Path because she wanted to enroll in the university's specifically developed modules and courses in science. These were developed collaboratively by professors in both the College of Arts and Sciences and the College of Education at the University of Nebraska-Omaha. Over 15 months, Sandra completed 18 graduate hours to enhance her content and pedagogical understandings in science. She selected modules based on her profiled learning needs, and for part of her 18 hours she enrolled in Earth Science for Educators and a geology field project. This led to her increased confidence in preparing for the new curriculum in Earth science.

As a result of CEMS professional development, Sandra described herself as a more inquiry-based teacher, one who is more a guide to discovery in the classroom than a lecturer and owner of the knowledge. She said, "I thought that I had to know everything in the science content area." However, she realized through her experiences that it was okay to learn along with her

Table 1. Impact on Achievement—CEMS University Cohort #2[a]

Grade	Discipline	Achievement Impact	Other
K–4	Science	Increased demonstration of conceptual understanding in journals	Positive impact on attitude
K	Science	School's CRT success above district average (86.2% vs. 82.1%). Participant's classes—100% success	
1	Science	Two CRTs administered—86% of students proficient or advanced	Students more involved and open to others' ideas
1	Science	School's first-grade CRTs above district average. Overall success rate is 83.9% vs. 77.2%	
1/2	Science	Less re-teaching required for CRT mastery. School's first- and second-grade CRTs significantly above district (first grade: 92.9% vs. 77.2%; second grade: 93.4% vs. 74.4%)	Higher-order questions asked; increased problem-solving without assistance
2	Science	Little re-teaching required for students to score Proficient or Advanced	Improved student motivation, collaboration, and creativity
2	Science	First CRT administered had 50% of students at Proficient or Advanced; last two CRTs had 100%	Increased engagement. Students' report understanding
2	Science	100% success on Standards 201 (Inquiry), 202 (Unifying Concepts/Processes), and 204 (Plants and Animals)	Improved student motivation
2	Science	93% of students Proficient or Advanced	Positive impact on attitude and participation
4	Science	90% successful on CRTs	Students more engaged
5/6	Math	School's fifth- and sixth-grade CRTs significantly above district average with increasing trend: 86.3% success (fifth grade) and 90.2% success (sixth grade). Participant's class—90% success	Increased confidence and enjoyment in mathematics
5/6	Math	92% mastered CRT	Positive attitude
7	Science	Positive impact on grades: 24% increase in Bs and 15% decrease in failures	Increase in higher-level questioning and responses to higher-level questions
7	Math	Improved mean score on problem-solving test	
8	Math	Average test grades increased from 75% to 86%; pretest mean score was 34.5% (no one scoring above 75%); on posttest, all but one student passed scoring 78% or higher	Improved attitudes about problem solving
HS Phys.	Science	Increased conceptual understanding; school's CRT success (84%) vs. district's CRT success (76%)	Improved attitude
HS Geom.	Math	Improved achievement on performance projects and traditional classroom assessments	Improved participation and behavior

[a] Sandra's action research findings are in the shaded row. CRT stands for Criterion Referenced Test.

students. First and second graders could discover science on their own. Sandra presented evidence of her students' mastery of the district content standards. She and her students have a greater understanding and enjoyment of the learning process.

Discovery was a critical teaching tool in Sandra's classroom. Her action research suggests that when students are engaged in cooperative learning groups there is an increase in the amount of higher-order questions in the categories of comprehension, analysis, and evaluation. Additionally, Sandra's research results showed an increased frequency of problem solving without the teacher's assistance. As a result, her classroom was more student-directed. Sandra said that her students were now drawing more details and labeling more accurately in their science journals. The videotape included in her portfolio also provided evidence of this finding. Students were achieving mastery. Table 1 summarizes action research findings by Sandra (shaded row) and the cohort of teachers with whom she participated in CEMS.

Vignette 2—The Team Path and a Leadership Team

Elementary School B, a diverse, Title I school, offers the only OPS multiage program. In 2001, the principal, Mary, committed to her school's becoming a CEMS Developing School, and a few teachers began their work. During the year, other teachers voiced concern about teaching science, and Mary knew science was often omitted from the day's learning experience. With the advent of the district's Criterion Referenced Tests (CRTs) in science, it could no longer be ignored. Scaffolding was needed for teachers to teach science, and Mary responded to the Team Path option. Together with Barb, the instructional facilitator, she recruited teams and supported portfolio work with release-time occurring every 10 days. Also important is the fact that they committed to complete a Leadership Team Portfolio. Barb said, "When I approached Mary with the idea of … completing a portfolio together, she was very willing. This process takes a great deal of time and as a building administrator, she has no extra time. This was a huge commitment for two very busy people."

The leadership team's commitment was integral to the eventual success of the program—Barb and Mary modeled their expectations of the staff. The teachers responded positively; staff participation resulted in the required 70% of fourth- to sixth-grade teachers and preK–fourth-grade teachers also becoming involved.

We worked closely with Barb and Mary that fall; their commitment was evident from the first day. This very busy pair spent a full afternoon with their PDS to complete the online profile, focus on profiled needs, and plan the next steps. They accessed CEMS online resources aligned with learning goals and tested the interactive online environment so they knew how to find our feedback. The leadership portfolio required them to learn about inquiry-based teaching, design professional development (in lieu of a unit of instruction), provide that professional development, and analyze its impact on teacher and student learning.

Barb and Mary immersed themselves in learning about inquiry and the nature of science, both needs indicated by their profiled results. At times they were overwhelmed, but when they encountered barriers, they immediately requested support, resulting in a *mix of internal and external expertise*. We interacted online, by phone, and face-to-face to map the sequence of their professional development sessions and develop their action research methodology.

The first professional development session was held on a "Science Saturday" during the second semester. Attendees included CEMS teachers and others who were not working on portfolios. While well received, it became apparent that the staff had many other needs. Feedback from teachers (part of the leadership team's action-research data) indicated a greater need for content knowledge and a need to organize the school's science materials in ways that would support science instruction. Two district elementary curriculum consultants were invited to the remaining Science Saturdays to focus on content learning, organization of science materials, and hands-on experiences of the lessons; teachers would then teach students. Barb and Mary co-presented these sessions.

Between sessions, the leaders completed three-minute walk-throughs (Downey 2001) in 16 classrooms to look for evidence of inquiry-based instruction. We did the first walk-through together, modifying the instrument for further work. Barb also felt that science was not evident in the classrooms, so she provided each room with standards posters and 5E learning cycle (Bybee 1997) posters and encouraged teachers to create other evidence of science instruction (e.g., bulletin boards and centers).

After months of work to enhance hands-on, minds-on science, it became evident that the efforts were leading to change. The leaders saw teachers begin to teach science, whereas they had ignored it in the past. They also saw evidence of science on the walls, in student dialogue, and in science centers. Table 2 shows the pre- and post-survey results gathered from second-through sixth-grade students and from the 20 teachers involved in CEMS. These data demonstrate the changes in students' and teachers' attitudes and efficacy.

Table 2. Action Research Pre- and Post-Survey Results for Teachers and Grades 2–6 Students

Focus of Survey Question	Initial Survey % Response	Final Survey % Response
Teacher level of comfort with inquiry-based science	15%	76%
Teacher love of teaching inquiry-based science	5%	72%
Student level of "liking" science	55%	90%
Student response—whether their teacher liked teaching science	40%	89%
Students thought they would pass their CRT	30%	80%

In her portfolio, Mary summarized the learning she and Barb had gained and the impact they felt their efforts had had on their school:

Reading the variety of articles was especially helpful for me since they seemed to inform me about the freedom of teaching science using the inquiry approach. Discussions with my partner enabled me to examine my beliefs and understandings from a different viewpoint in some instances. Surveys of staff and students were a key component of the success of my unit. The opportunity to learn what the students and teachers thought about science and the inquiry approach dictated the direction that I could take to improve science instruction in this school. Teachers were frank in telling what they wanted and needed to do a better job of teaching science. The three-minute walk-throughs provided the evidence I needed to see that teachers had indeed learned how to teach using the inquiry method and that students enjoyed science more when learning in an inquiry-based classroom setting. This project has served as a wonderful starting point for continual growth in my mission to provide students with fun and meaningful science lessons.

School B has begun a journey to improve science teaching and learning. In fact, the improvements in student achievement at the school qualified it as an Exemplary School, which resulted in its receiving additional resources to continue its work. Data upon which the exemplary status was determined are presented in Figures 1 and 2 and Table 3.

Vignette 3—The Schoolwide Path

The Middle School C (fifth–eighth grades) principal was interested in professional development tailored to the needs of all science teachers. Each grade-level science team participated in the Schoolwide Path, using the lesson study process to complete a school portfolio. The decision

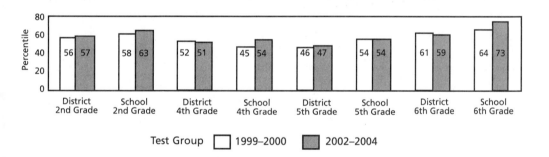

Figure 1. District Schools and Exemplary School California Achievement Test (CAT) Percentiles—Computation

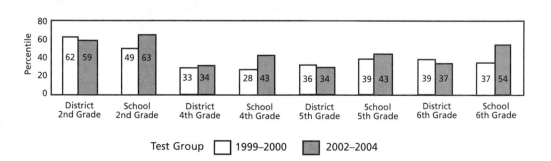

Figure 2. District Schools and Exemplary School California Achievement Test (CAT) Percentiles—Concepts and Application

Grade	Math District	Math School	Difference	Science District	Science School	Difference
K	92.1	95.0	+2.9	82.1	79.1	-3.0
1	95.5	95.9	+0.4	77.2	92.9	+15.7
2	90.7	93.2	+2.5	74.4	93.4	+19.0
3	78.7	78.7	—	64.8	97.7	+32.9
4	76.7	84.9	+8.2	73.9	85.5	+11.6
5	80.0	86.3	+6.3	62.0	70.5	+8.5
6	73.7	90.2	+16.5	66.8	87.1	+20.3

Table 3. District CRT Results vs. Exemplary School CRT Results

to include all science teachers in this schoolwide effort was made only after careful assessment of the teachers' needs, including a series of classroom observations. Our work began during the spring 2003 semester with three full-day workshops, each separated by a month during which teachers implemented their learning in their classrooms and reflected on it; their work continues to date. This vignette shares the story of teachers' learning during the first semester's work.

The fifth-grade team includes two novice teachers with high enthusiasm. The two sixth-grade teachers brought more experience to the group but both entered the experience as more traditional science teachers. The seventh- and eighth-grade teams include experienced teachers, the planetarium director, and one permanent substitute with a background in special education. These two teams represent a mix of traditional and constructivist teaching. While there was skepticism and even a hint of cynicism among the seventh- and eighth-grade teams, the overall reception was positive.

During the first session we conducted a needs dialogue to identify the gap between teachers' aspirations and their perceived reality of students. The teachers also completed the Profiler online. Based on these data, the focus of the portfolio and lesson study was defined—to "promote curious, responsible students through real-world inquiry experiences that require critical thinking and collaborative learning." Teacher learning around inquiry-based instruction was guided by the goal, and progress toward the goal was measured during action research. Lesson study was used to help teachers close the gap between their aspirations and the perceived reality of students.

Each team identified a standard they would teach that spring. Using the *National Science Education Standards* (NRC 1996), the *Atlas of Science Literacy* (AAAS 2001), and grade-level appropriate versions of the *NSTA Pathways to the Science Standards* series (Texley and Wild 1996), they explored the content of the standard. They were asked to complete additional readings prior to the next session and compile journal entries about how their instruction might or might not help develop the students of their aspirations.

At the next session, teachers learned more about process skills and how to enhance lessons to promote students' process abilities. A specific lesson was targeted and developed using the lesson study process. Grade-level teams shared their detailed lesson, including the inquiry strategies previously learned, and received constructive critique from other teams. This helped *focus on student understanding and use of scientific knowledge, ideas, and inquiry processes*. One member of each team volunteered to have the lesson he or she taught videotaped. Teachers were provided additional readings and prepared to videotape before the next session.

During the third meeting, grade-level teams used analysis instruments to critique the videos and, led by a CEMS facilitator, reflected on the analysis. As we closed the third session, plans were made to re-teach these lessons upon school start-up in the fall.

It was during this third session that the remaining "resisters" began to more fully collaborate in the process and see the benefits of our efforts. Feedback from the teachers at the end of the semester exemplifies the impact this experience had on their learning. Among their comments were the following:

> *I was apprehensive because I thought the experience would be more of a critique of my teaching style. I now realize this isn't about criticism, but different ways to make lessons work better for the student.* (More Emphasis condition: *understanding and responding to individual student's interests, strengths, experiences, and needs*)

> *Our work was effective because we were given time to plan and reflect. We were also given time to analyze and make changes.* (More Emphasis condition: *selecting and adapting curriculum*)

> *I was able to collaborate with my peers to study instructional practices. I feel I have grown five years as a professional educator.* (More Emphasis condition: *working with other teachers to enhance the science program*)

In May, School C's science coordinator shared his perceptions of teachers' changed attitudes with us. He felt that the teams had became more cohesive and were excited about ongoing lesson study in the fall and the potential it held for their school. At the time of this writing, the teachers' work continues.

More Emphasis on Reform in the Omaha Public Schools

The Urban Systemic Program is integral to the broader district efforts in science. It supports content learning as aligned with the NSES, but also as aligned with school improvement plans (EXCELS Plus). These plans, when well implemented, require more emphasis on standards-based content, assessment, teaching, and staff development. The CEMS program is the support process for these plans.

CEMS staff participated in the alignment of district standards with state and national standards as well as in the articulation of standards across the grades. The priority district science goal is inquiry. Each grade level is responsible for particular physical, Earth and space, and life science standards. Infused in each of these content standards are the other five content standards. This organizational structure provides the framework for *understanding scientific con-*

cepts and developing abilities of inquiry; learning subject matter disciplines in the context of inquiry; technology; science in personal and social perspectives; history and nature of science; integrating all aspects of science content; studying a few fundamental science concepts; and *process skills in context.* However, the framework alone does not ensure implementation at the classroom level. Support during implementation is at the heart of CEMS professional development efforts.

We worked with the district to develop CRTs for Nebraska's accountability system (STARS [School-based, Teacher-led Assessment and Reporting System]) and, eventually, federal reporting. We also helped develop course guides using backwards design (Wiggins and McTighe 1998). In addition, our professional development specialists work with CEMS teachers as they learn standards, improve classroom assessment, and administer CRTs (required of action research). As a result, we are moving toward *assessing what is most highly valued, assessing scientific understanding and reasoning, assessing to learn what students do understand,* and *assessing achievement and opportunity to learn.*

As demonstrated in the vignettes, the CEMS professional development model exemplifies all of the NSES Professional Development *More Emphases* conditions and our participants demonstrate the *More Emphasis* conditions of the Teaching Standards. Our additional work in the Curriculum and Learning Department at the Omaha Public Schools helps promote most of the *More Emphasis* areas of the Program Standards. CEMS currently funds the BSCS SCI Center's Analyzing Instructional Materials (AIM) process to facilitate our elementary science adoption (BSCS 2002).

Changes in Schools, Teachers, and Students

The true test of our program is its impact on teachers and students. Two cohorts have now completed portfolios with proficient or advanced ratings, indicating that they implemented the NSES *More Emphasis* conditions. All participants demonstrated in their action research that they had had a positive impact on student learning. A third cohort completed work in June 2004, and a fourth cohort has begun its work.

We named our first Exemplary School (see Vignette 2, above) and are very close to naming five to seven additional Exemplary Schools. We have fulfilled our first three years' agreements with the National Science Foundation for school and teacher involvement. More importantly, we anticipate an even broader impact because other Omaha public schools have indicated their intention to participate as CEMS Developing Schools in an effort to put more emphasis on Standards-based science learning.

References

American Association for the Advancement of Science (AAAS). 2001. *Atlas of science literacy.* New York: Oxford University Press.

BSCS: The SCI Center. 2002. *AIM: Analyzing instructional materials.* [Brochure]. Colorado Springs, CO: The SCI Center.

Bybee, R. W. 1997. *Achieving science literacy: From purposes to practices.* Portsmouth, NH: Heinemann.

Downey, C. J. 2001. Walk-throughs with reflective feedback. Presentation at the annual meeting of the National Staff Development Council, Denver, CO.

Fullan, M., and S. Stiegelbauer. 1991. *The new meaning of educational change*. 2nd ed. New York: Teachers College Press.

Hargreaves, A., and M. Fullan. 1998. *What's worth fighting for out there?* New York: Teachers College Press.

Koba, S., and W. Clarke. 2002. Action research: A tool to promote inquiry-based teaching and learning. In *Action research in science education,* eds. D. L. Jordan and J. T. Sutton, pp. 1–40. Aurora, CO: McREL.

Lortie, D. 1975. *Schoolteacher: A sociological study*. Chicago, IL: University of Chicago Press.

National Research Council (NRC). 1996. *National science education standards*. Washington, DC: National Academy Press.

Texley, J., and A. Wild. 1996. *NSTA pathways to the science standards: High school edition*. Arlington, VA: NSTA Press.

Wiggins, G., and J. McTighe. 1998. *Understanding by design*. Alexandria, VA: Association for Supervision and Curriculum Development.

Filling the Void in the Professional Development Continuum:

Assisting Beginning Secondary Science Teachers

Julie A. Luft
University of Texas at Austin

Gillian H. Roehrig
University of Minnesota

Nancy C. Patterson
Bowling Green State University

T he first years of teaching are generally regarded as the most difficult and challenging of an educator's career. One must learn school and district policies, locate curricular materials, organize lessons, practice instructional skills, develop and enact management plans, and motivate students. Some new teachers manage their first few years with ease, and experience relatively few problems. The majority, however, find the transition difficult on many levels. The recent nationwide dialogue on beginning teachers acknowledges the challenges they face and has reconfirmed the need for programs that foster the continual development of teachers. Such programs can help beginning teachers retain and enact their reform-based practices and ideologies, as well as contribute to their retention (Gold 1996).

Beginning teachers deserve and need induction programs that are as carefully crafted as their preservice or inservice programs. Induction programs should be situated within the discipline and foster the ongoing development of the teacher in a manner that is conducive to student learning and to teacher growth and development. In science education, two significant documents, *Before It's Too Late* (National Commission on Mathematics and Science Teaching for the 21st Century 2000) and *Educating Teachers of Science, Mathematics, and Technology: New Practices for the New Millennium* (Committee on Science and Mathematics Teacher Preparation 2000), state the importance of fostering the ongoing development of science teachers. The authors of both documents offer few specifics related to the design and planning of such programs, but they suggest that beginning teachers should enter learning communities, continue to learn about essential local and state standards, and participate in programs that are appropriate for their level of experience.

This chapter describes an induction program for secondary science teachers. Because there were not enough new teachers in secondary science at a school or in a district to warrant a program that was crafted to foster their professional development, the decision was made to work within a region to create a community of beginning secondary science teachers. The program was open to any first-, second-, or third-year secondary science teacher in the region, an area that ultimately covered several hundred miles. Science teachers from rural and urban middle schools and high schools, from low and high socioeconomic backgrounds, and from diverse and homogeneous schools were all invited and encouraged to participate in the program.

Guiding the Development of the Induction Program

Several documents informed decisions related to theory and practice in the development of our induction program. Two documents are important enough to briefly discuss here. The first document, a study conducted in 2001 (Luft and Cox 2001), described the state of induction programs in Arizona. The authors found limited numbers of beginning science teachers who had participated in a discipline-specific induction program and few beginning science teachers who were being mentored by science teachers. They also found that most beginning science teachers wanted more assistance than they experienced in their induction program. In light of the goals for the ongoing development of beginning science teachers, it was evident that a suitable program was not in place.

The second document, the *National Science Education Standards* (NRC 1996), provided important recommendations for the focus of our induction program. Specifically, the Standards state how important it is for students to know and explore the natural world, discuss their newfound understanding of the natural world in ways that demonstrate an understanding of science as inquiry, and link their new understanding, knowledge, and skills to their daily lives. To accomplish these goals, the Standards recommend that science teachers have sound learning experiences in science as inquiry and that their professional development experiences be developmentally appropriate. Our induction program sought to assist beginning teachers to consistently implement science as inquiry in their science classrooms. We emphasized a long-term learning process centered around three key ideas: the use of a variety of professional development activities that were developmentally appropriate; a mix of both university and school district experts who worked with the beginning teachers; and respect for the beginning teachers as intellectual, knowledgeable, and reflective practitioners who were part of a collegial community.

Our Program

Alternative Support for Induction Science Teachers (ASIST) was developed to bridge the gap between the graduation of teachers from science teacher preparation programs and the first years in the science classroom. The program, which ran for four years, was developed by Julie Luft with the assistance of mentor teachers and local administrators in the region. Any first-, second-, or third-year secondary science teacher was eligible to participate in the ASIST program. It is important to note that all beginning science teachers in the region could participate in the program, not just teachers who were graduates of the University of Arizona teacher education programs. To encourage participation, beginning teachers received either graduate credit at the university or district recertification credit. ASIST was initially funded for three years (1998–2001) through the Arizona Board of Regents' Eisenhower Mathematics and Science Program. Eventually, school districts and other grants provided the resources needed to administer the program.

Two groups of personnel were associated with the ASIST program. Overseeing the program was an advisory board made up of program staff, various school district staff-development specialists, and superintendents. The advisory board reviewed program format, checked the alignment of the program with district and state standards, and provided feedback on the implementation of the program. Six staff members worked directly with up to 20 beginning teachers each year. The program staff typically included one university science educator experienced in working with preservice and inservice teachers; three experienced science teachers, who were trained as mentors, were knowledgeable about Standards-based instruction, and were able to clearly explain their instruction; and two graduate assistants, who worked in various capacities with the beginning science teachers and were responsible for classroom support, observations, and data collection.

The ASIST program had several components that were designed to meet the expressed needs of beginning secondary science teachers in southern Arizona (see Luft and Cox 2001). These components were monthly Saturday meetings that allowed teachers to work in small- and large-group settings; electronic communications; classroom visits by program staff or peers; and a trip to a state or national science teachers' conference. Collectively, these components facilitated the professional development of the participating beginning science teachers. A more comprehensive discussion regarding the program can be found in Luft and Patterson (2002).

Our Teachers

The teachers who participated in ASIST came from a variety of backgrounds and taught various courses (Table 1). While it would be difficult to describe a typical teacher in the program, there were a few trends that were consistent over the years—the participation of university-certified teachers was typically high, most teachers taught general science classes, several teachers were teaching out of their major, and both middle and high school teachers participated in the program. The schools in which the teachers taught varied also, but again there were some distinct trends. Most of the ASIST teachers were from urban schools, with only five teachers coming from rural schools. In addition, most of the teachers worked in schools in which a majority of the students were Hispanic, while 10 teachers worked in schools that consisted primarily of Anglo students. In southern Arizona schools with a predominantly Hispanic student population, a majority of the students qualify for free or reduced lunch, and they struggle to achieve high levels of student performance per the state assessments.

	Year 1 (n = 13)	Year 2 (n = 17)	Year 3 (n = 21)	Year 4 (n = 19)
Middle school teachers	8	7	13	9
High school teachers	5	10	8	10
Science fields:				
• Biology	0	2	1	5
• Chemistry	0	0	2	2
• Physics	3	4	0	2
• Earth science	1	1	2	1
• General science	9	10	16	9
Returning teachers	NA	8	2	6
Teaching outside of major	4	7	12	12
Nonscience major	3	1	1	6
Emergency certified	1	0	1	1
University certification	9	11	13	16
Alternative certification	3	6	7	1
Uncertified	0	0	1	1

Table 1. The Background of Beginning Teachers in Years 1, 2, 3, and 4 of the ASIST Program*

* All participating teachers.

ASIST as an Exemplary Program

In the last two years, several articles describing the ASIST program have been published in various journals and books. An early publication by Luft and Patterson (2002) described the design and structure—the "nuts and bolts"—of the program and presented illustrative vignettes of various ASIST components. A later book chapter by Patterson et al. (2003) discussed the underlying theoretical assumptions of the program. That extended discussion focused on the discipline-specific and reflective nature of the ASIST program, two essential features for the creation of a continuum that supports science teacher development. A more reflective paper, describing the pathways and barriers that existed in the planning, development, and enactment of the ASIST program, was written by Luft, Roehrig, and Patterson (2002). This paper provided a glimpse into the entire process surrounding the development of the program and proposed a model for those interested in creating such a program themselves. Together, the articles are resource materials for science teacher educators who are interested in developing their own discipline-specific induction programs.

While the background and process of the ASIST program have been well described, the alignment of the program to the National Science Education Standards has not. Such an extended discussion is important if science teacher educators are going to start implementing aspects of the program. A solid connection to the Standards can demonstrate the applicability of this model in different settings, as well as offer a guiding framework that extends beyond our region. Our approach here will focus on the Professional Development Standards and the Teaching Standards. Though these Standards were touched upon in an earlier discussion, a more extensive explication will demonstrate the purposefulness in the design and implementation of the program and show how the program represents a change in emphasis in regard to professional development and teaching.

The Professional Development Standards emphasize learning opportunities that draw on the knowledge and abilities of the teacher in a manner that is conducive to the ongoing development of the teacher. While the ASIST program attended to the growth of the teacher, it did so in a manner that was developmentally appropriate. After all, these were first-, second-, and third-year teachers who were just beginning their careers in education. To foster the development of each teacher, we attempted to create a group that was actively engaged in understanding and exploring classroom practices. All individuals in the group frequently examined their enactment of science as inquiry in the classroom, as well as classroom management and lesson planning, with the assistance of university faculty and mentor science teachers.

While the ASIST program demonstrated several ideas from the area of professional development referred to as "changing emphases" (NRC 1996, p. 72), it also embraced new concepts in supporting the development of beginning science teachers. One concept used in the program was the *mix of internal and external expertise* (NRC 1996). In the ASIST program, there were several levels of expertise. Beginning teachers brought their current experiences and knowledge of students and schools to the program. For example, the beginning teachers often talked about locating materials or discussed how they worked with students who were frequently absent. Beginning teachers and experienced teachers resolve these matters differently, and it was important for the beginning teachers to share how they tackled these issues. Joining the beginning teachers were mentor teachers and university faculty and staff. Beginning teachers were viewed as experts in terms of their current situation, while the mentor teachers and university faculty and staff brought their own expertise. The mentor teachers were fluent in current district and school policy, lesson planning, and classroom management. University faculty and staff often brought a perspective that focused on developing beliefs and practices conducive to reform-based practices. Collectively, all three groups of individuals worked together to ensure the success and the ongoing development of the beginning science teacher.

The program also emphasized the *teacher as member of a community that can ultimately create change* (NRC 1996). Rather than targeting an individual teacher for change, ASIST staff viewed the beginning teachers as a community that was committed to improving the education of students. In creating this community, ASIST staff emphasized collaboration and communication among the beginning teachers, and they provided opportunities for the beginning teachers to join the larger science education community. For example, once a month, all of the beginning teachers met for a three- to six-hour session during which they discussed their current classroom successes and frustrations. While the beginning teachers were sharing their experiences, mentor teachers and university staff guided the conversation so that the beginning teachers could learn to discuss their experiences with one another, with the goal of understanding the situation or their actions. Mentor teachers and university staff were attempting to foster avenues for communication that would ultimately continue in the group's electronic communications. Throughout the year there was a strong focus on discussing, exploring, and articulating classroom experiences in a variety of settings. Ideally, as they purposefully discussed their experiences with each other, beginning teachers could start to understand their place in a community focused on creating reform-based classrooms.

The notion of science as inquiry was also emphasized in the National Science Education Teaching Standards. In our approach to science as inquiry, we encouraged teachers to consider how in-class investigations emerged from students' observations of natural phenomena, how students were encouraged to collect and analyze data, and how students could draw conclusions that explained their observations. Throughout the ASIST program, the beginning teachers were asked to explore their use of scientific inquiry in their classes and to reflect upon how such an approach was conducive to student learning and the process of science. The teachers in ASIST were well versed in traditional forms of instruction (as most had experienced traditional instruction in their undergraduate programs), and most had only recently learned about science as inquiry during their teacher education programs. To foster an inclination toward this form of instruction, program staff encouraged the beginning teachers to share their experiences in scientific inquiry and to explore the impact of this instructional approach on themselves and their students. Furthermore, mentor teachers and university staff often provided assistance in planning lessons that aligned with inquiry, and university staff frequently visited the classrooms of beginning teachers to offer specific feedback on their lessons. Beginning science teachers need countless opportunities to develop a way of thinking that is aligned with science as inquiry; this is best done in a community, with a focus on student learning, and in the presence of peers and external experts.

The Impact of the ASIST Program

To document the impact of ASIST, various measures were taken in regard to the development of the teachers. Such measures included the documentation of beliefs, the recording of classroom practices, and the monitoring of dialogue between the teachers and the program staff. These measures have been combined to build cases of teacher development. For example, Roehrig and Luft (forthcoming) developed cases of 14 teachers and explored the constraints they felt when trying to implement inquiry-based lessons; the cases also look at how the induction program mitigated these concerns. The authors found that an understanding of the nature of science and scientific inquiry, content knowledge, pedagogical content knowledge, teaching beliefs, and concerns about management and students all had an impact on a beginning teacher's ability to enact inquiry-based lessons. Yet an induction program was able to reduce their management concerns so that they could focus on other areas related to teaching inquiry lessons. These measures have also been quantitatively examined in order to understand the trends between different groups of beginning secondary science teachers. For example, Luft, Roehrig, and Patterson (2003) compared the beliefs and practices of ASIST teachers, beginning teachers in a general induction program, and teachers who did not participate in any induction program in order to understand the impact of a discipline-specific induction program. From the study, they concluded that a science-focused induction program supported student-centered beliefs and practices more than the other two types of experiences.

To shed light on the impact of ASIST as a program that demonstrates the goals of the National Science Education Standards, it is important to consider the development of the beliefs and practices of beginning science teachers. Beliefs are considered to influence class-room practices, but it unclear how beliefs and practices are directly related (Richardson 1996). Furthermore, it seems that the beliefs of beginning teachers are more tentative than the be-liefs of experienced teachers. Simmons et al. (1999) found that beginning teachers typically held idealist and reform-based beliefs when they graduated from their preservice programs. However, the reality of the classroom often led beginning teachers to enact traditional prac-tices while holding reform-based beliefs. Over time, their beliefs and practices aligned and often became more teacher centered.

In the ASIST program, all beginning science teachers were interviewed twice a year in order to understand their beliefs toward teaching science (see Luft et al. 2003). The interviews specified whether teachers held beliefs that were student centered or teacher centered. Pre- and post-interviews were analyzed and compared, and the variations in beginning teachers' beliefs were noted as maintained or shifting. Teachers who maintained their beliefs held consistent beliefs throughout the year and from year to year. Teachers with shifting beliefs moved toward student-centered or teacher-centered ideologies. The majority of teachers maintained their stu-dent-centered beliefs as they participated in the induction program, yet belief shifts toward more student-centered philosophies occurred among 12 participants (Table 2). Nine of these shifts in

Table 2. Belief Changes of ASIST Program Participants ($N = 55$)*

	Teachers With University Certification (coherent with induction program) ($n = 24$)	Teachers With University Certification (not coherent with induction program) ($n = 18$)	Teachers With Alternative Certification ($n = 10$)	Teachers With Emergency Certification or Uncertified ($n = 3$)
Beliefs shift toward student-centered	3	3	4	2
Beliefs maintained	19	15	5	0
Beliefs shift toward teacher-centered	2	0	1	1

*Participating teachers with a complete data set.

beliefs occurred in one group of teachers—those teachers who did not complete their preservice training at the institution coordinating the induction program. With two exceptions, these teachers were alternatively or emergency certified and had no science methods course during their preservice training. The two teachers in this group who were university certified had participated in science methods courses; however, the courses were not focused on the guidelines espoused in the National Science Education Standards. The two teachers who completed a preparation program from the institution coordinating the induction program did not demonstrate shifts in their beliefs until their third year in the program. From these data, it is possible to conclude that the ASIST program was important in maintaining beliefs and essential in the development of student-centered beliefs for teachers who did not participate in a university certification program. This is in contrast to Simmons et al. (1999), who found that teachers tended to shift their beliefs toward teacher-centered or student-centered ideologies in the absence of an induction program.

The emphasis of the ASIST program on working with beginning science teachers in their classrooms resulted in extensive records describing the practices of these teachers. These records have been examined and reveal the type of instruction that was prevalent among the teachers. More importantly, there is evidence that student-centered strategies that were modeled in the program were successfully implemented by more than 40 participants (Table 3). In looking at the data, it was evident that the longer a teacher participated in ASIST (two or more years), the greater the likelihood of the use of a student-centered strategy. More intriguing was the link between the educational background of a teacher and the use of such practices. While teachers from each certification program implemented student-centered practices in their classrooms, the degree of sophistication of the lessons was markedly different. Teachers completing a university preparation program aligned with the induction program were able to enact strategies that were more consistent with the practices espoused in the Standards. Teachers from other certification programs, however, had a more mechanistic or basic approach toward instruction.

Mike, a teacher from an alternative certification program, and Jennifer, a teacher from a university certification program (pseudonyms), illustrate the contrast between the two groups.

Table 3. Teaching Practices Used by ASIST Participants That Were Modeled by the ASIST Program (N = 55)*

	Teachers With University Certification (coherent with induction program) (n = 24)	Teachers With University Certification (not coherent with induction program) (n = 18)	Teachers With Alternative Certification (n = 10)	Teachers With Emergency Certification or Uncertified (n = 3)
Student-directed inquiry	11	4	4	1
Guided inquiry	10	3	2	0
Vee maps	7	1	4	1
Concept maps	9	2	1	2
Cooperative learning	7	5	1	0

*Participating teachers with a complete data set.

Mike and Jennifer developed an inquiry lesson together at an ASIST meeting that pertained to growing crystals. They worked diligently to plan a series of lessons that allowed students to identify questions, develop a plan to answer their questions, and then analyze their findings and share their results. When the lesson was enacted in the classroom, Mike emphasized the science processes of observing and inferring, while Jennifer had the students draw conclusions about variables that affected crystal formation. She also had students contemplate the role of models in science, which demonstrated her commitment to having students understand the nature of science rather than limiting the discussion to process skills.

This example reinforces the importance of a preservice program, and it also supports the role of subject-specific induction programs in terms of promoting student-centered practices in the classrooms of beginning teachers. The science teachers in the ASIST program had an ongoing opportunity to learn about practices that were conducive to student learning, and more than half were able to translate these experiences into classroom practice. Again, this is in stark contrast to the findings of Simmons et al. (1999), who reported a proliferation of traditional practices among beginning science and mathematics teachers.

At the end of each year, participants were asked to evaluate the ASIST program. While this is noted as self-report data, all of the participants valued the opportunity to share their experiences and ideas with mentor teachers and each other. The beginning teachers often felt that the suggestions of their peers and the mentor teachers helped them understand that all teachers have difficulties in their first few years. When participants were asked what affected their ability and confidence in trying new practices, they often spoke about the specific methods and activities that were provided throughout the program, as well as the ongoing support from program staff. Another interesting finding was that approximately 75% of the participating teachers felt the program had significantly challenged their ideologies about teaching science. Monthly meetings and classroom visits were most often mentioned by beginning teachers as events that fostered such challenges. The interaction with peers and program staff resulted in beginning teachers seriously considering and understanding constructivist views toward teaching and learning.

Conclusion

Rather than a general approach that addresses surviving the first year and classroom management, beginning science teachers need opportunities to explore a science as inquiry approach. The underlying goal of ASIST was to cultivate that approach. In addition, it was important to develop a program that situated the beginning teacher in a learning community. Such a community not only helps beginning teachers to negotiate the range of experiences during the early years, it can also allow beginning teachers to understand the contributions they can make to the profession as intellectuals and reflective practitioners. ASIST created a regional community that enabled teachers to build their practices and refine their beliefs about teaching. While these may seem like small developments along the continuum of science teacher development, ASIST ultimately provided beginning science teachers with the opportunity for ongoing and purposeful development that will encourage *all* students to learn science.

References

Committee on Science and Mathematics Teacher Preparation. 2000. *Educating teachers of science, mathematics, and technology: New practices for the new millennium.* Washington, DC: National Academy Press.

Gold, Y. 1996. Beginning teacher support: Attrition, mentoring, and induction. In *Handbook of research on teacher education,* ed. J. Sikula, pp. 548–594. New York: Macmillan.

Luft, J. A., and W. E. Cox. 2001. Investing in our future: A survey of support offered to beginning secondary mathematics and science teachers. *Science Educator* 10(1): 1–9.

Luft, J. A., and N. C. Patterson. 2002. Bridging the gap: Supporting beginning science teachers. *Journal of Science Teacher Education* 13(4): 287–313.

Luft, J. A., G. H. Roehrig, T. Brooks, and B. Austin. 2003. Exploring the beliefs of secondary science teachers through interview maps. Paper presented at the National Association for Research in Science Teaching, Philadelphia, PA.

Luft, J. A., G. H. Roehrig, and N. C. Patterson. 2002. Barriers and pathways: A reflection on the implementation of an induction program for secondary science teachers. *School Science and Mathematics* 102(5): 222–228.

Luft, J. A., G. H. Roehrig, and N. C. Patterson. 2003. Contrasting landscapes: A comparison of the impact of different induction programs on beginning secondary science teachers' practices, beliefs, and experiences. *Journal of Research in Science Teaching* 40(1): 77–97.

National Commission on Mathematics and Science Teaching for the 21st Century. 2000. *Before it's too late.* Washington, DC: U.S. Department of Education.

National Research Council (NRC). 1996. *National science education standards.* Washington, DC: National Academy Press.

Patterson, N. C., G. Roehrig, B. Austin, and J. A. Luft. 2003. Meeting the needs of beginning science teachers. In *Issues in science education: Science teacher retention: Mentoring, and renewal,* eds. J. Rhoton and P. Bowers, pp. 113–121. Arlington, VA: NSTA Press.

Richardson, V. 1996. The role of attitudes and beliefs in learning to teach. In *Handbook of research in teacher education,* ed. J. Sikula, pp. 102–119. New York: Macmillan.

Roehrig, G. H., and J. A. Luft. Forthcoming. Constraints experienced by beginning secondary science teachers in implementing scientific inquiry lessons. *International Journal of Science Education.*

Simmons, P. E., A. Emory, T. Carter, T. Coker, B. Finnegan, D. Crockett et al. 1999. Beginning teachers: Beliefs and classroom actions. *Journal of Research in Science Teaching* 36: 930–954.

Knowing and Teaching Science: Just Do It

Eddie Lunsford
Southwestern Community College

Claudia T. Melear
University of Tennessee, Knoxville

Leslie G. Hickok
University of Tennessee, Knoxville

Setting

About five years ago, an unusual course—Knowing and Teaching Science: Just Do It—was launched at the University of Tennessee, Knoxville. This state university, founded in 1794, is located in Knox County at the southeastern border of the state. About 28,000 students are enrolled in various programs. "Just Do It" is the product of an atypical partnership between two departments in two different colleges in the university—the Department of Theory and Practice in Teacher Education within the College of Education, Health, and Human Sciences and the Department of Botany within the College of Arts and Sciences. Together, they work to make "Just Do It" a success.

Background

Dr. Leslie G. Hickok, professor of botany/genetics, collaborated with Dr. Claudia T. Melear, associate professor of science education, to design a course in which the emphasis is on long-term scientific inquiry. The result, "Just Do It," is a graduate-level botany course focusing on research. Professors team up with doctoral students to teach the semester-long course. Any student with at least eight semester hours of college-level science credits is eligible to enroll. However, "Just Do It" was designed especially with preservice secondary science teachers in mind. Consistent with recommendations from the Holmes Group (1995), students must hold or complete a bachelor's degree in science before beginning their fifth-year teaching internship. According to state licensure standards, they must further engage in a long-term, open-ended inquiry activity. Because so few students have firsthand, quality experience in scientific research before graduate school (Lave and Wenger 1991; Roth 1995), the preservice teachers are directed by Dr. Melear toward the "Just Do It" course. It is the main means for students to rectify their deficits in scientific experimental design. The course is taught entirely within the botany department, in a laboratory classroom. Students have ready access to basic equipment and supplies for their research projects and may use other equipment within the department as necessary. Careful scheduling of lab facilities usually allows "Just Do It" students to have free access to their classroom at any time, including weekends.

Goals of Science Education and *More Emphasis* Conditions of the National Science Education Standards

The "Just Do It" course was designed to address the four primary goals of science education as listed in the National Science Education Standards (NSES) (NRC 1996):

The goals for school science that underlie the National Science Education Standards are to educate students who are able to

- *experience the richness and excitement of knowing about and understanding the natural world;*
- *use appropriate scientific processes and principles in making personal decisions;*
- *engage intelligently in public discourse and debate about matters of scientific and technological concern; and*
- *increase their economic productivity through the use of the knowledge, understanding, and skills of the scientifically literate person in their careers.* (p. 13)

"Just Do It" is also designed to prepare science teachers to place more emphasis on particular National Science Education Standards (NRC 1996). The course addresses the *More Emphasis* conditions of the Teaching, Assessment, and Content and Inquiry Standards.

Teaching Standards

At least six of the NSES science teaching *More Emphasis* conditions have been met in "Just Do It." (See p. 219 for the science teaching *More Emphasis* conditions.) Students grow in knowledge and understanding of the world due to more emphasis being placed on scientific inquiry and the process skills of science. Students actively use these skills in their work. They constitute a cooperative, respectful community of learners in which scientific discussion among students and teachers is the norm. Continuous assessment fosters and enhances all these processes. Finally, because teachers from different departments work together to enhance the content of the course, students understand that shared responsibility and cooperation extend beyond the classroom.

Assessment Standards

No fewer than five NSES assessment *More Emphasis* conditions have been satisfied in the course. (See p. 221 for the assessment *More Emphasis* conditions.) Students become scientifically literate and able to engage in meaningful dialogue because assessment in "Just Do It" is continuous. Students are given multiple opportunities to critique their own work and the work of others. The primary emphasis is on encouraging the ability to reason and to understand both content knowledge and scientific skills. The goal is for students to achieve a deep and well-structured understanding in a few of these areas.

Content and Inquiry Standards

Content and inquiry standards (see p. 222 for the content and inquiry *More Emphasis* conditions) are the central focus in "Just Do It." The four goals of science education (NRC 1996, p. 13) are nourished as a result. Students engage in multiple long-term inquiry activities to answer scientific questions, mostly of their own design. They learn subject matter but they also study the nature of science, hone scientific process skills, and use a variety of investigative and learning strategies within the context of actual scientific investigations. Students communicate results of their experiments to instructors and to each other. Results are used to formulate sound scientific explanations and arguments, to design further investigations, and to revise previous ideas. In short, students are actively immersed in real science.

Unique Features of "Just Do It"
Teaching, Content, and Inquiry Activities

The first major portion of the "Just Do It" course centers on learning to design experiments with a professional scientist (Melear et al. 2000). The goal is to provide students with opportunities to engage in long-term inquiry activities that closely resemble those encountered in actual scientific practice. These activities include engaging in extended inquiry activities; developing process and inquiry skills and strategies; communicating scientific evidence, arguments, and conclusions; and working in groups to evaluate and synthesize experimental data. Similar experiences have been shown to improve high school students' inquiry process skills (Bell et al. 2003).

On the first day of class, "Just Do It" students are given 10-mg samples of spores from an organism known as C-Fern, a cultivated variety of the tropical fern *Ceratopteris richardii*. Wild-type organisms, as well as a variety of others with all sorts of genetic variations, are readily available from biological supply companies (e.g., Carolina Biological). A website is available to assist teachers with use of C-Fern in their classrooms (*http://cfern.bio.utk.edu*). The organism is very easily cultured and requires nominal care. Details from the life cycle are easily observed with minimal magnification. C-Fern completes its life cycle, under ideal conditions, in as few as 90 days (Hickok et al. 1998).

In addition to the C-Fern, students are supplied with nutrient agar, culture containers, and other basic supplies. They are given few guidelines for the activity; they are asked simply to "find out something about the organism." They mostly use common materials and supplies within the lab, such as light microscopes, dissection scopes, petri dishes, and growth lights. However, students are told to consider their supplies and materials unlimited, unless instructed otherwise. From these rudimentary beginnings, students embark on an eight-week-long series of individual and group experiments during which they mostly pose and answer their own questions.

For example, students may elect to study the life cycle of the fern. They may design investigations to explore reasons for the presence of the two different growth forms of the plant (male and hermaphroditic gametophytes) or they can study the effect of temperature, growth density, or other environmental variables on the life cycle of C-Fern. Some students, depending on their research questions, may be covertly given genetic mutants of C-Fern, such as salt-tolerant varieties, to enrich their research activities.

During the course of their investigations, students learn a variety of science content. In a typical class, students and instructors consider evidence from the C-Fern inquiry activities as they build knowledge about, for example, life cycles of organisms, growth requirements of ferns, genetic variation and transmission, and pheromones. The important point to remember is that the students' own experimental evidence must be used to make and support claims and conclusions.

Through their work with Dr. Hickok and their collaboration with one another, students also learn many process skills and techniques. A research scientist places a great deal of emphasis on how traditional scientific paradigms (Guba 1995) deal with evaluation of evidence and scientific claims. In "Just Do It," students are taught, within the contexts of their investigations, about sample size, replication of findings, what counts as evidence, good and bad scientific practices, and so forth. Specific laboratory skills are acquired as the need arises. Students learn how to properly use a microscope and prepare slides, how to prepare laboratory solutions, how to sterilize spores and equipment, and how to prepare culture media. A case in point is the procedure for sterilizing C-Fern spores. Students are initially given nonsterilized spores that will almost invariably produce cultures rampant with mold contamination. As students discover the presence of both mold and fern gametophytes in their culture dishes, they are led by the instructor to consider their results (Which organism is the unknown? Are you sure that is mold? How do you know that? How could you provide evidence that it is contamination?). Then, a few students are taught to sterilize spores with a bleach solution and to teach others to do so.

About midway through the course, the focus begins to shift slightly. Students use their growing competence in designing and carrying out scientific investigations to consider the role of inquiry in their future careers as teachers. The science educator, Dr. Melear, provides students with new choices of research organisms. She asks students to begin inquiry activities with these organisms and to use their experiences to design inquiry-based lessons appropriate for high school students. In most cases, simplicity of materials is the key. As a rule, the organisms that are selected for use have short life cycles and quick germination times and are easily maintained and/or require little in the way of expensive care. Students are often given a supply of cups and other containers, potting soil and seeds of various types (ryegrass, wheat, clover, sunflower, and many others) and asked to go to work. Materials of these sorts are widely available from biological supply companies, garden centers, and shopping centers. Students may use these supplies to study environmental effects on the growth, germination, and reproduction of plants; to compare the growth of various plant species under varying treatments; or to explore other areas of interest to them. Class instructors often supplement these inquiry opportunities with other organisms. Mealworm (*Tenebrio molitor*) larvae, isopod cultures, earthworms, and other types of organisms may be made available. In some cases, students supply their own organisms if they have particular interests they would like to explore. In short, students are free to choose their research organisms, research questions, and methods. Once again, they learn content, skills, techniques, and methods collaboratively and within the context of their research.

Assessment Methods

Assessment is designed to match the students' "Just Do It" experiences and to be typical of assessments encountered by professional scientists. There is a shift from summative (end of activity) paper-and-pencil tests toward formative (ongoing and guidance-providing) assessments. Two categories of evaluation, described by Enger and Yager (1998), are central to the "Just Do It" assessment philosophy. First is authentic assessment, in which the assessment activity is tied to the learning activity and may be performed by actual practitioners. Second is performance assessment, in which the assessment activity requires that the student transact some skill or task related to his or her learning. As a general example, students who have completed an inquiry activity concerning sound may be asked to build and demonstrate a musical instrument as an authentic and performance-based assessment. Throughout the course, numerous authentic and performance-based assessments are used to provide a clearer picture of student achievement and progress. Because the goal of "Just Do It" is to help students become adept at inquiry, with process skills, and in scientific reasoning, the assessments are selected with these outcomes in mind.

Students are almost constantly involved in the critical evaluation of scientific research during the course. This begins, of course, with the instructors' insistence that students present evidence from their own experiments to back up their claims and conclusions. This quickly spreads to self- and peer evaluation of the evidence. Formal and informal discussions about the students' ongoing research make up much of the formative assessment. A typical exchange between students and one of the course instructors, Dr. Hickok, is represented below. It is noteworthy that students are encouraged to develop their own terminology as they discover aspects of the C-Fern life cycle (Lunsford 2002/2003). (All student names are pseudonyms.)

Alice: We've found there are two growth forms, the rice [male gametophyte] and the cornflake [hermaphroditic gametophyte].

Dr. Hickok: A genetic difference? Has anybody proven that?

Alice: You'd see a developmental difference if it was. We didn't.

Sara: It seems to be environmental, the difference.

Greg: How many did you do?

Alice: We used 18 spores.

Dr. Hickok: Do you think that's enough?

Greg: Well, according to our results it would be. It was consistent.

Dr. Hickok (turning to another group): What was the sample size and treatment in Alice's group?

Richard: Their treatment was 1 spore in a dish of agar by itself. They had 18 individual dishes. Ours was 10 spores in 6 dishes. We put sterilized spores in each dish.

No grades are assigned to these informal but critical discussions of evidence. More formal types of evaluation, summative and graded, also are used. As the students come to a better understanding of the nature of science, they are asked to seek out and critique a scientific research paper that is of interest to them. Other students join the discussion as the evidence, methodology, and claims from the paper are considered with the critical eye of science. Students also

Figure 1. Rubric for Evaluating Written and Oral C-Fern Reports

Components of Report	Points 4	3	2	1
Introduction—*justification and background*	Clearly presents the basis and rationale of the experiment, along with any background material that is appropriate.	Only partially presents the basis and rationale of the experiment.		Does not present the basis and rationale of the experiment.
Materials and Methods—*experimental design*	All variables are properly identified and dealt with. The experimental design is adequate; it includes data to be collected, controls, techniques used, and an adequate number of replicates.	Only some of the variables and design issues are correctly identified and dealt with.		None of the variables and design issues are properly identified and dealt with.
Results—*presentation of data*	Complete and adequate. Tabular and/or graphic representation of data where appropriate.	Only partially adequate; graphic and/or tabular data are not clearly represented. Some components are omitted or improperly identified and/or presented.		Description of results is totally inadequate.
Discussion—*analysis and interpretation of outcomes*	Appropriate interpretation and discussion of the outcomes of the experiment. Possible implications/further experiments are proposed.	An adequate interpretation of the data is presented, but it is not related to possible implications or additional experiments are not suggested. . . OR vice versa.		The data and implications are not adequately discussed.
Oral—*overall verbal and visual presentation*	Excellent use of visuals and clear, well-rehearsed, and enthusiastic presentation.	Presentation adequate, but there is considerable room for improvement of verbal and/or visual portions.		Unorganized verbal presentation with ineffective use of visuals.
Written—*grammar and language use*	Grammar/language use is very adequate.	Grammar/language use is inconsistent or somewhat inadequate.		Grammar/language use is generally poor.

present, orally and in writing, formal accounts of their research with C-Fern. A rubric is used by the instructor to help quantify various components of written and oral scientific presentations (Figure 1). The presentations allow students to publicly communicate, evaluate, and synthesize their scientific findings and knowledge, and often lead to further investigations. Students are allowed to revise their written papers as many times as they wish.

Formative assessment, of the types described above, also continues as the students engage in their second round of inquiry activities, using other organisms. Summative assessment of this activity requires that all student groups present to their peers an inquiry-based science lesson, suitable to high school students and based on their lab work. Students must use the 5E learning cycle (Trowbridge and Bybee 1995) as they design and carry out their inquiry lessons. During these lesson presentations, students may involve other members of the class by asking them to prepare laboratory solutions, evaluate data from an experiment, graph class data, or make recommendations as to how inquiry results may be applied to real life. In one case, for example, students grew ryegrass (*Lolium multiflorum*) in varying concentrations of urea to simulate runoff from fertilizer. They presented the plants to the class, along with the map shown in Figure 2. Students were asked to correlate the ryegrass samples with growth locations on the hypothetical map. This led to discussions of land use within the context of the students' evidence.

Figure 2. Alice and Veronica's Lesson Presentation Map

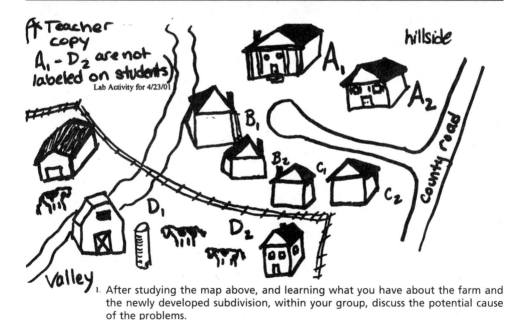

1. After studying the map above, and learning what you have about the farm and the newly developed subdivision, within your group, discuss the potential cause of the problems.

Another major component of assessment in the course involves the notion of scientific inscriptions. Inscriptions are written, electronically produced, hand-drawn, or otherwise preserved representations of scientific knowledge and thought (Latour and Woolgar 1979; Roth and McGinn

Figure 3. Rubric for Evaluating Student Inscription Notebooks

Evaluation Sheet
Laboratory-Inscription Notebook

Your laboratory-inscription notebook will account for 10% of your total course grade. Listed below are the criteria upon which your notebook will be evaluated. Your completed notebook will be due _____. At that time, please hand in all carbon copies to me, along with this sheet. I would like to look over your notebook periodically, at least two or three times, throughout the course as well. I encourage you to frequently exchange and share your carbon copies within and between your lab groups too. Be sure to get all of your own carbon copies back, and organized into a completed notebook, before the due date. Please feel free to ask me any questions concerning this assignment that you have. You may ask me in person or by e-mail.

Criteria	Absent	Poor	Fair	Adequate	Good	Excellent
Total number of Inscriptions (50 inscriptions = adequate)	0	2	4	6	8	10
Neatness and Clarity (e.g., labeling of figures, listing names of partners, dates, references to other pages, units of measurement)	0	2	4	6	8	10
Transformation Cascades Combining simpler and less abstract inscriptions (e.g., lists, Vee diagrams, sentences, drawings, photographs, maps, tables) into more complex and abstract ones (e.g., concept maps, graphs, composite drawings, equations) (8 cascades = adequate)	0	6	12	18	24	30
Social Use of Inscriptions Share ideas, data, methods. Document meetings within and between groups. Use others' ideas in your own inscriptions. (8 uses = adequate)	0	6	12	18	24	30
General Improvement Over Time (e.g., choice of material for inscriptions, better quality, increasing incidence of social use, and transformation of inscriptions)	0	4	8	12	16	20

Total Points (100 points max) _____

1998). They may take the form of lists, photographs, graphs, tables, charts, and maps, for example. Early in the course, students are given minimal instructions about the various types of scientific inscriptions and their uses in professional science. They are required to maintain a notebook of inscriptions in order to document their observations, methods, results, and conclusions throughout their inquiry experiences. The laboratory notebooks are constructed to allow students to make at least one carbon copy of each handwritten inscription they generate. They may then easily share their inscriptions with others in the learning community, fostering the collaborative nature of the class and helping students and instructors to monitor progress in scientific reasoning. The students use their inscriptions to display, summarize, and evaluate their evidence; to consider future experiments; and to argue their claims in class discussions, presentations, and written papers. Students are graded on the total numbers of inscriptions, on the social generation and sharing of inscriptions, and on transforming (Roth and McGinn 1998) basic, concrete inscriptions (such as written statements, tallies, and basic diagrams) into more complex, abstract inscriptions (tables, graphs, equations, complex diagrams) as the course progresses. The rubric used to evaluate student-generated inscriptions is shown in Figure 3.

Students also maintain a reflective journal in which they make at least weekly entries about affective experiences in the course. They are asked to consider if/how their thinking changes regarding the nature of science, science process skills, abilities to work with a group, and so forth. They are often given writing prompts such as, "How much do you understand about what you are supposed to be doing?" and "Is this course similar/dissimilar to previous science courses?" The reflective journal helps students monitor their understanding of science and of process skills. Entries are regularly shared with an individual (usually a science education graduate student) who provides feedback and suggestions. The science instructor does not have access to the reflective journals until after the class has ended.

A summary of the assessments used in "Just Do It" is presented in Figure 4. Figure 5 presents a summary of some of the students' thoughts on how they were assessed. Data were derived from reflective journal entries and from interviews (Lunsford 2002/2003).

Figure 4. Summary of Assessment Methods Used in "Just Do It"

Summative Assessment
(assigned a numerical point value)

- Presenting summaries of scientific research papers
- Keeping a reflective journal (also used as formative assessment during the course)
- Giving a written and oral presentation on C-Fern
- Maintaining a Laboratory-Inscription Notebook (also used as formative assessment during the course)
- Designing and presenting an inquiry-based science lesson

Formative Assessment
(not assigned a numerical point value)

- Defending methods and conclusions to course instructors

Figure 5. Summary of Affective Comments Relating to Assessment

- "Having to defend your work to a fellow scientist is not a personal attack on you. It feels natural with practice. Also you should look at your own work and the work of others more critically."
- "I think the assessment really reflects my work."
- "There were no tests like in my other classes."
- "What we did was more valid that a test would have been."
- "The laboratory-inscription notebook was very valid. It was hard to know what to record at first and I was worried about having enough inscriptions. As time went on, it became more natural to record inscriptions."
- "I liked the rubrics."

Evidence for "Just Do It" Effectiveness

Figure 6 provides a general summary of the sorts of things students learn during their "Just Do It" experience. Some examples of, and evidence for, student learning in the course have already been presented. To review, students use actual laboratory experiences to gain an understanding of basic laboratory skills such as the preparation of reagents. During the course of their observations and investigations, they study topics such as metamorphosis, plant reproduction, and plant growth requirements. The course focuses on science as inquiry, unifying concepts and process skills, the nature of science, and science in personal and social perspectives. Since the course uses living organisms for inquiry purposes, it naturally provides opportunities for students to study a variety of content from the life sciences; other content standards, such as Earth and space science, science and technology, and physical science, are often studied in the context of inquiry as well. For example, past "Just Do It" students have considered soil profiles, light, weather patterns, chemical reactions, and biogeochemical cycles in conjunction with their inquiries. Students routinely use computer technology to assist them with the production of graphs and other inscriptions. Also, the class frequently maintains an internet website, allowing for discussions and the posting of results discussion. Some lines of evidence for the effectiveness of the course are quite surprising, considering that students in the course almost invariably hold a degree in science. Many of these graduate students are unable to correctly use a microscope when they enter "Just Do It" (Melear et al. 2000). In another surprising case, one student reported that he thought "bugs" might have been inexplicably falling into his mealworm culture. This good student could have recited a brilliant definition of *metamorphosis* on entering the course. However, he and others made great strides in correcting their misconceptions by the end of the class (Lunsford 2002/2003).

> *Morgan:* I learned some valuable information about my mealworms. For the longest time, I have thought that my worms have been drying out and dying. This was so wrong. They shed their exoskeleton in order to grow. I had never considered that to be what was going on.

Other students built inscriptions concerning their observations of their mealworm cultures. They correctly worked out the life cycle by way of collaboration and sharing of evidence. Phillip

Figure 6. Summary of Student Learning in "Just Do It"

Content (Partial List)
- C-Fern life cycle
- Alternation of generations
- Pheromone signals in development
- Plant growth requirements
- Preparation of laboratory solutions
- Preparation of wet mounts with stains
- Use of microscope
- Metamorphosis
- Biogeochemical cycles
- Effect of chemicals on plant growth
- Effect of soils on plant growth
- Effect of other environmental variables on plant growth
- Sterile technique
- Genetic transmission of traits
- Careers in biology
- [Many others depending on student inquiry projects]

Scientific Skills
- Posing good scientific questions
- Designing and carrying out an experiment
- Interpreting evidence in science
- Importance of replication, control, and operational definitions
- Communicating scientific evidence
  - Preparation and use of inscriptions
  - Writing a scientific research report
  - Oral presentations of evidence
- How to do a literature review
- Recognizing good and bad scientific practices

Pedagogical Skills
- Preparing inquiry lessons
- How to teach by way of inquiry
- Using group work and cooperative learning
- Teaching techniques in lieu of lecturing

made a discovery that tied all the evidence together and ended the mystery: "Pupae are starting to emerge. They look like little white beetles" (Lunsford 2002/2003). Contrary to results reported by researchers such as Barnett et al. (2001), "Just Do It" students routinely used their own inscriptions to argue the efficacy of their results and to share their findings during formal and informal presentations. They made, used, and understood inscriptions that were a mirror of their research. Some inscriptions, such as graphs, were abstract representations of the students' experimental data but were used in ways that linked them with the students' work.

One of the most obvious lines of evidence for the effectiveness of "Just Do It" lies in the students' improved ability to design, carry out, and interpret sophisticated experiments with the passage of time in the course. By the end of the typical "Just Do It" experience, students are able to design experiments that use evidence to demonstrate such things as various aspects of plant life cycles, transmission of genetic traits, chemical developmental signals, and the effects of varying environmental conditions on plant growth (Hickok et al. 1998; Lunsford 2002/2003).

Students typically enter the course with the ability to verbalize well-articulated notions of experimentation, sample size, control, and replication. However, despite their extensive academic backgrounds in science, they almost invariably fail in their initial attempts to actually "do it." In other words, the students can talk about doing an experiment, but initially lack the ability to do so. In a recent analysis of "Just Do It" students, Lunsford (2002/2003) found that the students' ability to design and carry out sound and successful experiments increased during the course. Multiple experiments were evaluated from 10 students, organized into four cooperative work groups. In the first experiments, only one group had a control and none had a well-designed research question. Most students left operational definitions and details on methods open to the imagination. By the end of the class, however, students had improved these abilities dramatically. Students' final experiments all included replicated controls and focused on a single, well-stated research question. The students included detailed operational definitions that would allow for easy replication of their procedures by other researchers. They also used multiple replicates in their experimental groups.

The students attributed this dramatic shift in their ability to engage in inquiry to several factors. They all agreed that their experience with Dr. Hickok was a primary factor. Further, they stated that the ability to actually do real science helped as well. They also identified the collaborative nature of the class and their production and use of scientific inscriptions as benefits toward their gaining competence in inquiry. Many students related that they began to "think like a scientist." Some additional student comments are shown below (Lunsford 2002/2003).

Alice: [Dr. Hickok] was able to direct us throughout the experiment. He knew the right questions to ask. He would direct us [but] really forced us to do it on our own.
Veronica: You don't get answers to your questions, you get questions to your questions. We are so used to…having the cookbook recipe of an experiment and not having to actually think on our own.
Sara: The journal club presentation was a great idea because we got to see exactly what a real scientific paper is and what research should look like.

One other critical measure of the success of "Just Do It" remains to be thoroughly evaluated; it will be the subject of future research by the authors and others. A primary goal of the course is to prepare preservice science teachers to teach their own students by inquiry. Since the course is relatively new, detailed data on this measure of success are scant. "Just Do It" students clearly learn inquiry techniques and skills. However, the question regarding their ability to transfer these skills to their own classrooms remains completely unanswered at this time. Brown (2002) has completed the only longitudinal study of the effects of "Just Do It." She evaluated eight students who took the course in the first three cohorts. These individuals, now teachers, had one to three years of teaching experience at the time of her study. Two instruments are pertinent: the Salish I Research Project's Secondary Teaching Analysis Matrix (STAM) (Simmons et al. 1999) and the Teacher Pedagogical Philosophy Interview (TPPI) (Richardson and Simmons 1994). Simmons et al. (1999) document the three-year national study of science teacher preparation programs (Salish I Research Collaborative [1997] and Salish I Research Project Supplement [1997]). Using the STAM, an instrument that measures actual classroom behavior of teachers with a schema drawn from both teacher-centered *conceptual* inquiry and the TPPI, Simmons et al. (1999) reported a stark contrast between new teachers' ($N = 60$) student-centered beliefs and their teacher-centered actions. The teachers espoused their belief in inquiry, student-centered teaching, but their behaviors did not support their beliefs. Even though some reported a traditional research experience in the laboratory of a scientist, prior to the study, Salish I teachers had no comparable research experience like that in the "Just Do It" course.

Brown (2002) found that "Just Do It" teachers, while also showing mostly teacher-centered teaching behaviors, were aware that they were teaching in this *conceptual* rather than inquiry-oriented manner. We believe that it is too early in the teaching careers of these participants to accurately measure what effects their preservice preparation (i.e., the "Just Do It" experience)

Figure 7. Ways in Which "Just Do It" Meets NSES Science Teaching, Assessment, and Content and Inquiry *More Emphasis* Conditions

Science Teaching
- Course consists of long-term inquiry with living organisms.
- Students present and debate the results of their own experiments.
- Assessment occurs throughout the course.
- Group work is emphasized.
- Scientists and science educators designed the course.
- Research questions come mostly from students' interests and needs.

Assessment
- Students assess their own work and that of peers.
- Evidence from inquiry activities is used to back up claims and conclusions.
- Emphasis is on process skills of science.
- Content learned relates to inquiry activities.
- Inscriptions are based on inquiry activities.
- Both formative and summative assessments are used.

Content and Inquiry
- Most class time is devoted to student-generated experiments.
- Students use and contribute to a course website.
- Emphasis is on life science with opportunities to explore other content areas within the inquiries.
- Students communicate, synthesize, and defend their findings.
- New questions are generated from the students' own work.

might have on teaching by inquiry. The fact that these new teachers are more aware of the match between their teaching philosophy and their teaching behavior is an indication that, if they choose to move toward more inquiry-based instruction, they have the skills to do so. That is, they have the self-awareness necessary for deliberate behavioral change.

Summary

Knowing and Teaching Science: Just Do It is a unique and effective learning experience in teacher preparation. The semester-long course provides students with the firsthand, detailed, long-term exposure to scientific inquiry that is so often lacking in their other science courses. By "just doing it," students become adept at planning and carrying out scientific investigations. They learn scientific content and are assessed by methods that are more closely in line with the work of an actual scientist. Students learn about alternative ways to teach and assess their own future students. A summary of the ways in which "Just Do It" helps to make the NSES *More Emphasis* visions come to life is offered in Figure 7.

References

Barnett, M., J. MaKinster, S. Barab, K. Squire, and C. Kelly. 2001. Addressing the challenges of designing an on-line environment to support student learning through the use of inscriptions and technology-rich resources. Paper presented at the annual conference of the National Association of Research on Science Teaching, St. Louis.

Bell, R. L., L. M. Blair, B. A. Crawford, and N. G. Lederman. 2003. Just Do It? Impact of a science apprenticeship program on high school students' understandings of science and scientific inquiry. *Journal of Research in Science Teaching* 40 (5): 487–509.

Brown, S. L. 2002. *A study of science teachers' pedagogical practices as measured by the Science Teacher Analysis Matrix (STAM) and Teacher Pedagogical Philosophy Interview (TPPI)*. Doctoral diss., University of Tennessee, Knoxville.

Enger, S. K., and R. E. Yager, eds. 1998. *The Iowa assessment handbook*. Iowa City, IA: University of Iowa.

Guba, E. G., ed. 1995. *The paradigm dialog*. London: Sage Publications.

Hickok, L. G., T. R. Warne, S. L. Baxter, and C. T. Melear. 1998. Sex and the C-Fern: Not just another life cycle. *BioScience* 48: 1031–1037.

Holmes Group. 1995. Tomorrow's schools of education: A report of the Holmes Group. Paper presented at the South Central Region Holmes Group Conference, Austin, Texas.

Latour, B., and S. Woolgar. 1979. *Laboratory life: The social construction of scientific facts*. London: Sage.

Lave, J., and E. Wenger. 1991. *Social learning: Legitimate peripheral participation*. Cambridge, UK: Cambridge University Press.

Lunsford, B. E. 2002/2003. Inquiry and inscription as keys to authentic science instruction and assessment for preservice secondary science teachers. Doctoral diss., University of Tennessee. *Dissertation Abstracts International* 63 (12): 4267.

Melear, C. T., J. D. Goodlaxson, T. R. Warne, and L. G. Hickok. 2000. Teaching preservice science teachers how to do science: Responses to the research experience. *Journal of Science Teacher Education* 11 (1): 77–90.

National Research Council (NRC). 1996. *National science education standards*. Washington, DC: National Academy Press.

Richardson, L., and P. Simmons. 1994. *Self-Q research method and analysis, Teacher Pedagogical Philosophy Interview (TPPI): Theoretical background and samples of data*. Athens, GA: Department of Science Education, University of Georgia.

Roth, W.-M. 1995. *Authentic school science: Knowing and learning in open-inquiry science laboratories*. Boston: Kluwer.

Roth, W.-M., and M. K. McGinn. 1998. Inscriptions: Toward a theory of representing science as social practice. *Review of Educational Research* 68 (1): 35–59.

Salish I Research Collaborative. 1997. *Secondary science and mathematics teacher preparation programs: Influences on new teachers and their students*. Iowa City, IA: Science Education Center, University of Iowa.

Salish I Research Project Supplement. 1997. *Secondary science and mathematics teacher preparation programs: Influences on new teachers and their students; Instrument package and user's guide*. Iowa City, IA: Science Education Center, University of Iowa.

Simmons, P. E., A. Emory, T. Carter, T. Coker, B. Finnegan, D. Crockett et al. 1999. Beginning teachers: Beliefs and classroom actions. *Journal of Research in Science Teaching* 36: 930–954.

Trowbridge, L., and R. Bybee. 1995. *Becoming a secondary school science teacher*. Upper Saddle River, NJ: Prentice Hall.

Emphasizing Inquiry, Collaboration, and Leadership in K–12 Professional Development

Andrew J. Petto, Michael Patrick, and Raymond Kessel
University of Wisconsin

The Wisconsin Teacher Enhancement Program (WisTEP) at the University of Wisconsin-Madison is a professional development program for K–14 science and health educators (including those who teach in the two-year colleges in the University of Wisconsin system) (*www.wisc.edu/wistep/about/about.html*). WisTEP is designed to promote curriculum and professional development through investigation and hands-on inquiry based on the active collaboration of an instructional team that integrates contemporary scientific research with the classroom expertise of seasoned teachers. The WisTEP Summer Institute awards one to three graduate credits as teachers work collaboratively with colleagues from the Upper Midwest and from elsewhere in the United States and abroad. The instructional team is made up of a scientist-instructor (a research scientist from a postsecondary institution or from an independent research lab) and a lead teacher (a classroom teacher who has completed one or more Summer Institute modules in the past and who leads the integration of scientific knowledge with classroom practice in the module).

The WisTEP Summer Institutes typically provide up to 40 short, intensive modules that combine guest lectures, laboratory investigations, field trips, resource and curriculum development, and collaboration among participants. These features encourage learning science through investigation and inquiry, the integration of science and teaching knowledge, collaborative and collegial learning, and varied professional development activities. The modules also model a classroom in which the roles of "question poser" and "explanation provider" are shifted from those conducting the class to those "taking" the class (Gilbert, Butler, and Rutherford 2000).

To date, over 2,000 teachers have participated in this program, with most drawn from school districts in Wisconsin and bordering states. The teachers come from urban, suburban, and rural districts, as well as tribal schools from some of Wisconsin's reservations. WisTEP also has special ongoing projects with the Milwaukee Public Schools and the Oneida Tribal Schools.

History of WisTEP

WisTEP began in 1985 in response to a typical guest-lecture to a class of preservice teachers. Like many such lectures, it consisted of a university scholar talking to a class of preservice teachers about an area of research—without the research being integrated into the course or otherwise connected to the students' preparation, needs, or interests. From that unfruitful experience, the founders conceived a program of professional development for science teachers based on a collaborative effort between educators and scientists. That program recognized teachers as leaders in the professional development process and as active partners in integrating scientific knowledge into the practice of teaching. Current projects in professional and curriculum development that grew from that program are organized around Wisconsin's Model Academic Standards for Science (WI DPI 1998) and the National Science Education Standards (NSES) (NRC 1996).

The guiding principle of all WisTEP activities is the collaboration among teacher-participants and the instructional team. The collaboration is built on hands-on laboratory and field inquiries as the foundation for curriculum development and teacher leadership in K–14 schools. WisTEP is constantly evolving both to serve the interests of K–14 science teachers and to broaden the participation of the research community in science education. The annual Summer Institute embodies 10 of the 14 NSES Professional Development *More Emphasis* conditions; the other 4 are addressed outside the Summer Institute in follow-up activities throughout the academic year (see Table 1)

The overall goal in the Summer Institute is for teachers to experience the four goals of science education in the NSES (NRC 1996, p. 13) and to learn from the lead teachers how to generate these experiences in their own classrooms. Through hands-on laboratory and field inquiries, teacher-participants "experience the richness and excitement of the knowledge about, and understanding of, the natural world" (NRC 1996, p. 13) within the context of a particular scientific discipline relevant to their own teaching. Through these inquiries, teachers develop appropriate curricula and learning activities that will help their own students apply scientific processes and principles in making social and personal decisions. Through their collaborations with other teachers and program leaders, participants also "engage intelligently in discourse and debate about matters of scientific and technological concern" (NRC 1996, p. 13), using these discussions to shape the curriculum they take back to their schools. In this model, scientific literacy emerges from the active, intellectual collaboration among teachers and researchers in the context of providing a classroom experience for K–14 students that will lead them toward the NSES goals. In all the course modules, the expectation is that teachers will apply their experiences to the development of new instructional materials or approaches. In most cases, the final course outcome for WisTEP partici-

Table 1. National Science Education Standards *Changing Emphases* for Professional Development

Less Emphasis on	More Emphasis on [a]
Transmission of teaching knowledge and skills by lectures	*Inquiry into teaching and learning*
Learning science by lecture and reading	**Learning science through investigation and inquiry**
Separation of science and teaching knowledge	**Integration of science and teaching knowledge**
Separation of theory and practice	*Integration of theory and practice in school settings*
Individual learning	**Collegial and collaborative learning**
Fragmented, one-shot sessions	*Long-term coherent plans*
Courses and workshops	**A variety of professional development activities**
Reliance on external expertise	**Mix of internal and external expertise**
Staff developers as educators	**Staff developers as facilitators, consultants, and planners**
Teacher as technician	**Teacher as intellectual, reflective practitioner**
Teacher as consumer of knowledge about teaching	**Teacher as producer of knowledge about teaching**
Teacher as follower	**Teacher as leader**
Teacher as an individual based in a classroom	*Teacher as a member of a collegial professional community*
Teacher as a target of change	**Teacher as source and facilitator of change**

Source: National Research Council. 1996. *National science education standards.* Washington, DC: National Academy Press, p. 72.

[a] The *More Emphasis* items in bold type are embodied in the WisTEP Summer Institute. The *More Emphasis* items in italics are addressed in follow-up activities with teachers throughout the academic year.

pants is a curriculum unit—lesson plans, field trips, laboratory investigations, and so on—for use in their own classrooms. These materials may be collected and later shared with current and future participants with the authors' permission.

The teachers in this program have typically participated in numerous professional and curriculum development programs throughout their careers. They are committed to active learning through hands-on inquiry in their classrooms and wish to develop more familiarity with contemporary scientific research in order to create more powerful and more effective classroom inquiry. The classrooms of the teacher participants run the gamut from modern, well-equipped science-teaching environments to much older, "standard-issue," general classroom spaces. What ties WisTEP together is not the classrooms from which the teachers are drawn, but the commitment of the teacher-participants to the type of teaching and learning embodied in the NSES, as well as their motivation to strengthen their content knowledge, learn new pedagogy, and reflect on their practices and outcomes.

NSES Professional Development *More Emphasis* Conditions

In this section we will report on the aspects of WisTEP that are designed specifically to promote the NSES Professional Development *More Emphasis* conditions. In the next section, "Evidence of Success," pp. 154–159), we will review data from a five-year retrospective survey of WisTEP teacher-participants to assess the extent to which WisTEP actually produces in the participants' classrooms any of the changes encouraged by the NSES.

A discussion of each of the 10 conditions addressed by the Summer Institute follows.

1. **Learning science through investigation and inquiry**

   Every Summer Institute module is based in a university research and/or teaching laboratory or comparable field site. Under the guidance of a scientist-instructor and in collaboration with an experienced lead teacher, teacher-participants use the methods and materials of scientific investigation in the context of one or more inquiries relevant to their classroom teaching. Later, the scientist-instructor and the lead teacher help teacher-participants analyze their experiences, relate them to curricular content, and develop strategies for integrating them into their own classrooms. For example, in a two-week module on cellular and molecular biology, teachers learn to integrate computer-based and physical modeling in order to understand biomolecular structure and function. The teachers explore and model cutting-edge research in structural biology; they are linked electronically with biomolecular researchers around the country to help them refine, assess, and reflect on their experiences.

2. **Integration of science and teaching knowledge**

   The dual goals of WisTEP are to provide the scientific knowledge that teachers need to develop hands-on, inquiry-based learning for their students and to model the inquiry experience for teachers. At each step in WisTEP, teachers are challenged to show how this knowledge can be incorporated into existing curriculum or developed into new curriculum. The teacher-participants learn to apply the tools of a scientific investigation at the same time that they work to incorporate new scientific knowledge into their classroom practice. For example, an award-winning course entitled Mosquitoes in the Classroom—based on an instructional book written by WisTEP's Dr. Francis Spray (1995)—creates for elementary and middle school teachers a "webbing" approach that ties together science, history, literature, and music through the common topic of mosquitoes. WisTEP also recently instituted a Science Teaching Intern program that provides opportunities for young researchers (graduate and postdoctoral students) to work in Summer Institute modules.

3. **Collegial and collaborative learning**

   All WisTEP modules feature collaboration on several levels. First, the scientist-instructor and the lead teacher are equal partners in the development of the summer module. Together, they work to align the course with the real needs of classroom teachers and to find inquiries and resources that connect well to the classroom environments from which teacher-partici-pants are drawn. Second, the teacher-participants work in teams, initially in carrying out the short-term inquiry, but later in finding and sharing resources for curriculum development, in critiquing lesson plans and activities, and in brainstorming ideas for multilevel collabora-tion in schools. For example, in courses on drug use and abuse, teachers, school nurses, social workers, and administrators often collaborate and come to recognize the different perspec-tives from which they see the problems in their schools and how different solutions may operate at these different levels. The goal is to produce more robust solutions.

4. **A variety of professional development activities**

   WisTEP modules are based primarily on hands-on inquiry. However, teacher-participants also engage in model building, library research, peer teaching and advising, professional pre-sentations, and curriculum writing. It is also common for WisTEP leaders to recruit former teacher-participants to share their experiences with the inquiry-based approach and to help plan field trips. WisTEP emphasizes that laboratory research is not the *only* route to inquiry-based learning. For example, teacher-participants in the Salad Bowl course module do their "research" at local supermarkets where they investigate the biology of fruits and vegetables and develop the supermarket as a teaching resource.

5. **Mix of internal and external expertise**

   One hallmark of WisTEP is the expectation that teacher-participants are responsible for the development of classroom practice, science pedagogy, and science curricula in their own school communities. The instructional team of the scientist-instructor and lead teacher models the interplay between external and internal expertise. Teacher-participants "own" the instruc-tional environment and curriculum in which they practice. The goal of WisTEP is to provide only the necessary external expertise to help the teachers meet their own goals of infusing their teaching with more inquiry-based learning. For example, a course on urban wildlife used the teachers' own knowledge of the geographic and ecological environs of their schools to construct wildlife monitoring projects that their students could carry out over many sea-sons and years. These courses were then presented and refined by discussions with other teachers (for the pedagogical impact) and wildlife biologists (for the types of data and analy-ses that might be most fruitful).

6. **Staff developers as facilitators, consultants, and planners**

   WisTEP provides for staff development mainly through the actions of teachers who have participated in various aspects of our programs. In the Summer Institute, the WisTEP staff helps to connect teachers with resources and people who can assist in their curricular plans. Sometimes this merely involves information and referral; sometimes it involves direct action, such as assisting with purchases or grant writing. However, WisTEP mainly serves to help teachers find and model exemplary practices and programs in their own planning and en-courages them to take on leadership roles in their own districts. For example, WisTEP staff worked closely with the information technology director of a local school consortium to de-termine the equipment needs that would allow the consortium's teachers to participate in a university-based internet learning project funded by a grant written by WisTEP staff (see the "Callicam" at *www.primate.wisc.edu/pin/marmoset/*)

WisTEP staff will also work directly with teachers and administrators in schools as consultants and facilitators through workshops, classroom visits, and cooperative planning sessions. For example, WisTEP staff worked collaboratively with a group of teachers in a local environmental education charter school to develop a middle school curriculum that integrated environmental science throughout all the disciplines in the school. WisTEP staff conducted workshops and problem-solving sessions to model the inquiry process for teachers and to help teachers in nonscience disciplines understand the foundations of the school's curricular theme.

7. **Teacher as intellectual, reflective practitioner**

The ultimate success of WisTEP is based on the practice of K–12 classroom teachers. In each WisTEP module, the strength of the curricular outcome relates to the willingness of the teacher-participants to explore new ideas about teaching and to reflect on their own classroom practices. While participating in WisTEP projects, teacher-participants are encouraged to use on-campus research collections on curriculum development in their reflections. The presentations of the teacher-participants' outcomes to their colleagues also generally include reflection on the units, both by the teachers who produced them and their colleagues. This process models the professional development goal of making reflection on one's classroom practice a regular part of the teachers' routine. For example, in a course on the skeleton for elementary teachers, the class learned to apply a four-part critical analysis to their models of the human skeleton. This analysis explored the materials and quality of construction, the extent to which the model illustrated significant aspects of the material being presented, the ability to integrate the hands-on inquiry with other parts of the curriculum, and how the model builder might proceed next time, perhaps with different materials or approaches, in order to produce a better outcome.

8. **Teacher as producer of knowledge about teaching**

WisTEP projects take as a given that the teacher-participants add value to WisTEP by sharing the knowledge they have acquired from their years of active teaching. Even in those modules in which teachers are working hard to learn new techniques and work with new materials, the most valuable discussions revolve around how the new scientific knowledge can enhance classroom teaching. This is exemplified in the role of the lead teacher as an equal member of the instructional team, without whose knowledge of and expertise in classroom practice WisTEP might be little different from a standard university summer course. The high profile that WisTEP gives to making sure that inquiry-based learning activities work in real life is one of the keystones of the program. For example, in the course on mosquitoes for elementary teachers, the module has evolved based on the expertise and feedback of classroom teachers about the equipment and supplies needed by their elementary students to complete the project successfully. This sort of interaction shows that the teachers' expertise has been taken seriously and can turn a good idea into a valuable inquiry project.

9. **Teacher as leader**

WisTEP directly encourages teacher leadership in several ways. The first is the lead teacher position in every summer module. Teachers who have participated in WisTEP modules in the past or have similar experiences with hands-on, inquiry-based learning are matched with scientist-instructors to produce a collaborative instructional team. Lead teachers may continue to collaborate with researchers for years, may collaborate with several researchers over a period of time, or may initiate their own courses and locate an appropriate scientist-instructor to serve as a resource person. Former lead teachers who have retired from classroom service are offered WisTEP Teacher Emeritus Fellowships to help mentor and develop inservice teachers. About one-third of WisTEP teacher-participants are invited to serve as lead teachers based on their outstanding motivation and leadership skills demonstrated in the Summer Institute.

WisTEP also encourages leadership through its advisory board. Teachers have the opportunity to advise WisTEP directors on the direction, content, curricular areas, and potential projects that might help WisTEP better serve its constituents. About one-sixth of WisTEP teacher-participants express an interest in serving on the advisory board.

10. **Teacher as source and facilitator of change**

WisTEP also encourages teachers to take leadership roles to produce change in their own schools in a variety of ways. One way is simply to initiate the NSES-related changes in their own classrooms. However, over half the former teacher-participants expressed interest in taking a variety of leadership roles in their own schools—from leading workshops to developing new curricula for their schools or districts. Although most of the teacher-initiated change is focused on the classroom, a number of WisTEP participants have reported that they have acted to promote curricular changes in some way in their districts and schools (see the next section, "Evidence of Success").

In addition to these 10 *More Emphasis* conditions, WisTEP indirectly promotes 4 others:

1. **Inquiry into teaching and learning**

WisTEP connects teacher-participants and their schools with professionals involved in active exploration of curriculum reform models. For example, Madison, Wisconsin, has a very active classroom action research program for K–12 teachers, and a number of participants in WisTEP projects took the additional step of making a more formal inquiry into the processes and outcomes of teaching and learning in their schools.

2. **Integration of theory and practice in school settings**

The goal of WisTEP is to model the hands-on, inquiry-based learning emphasized by the NSES. WisTEP provides academic-year support for teachers and schools implementing curriculum and classroom changes derived from WisTEP or similar programs. WisTEP participates in these programs by invitation from the school, and offers both on-site work with K–12 educators and information-and-referral services for programs undergoing reform. For example, teacher-participants who had completed a one-week module on the analysis and interpretation of human skeletal remains worked with the WisTEP staff to initiate a unit that integrated biology, mathematics, social studies, and literature.

3. **Long-term coherent plans**

Working with teacher-participants, WisTEP develops emerging expertise in a variety of science-related fields by providing programmatic tracks that group course modules by theme, subject, and grade level. Teacher-participants may take courses from within a single track or may choose to construct their own plans by combining course modules from different tracks depending on their own backgrounds and curricular needs. Originally, teacher-participants chose among four tracks: Cellular and Molecular Biology, General Biology, Human Biology, and Environmental Biology. Later, other tracks were added, including Integrated and Interdisciplinary Biology, Elementary School Biology, and Health Education. Most respondents in a recent five-year survey of WisTEP teacher-participants (see next section) took part in several courses—over 45% reported that they had participated in this program for more than two years; over 96% reported that they had participated in other similar programs for professional development.

4. Teacher as a member of a collegial professional community

WisTEP introduces its teacher-participants to a select group of colleagues who share an interest in, and motivation for, improving their students' learning through a hands-on, inquiry-based science curriculum. Teacher-participants regularly present their innovative course materials at statewide meetings of science teachers and in formal curriculum-sharing venues such as BioNet (see *www.wisc.edu/cbe/bionet*). Furthermore, teacher-participants are among the most important sources for recruitment of new WisTEP participants.

Evidence of Success

The examples in the preceding section show how WisTEP is designed to achieve the professional development goals laid out in the NSES. However, a well-designed program requires external confirmation that its goals are being met. In this section we report briefly on an extensive survey commissioned by WisTEP to collect evidence of the program's effects. The survey was developed and conducted independently by the Wisconsin Survey Research Laboratory (WSRL), which also scored and entered the original data. WSRL carried out a pretest of the survey questions with a subset of WisTEP participants before mailing out survey booklets to 1,000 participants who had attended over a five-year period. WSRL developed, tested, distributed, and analyzed the survey data, beginning in 1995. There were 605 valid responses, of which 411 were from those who primarily identified themselves as teachers. Further analysis was conducted subsequently by WisTEP staff to explore specific questions in more detail.

WisTEP commissioned a survey over a five-year period because it is often difficult to determine the long-term impact of professional development projects based only on teachers' reflections immediately after the end of a project (e.g., Peters 2002; Pritchard and Marshall 2002). Moreover, the survey was concerned not only with the participants' reactions to WisTEP, but also with the impact on classrooms and on student learning—an outcome that is likely to take some time to develop (see, e.g., Gibbons, Kimmel, and Shea 1997). As the data below will show, there is a difference between the teachers' motivations for taking the summer course modules and their wider impact on classroom practice.

The complete analysis of the structure of WisTEP and of the nature of the participants' experiences, especially in the Summer Institute, was concordant with the NSES *More Emphasis* conditions. In this section, we will present the parts of the survey data that relate to whether and how, as a result of their experiences in WisTEP Summer Institutes, teachers changed their (1) teaching methods, (2) assessment methods, (3) instructional materials, and (4) attitudes toward teaching and learning in the directions endorsed by the NSES.

In their responses to the survey, teachers acknowledged the contributions that WisTEP projects had made to their districts in those four areas (see tables and discussion below). Table 2 shows the most common reasons that teachers chose the WisTEP Summer Institutes. These respondents were most highly motivated by access to disciplinary content and ideas for classroom activities (in another part of the survey, over 26% of teachers noted that insufficient knowledge of disciplinary content significantly limited their success in the classroom, and over two-thirds reported a noticeable limitation).

Because the motivations behind seeking professional development are complex and multifactorial, we carried out a factor analysis to explore whether the answers on these individual questions formed any patterns that would help us to extract a more coherent explanation of key features underlying teachers' motivation and need for professional development. The partial results shown in Table 3 indicate that the teachers' answers form a number of coherent clusters (as indicated by factor scores greater than 0.5). All but one of the program features aligned with the NSES goals for

Table 2. Teachers' Reasons for Pursuing Professional Development by Participating in the WisTEP Summer Institutes

Feature[a]	Very Important (%)	Somewhat Important (%)	Slightly Important (%)	Not Important (%)
Refresher or New Content (401)	78.1	17.7	3.5	0.7
Classroom Activities (402)	66.2	20.6	9.5	3.7
Interaction With Colleagues (405)	59.8	31.6	6.9	1.7
University Credit (402)	57.5	23.1	10.4	9.0
Improved Command of Material (402)	55.2	33.6	8.5	2.7
Science Immersion Experience (386)	44.6	32.6	12.7	9.5
Resources for the Classroom (402)	44.5	32.6	13.9	9.0
Close to Home (404)	42.6	33.2	14.6	9.7
Explore New Subject Area (405)	41.1	36.7	13.6	7.4
Different Teaching Strategies (402)	39.3	40.0	14.2	6.5
Stipend (405)	38.3	36.3	9.8	5.7
Assistance in Instructional Materials Development (401)	36.2	38.9	18.2	6.7
Contact With Researchers (398)	35.2	33.9	19.8	11.1
New Pedagogy or Assessment (394)	27.4	37.3	27.2	8.1
Alignment With Standards and Benchmarks (386)	26.7	29.3	19.9	24.1
Living Expenses (402)	26.1	23.9	15.7	34.3
Residential Experience (379)	11.9	17.2	20.8	50.1

Note: Answers were compiled from 411 program participants who identified themselves primarily as teachers and returned program evaluation surveys. Percentages are calculated for the number of valid answers (*n* of valid answers in parentheses).

[a] The items in bold type align with the NSES Professional Development *More Emphasis* conditions (see Table 1).

professional development have high positive scores on the first three axes describing the teachers' expressed motivations for coming to WisTEP. The scores on these axes indicate that teachers' motivations primed them for the *More Emphasis* changes promoted by the NSES.

The WisTEP survey asked teachers to assess the impact of their experiences on their own classrooms and on their students' performance (Table 4) and on their own motivations to become leaders in professional development and science education reform (Table 5). Table 4 shows that these teachers felt that their command of, and comfort with, the disciplinary content was improved and that they developed or adapted instructional materials as a result of their experiences. However, most teachers rated these changes in the "somewhat" column, indicating that WisTEP projects helped them to achieve changes in instruction that they had already begun or were already interested in accomplishing. Table 4 also shows that the teach-

Table 3. Factors Underlying Teachers' Motivations for Participating in the WisTEP Summer Institutes

Axis	1	2	3	4	5
	Classroom Practice, Strategies, and Resources	Logistical Aspects	Collegiality and Collaboration	Stipend	Content
Assistance in Instructional Materials Development	.737				
Different Teaching Strategies	.712				
Improved Command of Material	.683				
Resources for the Classroom	.654				
New Pedagogy or Assessment	.640				
Alignment With Standards and Benchmarks	.604				−.564
Classroom Activities	.514				
Close to Home		.723			
Living Expenses		−.577			
University Credit		.527			
Contact With Researchers			.642		
Interaction With Colleagues			.580		
Stipend				.742	
Refresher or New Content					.600
Explore New Subject Area					
Science Immersion Experience					

Note: 347 nonmissing cases; first 3 axes account for 38.8% of variance; Varimax rotation with Kaiser Normalization.

[a]The Features in bold type are embodied in the WisTEP Summer Institute. The Features in italics are addressed in follow-up activities with teachers throughout the academic year.

Table 4. Teacher-Reported Instructional Impact of Participating in WisTEP Summer Institutes

Feature	Very Much (%)	Somewhat (%)	Only a Little (%)	Not at All (%)
Scientific Knowledge Increased (387)	48.6	47.0	3.1	1.3
Comfort Level Increased (382)	41.1	46.3	9.4	3.1
Teaching More Enjoyable (374)	36.9	46.5	13.4	3.2
Use WisTEP Materials (371)	36.4	43.7	16.7	3.2
Students Enjoy Class More (356)	36.2	47.2	14.0	2.5
Used or Developed New Materials (372)	32.8	46.2	18.5	2.4
Students More Interested (355)	32.7	46.2	17.2	3.9
Teacher Is Active Science Education Advocate (392)	29.1	43.9	17.9	9.2
Student Performance Improved (347)	19.0	55.6	21.3	4.0
Teacher Restructured Courses (363)	16.3	53.4	23.1	7.2
Students Conducted Research (349)	15.5	35.5	30.9	18.1
Teacher Changed Methods (361)	12.7	51.5	27.7	8.0
Curriculum Aligned With Standards or Benchmarks (334)	9.3	29.9	25.1	35.6
Teacher Changed Student Assessment Methods (355)	8.7	33.2	34.4	23.7
Teacher Restructured Curriculum (365)	3.7	23.0	27.0	46.3

Note: Answers were compiled from 411 program participants who identified themselves as teachers and returned program evaluation surveys. Percentages are calculated for the number of valid answers (*n* of valid answers in parentheses).

ers applied their WisTEP experiences throughout all levels—from the basic approach to materials and activities through re-alignment of the curriculum. However, the influence was greater in those areas in which teachers had the most discretion and control (e.g., instructional materials) and less in those areas that are the purview of district or state educational bodies (e.g., curricular structure).

Teachers who had participated in the WisTEP Summer Institute modules consistently reported that their students showed significantly more enjoyment and interest in science classes and that student performance had improved measurably. What is more, when their disciplinary knowledge and comfort levels increased, teachers found that teaching was more enjoyable. A factor analysis (not shown) found that the outcomes reflected in the responses could be organized into five categories, with student engagement the first and strongest outcome and strong associations with teacher knowledge and comfort, student performance, and teacher satisfaction (all factor scores > 0.8). Of the five factors extracted from the data in Table 4, no factor accounted for less than 15.5% of the variance, and the first axis accounted for 30.9% (if the impact of all five axes were equal, they would each have accounted for 19.5% of the variance). These results indi-

Table 5. Teacher-Reported Leadership Impact of Participating in WisTEP Summer Institutes

Feature	Yes (%)	No (%)	No Answer (%)
Teacher Is Resource for Colleagues	66.4	29.2	4.4
Teacher Is Interested in Academic-Year Programs	50.9	29.7	19.5
Teacher Is Interested in System Support	50.9	31.4	17.8
Teacher Is Interested in Instructional Materials Development	39.9	39.9	20.2
Teacher Is Interested in Becoming Lead Teacher	29.0	49.6	21.4
Teacher Is Interested in Serving on Advisory Board	17.3	61.8	20.9

cate that WisTEP had a strong and consistent impact in producing reforms in science education in many areas of both classroom practice and curricular reform.

Finally, Table 5 reports the effect of WisTEP participation on teacher leadership in science education reform. Almost two-thirds of the respondents reported that their experiences in WisTEP resulted directly in their becoming a resource for colleagues in their own schools and districts. As this function is essentially informal, we also asked about formal participation in several WisTEP-sponsored leadership roles. About half of the respondents indicated that they would be interested in ongoing programs that provided support for professional and curricular development to their classes, schools, or districts. These functions are provided by the WisTEP Academic-Year and System-Support projects. What is interesting in these results is that only about one-third of the respondents indicated that they were aware that these programs were available from WisTEP, but, on the basis of their experience with WisTEP, over half expressed an interest in bringing these programs to their schools. Both of these programs involve teachers in "long-term coherent planning" and a "mix of internal and external expertise" and provide WisTEP staff as "facilitators, consultants, and planners" (NRC 1996, p. 72).

About 40% of the respondents indicated that they would be interested in developing instructional materials, including contributing to collections of materials or field testing new materials. It is important to note that this interest refers to collaboration beyond the school or district in which these teachers work, and not to materials for use solely in their own classrooms. Despite the fact that only about 25% of respondents reported that they were aware that WisTEP supported development, collection, and field-testing of instructional materials, and that only 8% had participated in the past, many more expressed interest in participating in the future. This aspect of WisTEP incorporates and promotes the "integration of science and teaching knowledge," the "teacher as producer of knowledge about teaching," and the "teacher as a member of a collegial professional community" (NRC 1996, p. 72).

The last aspect of teacher leadership included in the survey involved taking leadership roles in WisTEP—participation in future modules as lead teachers or service on the WisTEP advisory board. Over 40% of participants were aware of the Lead Teacher Program and about 7% had previously served as lead teachers; 29% expressed an interest in participating in the future. Only 16% reported being aware of the advisory board, and 17.3% expressed an interest in being on the board; almost 8% reported that they had participated in the advisory board.

Summary

The Wisconsin Teacher Enhancement Program (WisTEP) is an ongoing professional and curriculum development program for K–14 science teachers. The design of WisTEP directly supports 10 of the NSES *More Emphasis* changes for teacher professional development. Teacher-participants are generally motivated to attend course modules by the desire to improve their classroom practice and their content mastery. These teachers also wish to improve their students' performance and understanding of the sciences. However, WisTEP also motivates teachers to take leadership roles in science education reform and to join with their colleagues in collaborative learning and curriculum development projects.

This outcome is consistent with outcomes reported by other programs based on collaborative models that value the expertise and leadership of classroom teachers (e.g., Peters 2002; Pritchard and Marshall 2002). It is also consistent with the assessment of other professional development programs that model hands-on, inquiry-based, process-oriented activities as a means to improve content mastery (Basista and Mathews 2002; NRC 1996, p. 63). In essence, WisTEP modeled the relationships that underlie Professional Development Schools (PDSs) (see, e.g., Sandoval 1996; Nelson 1998) but modified the PDS concept so that the university involvement included *practitioners* in scientific fields along with teacher educators in those fields—a variation that shows how broadly collaboration can be construed (Metcalf-Turner 1999; Snyder 1999).

Our assessment of these results is that WisTEP succeeded in instilling a sense of leadership among the teachers who participated in WisTEP. Most of the teachers directed their leadership activities to their own schools and districts. We are encouraged by this finding, since a major objective of WisTEP is to help teachers improve their science teaching and share their knowledge with colleagues. In this way, WisTEP participants become *de facto* leaders in science education reform.

In summary, the WisTEP Summer Institute is a successful program for teachers' professional development and an example of the power of the approach to professional development programs in science education laid out in the NSES (NRC 1996). Even though most participants expressed their motivation for attending WisTEP and similar programs in terms of improving their own classroom practice, WisTEP achieved many of the NSES *More Emphasis* expectations through the design of its program. Respondents to the WisTEP survey reported improved student learning, improved teacher motivation, more interesting and innovative classroom and laboratory activities, a redesigned curriculum, and revised methods of instruction and student assessment (see, e.g., Levitt and Manner 2001). By virtue of their own classroom practice and by working collaboratively with other teachers, WisTEP participants now lead their districts and their colleagues on the road to science education reform.

References

Basista B., and S. Mathews. 2002. Integrated science and mathematics professional development programs. *School Science and Mathematics* 102(7): 359–370.

Gibbons S., H. Kimmel, and M. Shea. 1997. Changing teacher behavior through staff development: Implementing the teaching and content standards in science. *School Science and Mathematics* 97(6): 302–309.

Gilbert J. K, C. J. Butler, and M. Rutherford. 2000. Explanations with models in science education. In *Developing models in science education*, eds. J. K. Gilbert and C. J. Butler. London: Kluwer.

Levitt, K. E., and B. M. Manner. 2001. An earth science summer institute for elementary teachers. *Journal of Geosciences Education* 49(3): 291–299.

Metcalf-Turner, P. 1999. Variable definitions of professional development schools: A desire or a dilemma? *Peabody Journal of Education* 74(3–4): 33–41.

National Research Council (NRC). 1996. *National science education standards*. Washington, DC: National Academy Press.

Nelson, M. D. 1998. Professional development schools: An implementation model. *NASSP Bulletin* 82(6006): 93–102.

Peters, J. 2002. University-school collaborations: Identifying faulty assumptions. *Asia-Pacific Journal of Teacher Education* 30(3): 229–242.

Pritchard, R. J., and J. C. Marshall. 2002. Professional development in "healthy" vs. "unhealthy" districts: Top 10 characteristics based on research. *School Leadership and Management* 22(2): 113–141.

Sandoval, P. A. 1996. How deep is collaboration? Teacher education curriculum, course curriculum, and the field. *Contemporary Education* 67: 233–236.

Snyder, J. 1999. Professional development schools: What? So what? Now what? *Peabody Journal of Education* 74(3–4): 136–144.

Spray, F. J. 1995. *Mosquitoes in the classroom*. New York: Kendall-Hunt.

Wisconsin Department of Public Instruction (WI DPI). 1998. *Wisconsin Model Academic Standards for Science*. Madison, WI: Wisconsin Department of Public Instruction. Also available online at *www.dpi.state.wi.us/standards/*.

The Oklahoma Science Project for Professional Development: A Road Taken

Philip M. Silverman
Oklahoma Medical Research Foundation

Education…is a Subject so vast, and the Systems of Writers so various and so contradictory: that human Life is too short to examine it; and a Man must die before he can learn to bring up his Children. The Philosophers [sic], Divines, Politicians and Pedagogues, who have published their Theories and Practices in this department are without number….
The Science has so long laboured with a Dropsy that it is a wonder the Patient has not long since expired…. —John Adams to Thomas Jefferson, June 19, 1815

There is no magic bullet or quick fix to the subtle, complex, and lengthy process of education. Even 190 years after Adams addressed the subject in his letter to Jefferson, conflict continues to swirl around basic expectations of what public education in the United States should primarily accomplish (Egan 1997). Given this history, it should not be surprising that eight years after the National Science Education Standards (NSES) (NRC 1996) were introduced as a road map to broaden science literacy in the United States, the NSES have yet to be fully accepted as the *de facto* benchmark against which pre-college science instruction is measured. This is especially so for the all-important area of professional development (Supovitz 2003), the subject of this book.

The science teacher has been referred to as "the single most important factor in the science education equation" (Wheeler 1998). Efforts to inculcate a Standards-based pedagogy among these teachers would therefore appear to be a prerequisite to widespread and meaningful acceptance of the NSES at all levels of the education establishment. I describe here an effective professional development model for secondary school science teachers in Oklahoma that aims to do just that.

The Oklahoma Science Project:
Origin, Context, and Relation to the NSES

Oklahoma is largely a rural state. Of its more than 550 school districts, serving 178,000 secondary school students (including 26,000 Native Americans), about 520 have fewer than 2,500 K–12 students in average daily attendance. These districts serve small communities, which lack the museums, universities, and other resources that elsewhere supplement the science instruction offered in schools. Providing innovative science instruction in these communities was the challenge undertaken by the Oklahoma Science Project (OSP).

Rural science teachers cite inadequate resources and isolation as the two major problems they face (Leslie 2001). Their urban and suburban colleagues also need material resources to do their jobs, but it is the isolation of rural teachers, from each other and from the larger scientific community, that makes their circumstances unique. The OSP was conceived in 1993, several years before publication of the National Science Education Standards in 1996, with the main objective to ameliorate the isolation of Oklahoma's rural high school science teachers. In the years since, formative changes to the OSP have brought it and the NSES Professional Development *More Emphasis* conditions into near congruence, as noted in italics throughout the text. One emphasis of the present report is the effects of these changes on teachers and, through them, on students.

Theory of Action: The Research Dynamic

From the outset, the OSP was based as much on how science is actually done as on how it should be taught. The desired outcome was a cadre of knowledgeable and confident teachers who could merge an authentic research dynamic with their pedagogical skills. (NSES Professional Development *More Emphasis* conditions: *inquiry into teaching and learning, integration of science and teaching knowledge, teacher as intellectual, reflective practitioner, and teacher as producer of knowledge about teaching*) By *research dynamic* I mean the essential features of how scientific research is actually conducted. The sociologist Robert K. Merton (1987) identified three practices common to the conduct of scientific research. First, the phenomenon to be studied must be established as a proper object of scientific investigation. Second, strategic materials, or model systems, are chosen to optimize analysis. The third practice is the most important for our purposes: It is the art of framing a problem in a certain way to highlight what is not known about the phenomenon but must become known for further progress, what Merton refers to as "the cognitively consequential practice" of specifying one's ignorance.

The concept of specified ignorance is often mentioned by scientists and educators. Richard Feynman (1998), the physicist and renowned teacher, referred to "the great value of a satisfactory philosophy of ignorance" not only to science but to a free society, for specifying our ignorance opens the way to constructive dialogue, civil as well as scientific. James Seago (1992), discussing the role of research in undergraduate institutions, also referred to specified ignorance using the phrase "the frontier of knowledge." In practice, specified ignorance as an essential part of a research dynamic entails ongoing, critical, peer interactions. These two elements, specified ignorance and peer interactions, are the components we identify with an authentic research dynamic. As such, they are also key components of the OSP professional development model

(McCarty 2003). Indeed, the first four NSES Professional Development Standards all touch upon these issues as they relate to classroom practice.

In the OSP professional development model, the experimental history of molecular genetics is used to template a research dynamic for the biological sciences (Silverman 2003). Why does the OSP rely on a historical approach? Morris Shamos (1995) has pointed out that the science at the origins of a discipline is generally much simpler and the reasoning involved is more transparent than in a contemporary example, which requires too much background information for a high school student (or teacher) to appreciate. This is certainly true of molecular genetics. After all, we did not arrive at our deep understanding of genetics in one or two class periods. It has taken numerous investigators building on decades of prior results to bring us to our current state of understanding. Why should we expect a 16 year old to achieve anything like comprehension of contemporary genetic science in an absurdly short time with no background whatsoever? Better to begin at the beginning and build comprehension over time.

The pedagogical value of recapitulating the acquisition of knowledge has been effectively championed by Kieran Egan (1997). Egan's major thesis is that individuals acquire intellectual tools as they develop in roughly the same order that these tools evolved in the human population. In discussing pre-college students' acquisition of intellectual tools based on abstraction, reasoning, and inference, Egan noted the importance of "embedding scientific achievements in their historical setting, particularly through discussing the passions, hopes, fears, and intentions of those who developed the scientific knowledge in the first place" (p. 222). We find that teachers respond well to this approach, in part because it is so much more engaging to them than the sterile textbooks and contrived laboratory exercises to which they are otherwise bound.

There appears to be deep resistance to the use of history as a pedagogical tool for science instruction (Duschl 1989). This is too bad. High school students bring to the classroom a remarkable body of misinformation that turns out to be notoriously difficult to change (Clough and Wood-Robinson 1985; Carey 1986; Kindfield 1991). The NSES acknowledge this fact (NRC 1996, p. 181). The pedagogical challenge is to reconfigure the central concepts around which young people organize "knowledge" that, while wrong, fit comfortably into their overall interpretation of the natural world (Posner et al. 1982; Carey 1986). Only then can students organize new knowledge effectively. History could be an effective lever to accomplish the necessary reconfiguration. By recreating simple experiments and transparent logic whose historical outcomes can be easily accessed, students have the opportunity to acquire and interpret knowledge in more or less the same way it was acquired and interpreted originally. Ideally, the specific content of the experiments can be connected to contemporary and familiar issues, so that students can begin to appreciate the flow of scientific discovery. Manifestly, this pedagogy requires teachers who are knowledgeable and confident and who themselves have experience with the give-and-take of a research dynamic. If the NSES Professional Development Standards were to be distilled into a few words, those words would be *knowledge* and *confidence*.

Practices

To inculcate teachers with a research-oriented approach to pre-college science education, we organized the OSP around three practices. The first was to provide teachers with an authentic and relevant research experience (Silverman 2003). This experience is conspicuously absent from most professional development efforts, where laboratory exercises tend to be ends in themselves, rather than elements of a rationally conceived investigation. It is difficult to see how teachers can be expected to understand the dynamics of scientific research without experiencing it directly. Absent such understanding, teachers can not be expected to pass on to their students the richness and excitement of discovering and exploring the phenomena of the natural world or how the processes and principles attached to such exploration apply to personal decisions these students will one day have to make. (NSES Professional Development *More Emphasis* condition: *learning science through investigation and inquiry*)

The second practice was to have teachers work together in the same laboratory to exploit peer interactions, which are essential components of a research dynamic. When this occurs, teachers see and discuss their research experiences in terms of their students and their classrooms (McCarty 2003). Since OSP staff participate in these discussions, the experience is a true partnership; each participant is an expert, albeit of different subjects. The experience has been transformative for both teachers and OSP staff. (NSES Professional Development *More Emphasis* conditions: *collegial and collaborative learning, mix of internal and external expertise, teacher as a member of a collegial professional community, teacher as a source and facilitator of change*)

The third practice was to choose research topics carefully. They should be logically transparent and conceptually focused; introduce the intellectual tools of inference and abstraction; be well suited to framing and testing hypotheses, and above all, engage teachers in significant and fundamental problems. (NSES Professional Development *More Emphasis* condition: *learning science through investigation and inquiry*)

Structure

Specific OSP components (Table 1) were developed to implement the project's organizing principles, as described in the preceding section. As was true of the principles, these components conform closely to the NSES *More Emphasis* components for professional development.

Table 1. Oklahoma Science Project Components and Expected Outcomes

Components	Expected Outcomes
Year-round stipends for teachers	Teacher as respected professional
Summer Research Institutes	Authentic and relevant research experiences; expanded content knowledge; development of mentoring and pedagogical skills; opportunities for teacher renewal and long-term development as science professionals
Classroom support	Improved student performance and interest in science; better student appreciation for the nature and value of science and scientific knowledge
Integrated, multiyear program	Concerted professional and curriculum development

Summer Research Institutes

Summer Research Institute I (SRI-I) is an eight-week research experience providing selected pre-college science teachers with an introduction to scientific research. Teachers are first introduced to key, enabling assays from which molecular genetics flowed (Silverman 2003). Modern molecular genetics derives from several lines of research, each associated with a quantitative, simple, and inexpensive assay method that defines the phenomenon to be investigated. Today, these assays stand out for their elegance and clarity. They emphasize the importance of constructing specific hypotheses with clear predictions, of observation, and of logical inference. I refer to these as "gateway" assays because once mastered, which requires no more than a week, they open up entire realms of biological investigation to teachers, just as they did to the investigators who originally employed them. A description of one such assay and how it is used in SRI-I has been published (Silverman 2003). All of the assays are technically simple, inexpensive, and can be tailored to specific classroom situations. (NSES Professional Development *More Emphasis* condition: *learning science through inquiry*)

Importantly, SRI-I employs a reflective pedagogy (McCarty 2003). The scientist who mentors the teachers during SRI-I assumes the same role that he or she assumes with beginning graduate students—colleague, mentor, and constructive critic. To the degree that teachers learn how to adopt this role with their students, the SRI-I combines action research relevant to the classroom with an authentic research dynamic based upon specified ignorance and peer interactions (McCarty 2003). (NSES Professional Development *More Emphasis* conditions: *inquiry into teaching and learning, integration of science and teaching knowledge, mix of internal and external expertise, teacher as member of a professional community, collegial and collaborative learning*)

Assays and related experiments and follow-on materials have been developed as curriculum modules collaboratively by OSP staff and teachers. The modules are layered, so that teachers can take each of them as far as his or her circumstances permit. Modules include "Viruses and Replication" (Silverman 2003), "Natural Selection in a Petri Dish" (McCarty and Marek 1997), and "Regulation of Gene Expression." (NSES Professional Development *More Emphasis* conditions: *integration of science and teaching knowledge, mix of internal and external expertise, teacher as member of a professional community, collegial and collaborative learning*)

Teachers completing SRI-I are provided with a laptop computer for easy communication during the school year among themselves and to request materials and assistance from OSP staff at the Oklahoma Medical Research Foundation (OMRF). (NSES Professional Development *More Emphasis* conditions: *mix of internal and external expertise, teacher as member of a collegial professional community*)

Realizing that professional development is best regarded as a long-term continuum, we instituted a second Summer Research Institute, SRI-II or Return to Science, in 1999. The Return is an opportunity for teachers who have taken SRI-I to return to OMRF in subsequent summers for periods up to one month. The Return, fully subscribed for the four years of its existence, was intended to reinforce habits of exploration and research. Most recently, returning teachers have been encouraged to develop their research experiences into curriculum modules that address fundamental biological questions as well as the impact of biology on society. (NSES Professional Development *More Emphasis* conditions: *long-term, coherent plans, teacher as pro-*

ducer of knowledge about teaching, teacher as leader, teacher as source and facilitator of change, integration of theory and practice in school settings)

Classroom Support

The Summer Research Institutes are an effective way to introduce teachers to a research dynamic, and there is evidence that teachers change their classroom practices as a result (see "Outcomes: Is It Working?" on p. 167). To encourage classroom application of teachers' SRI experiences, OSP provides supplies to SRI participants when they return to their classrooms. (NSES Professional Development *More Emphasis* condition: *integration of theory and practice in school settings*) Teachers do take advantage of this; in one three-month period, OSP shipped 1,600 items. Finally, we are developing a teacher support network, designated OSPNet, based on the use of the internet and videoconferencing to connect rural classrooms throughout the state to each other and to the OSP. (NSES Professional Development *More Emphasis* condition: *mix of internal and external expertise*) As one example of what OSPNet can do, we have introduced eLAB, electronic notebooks available from the OSP server over the web. Users view and modify notebooks through a standard web browser from any computer connected to the internet. Formatting and uploading of files can be as simple or complex as the user desires. eLAB is designed mainly to encourage and evaluate collaborations between students and teachers based on shared electronic notebooks. (NSES Professional Development *More Emphasis* conditions: *collegial and collaborative learning, a variety of professional development activities, teacher as leader, teacher as member of a collegial professional community*)

Integrated Multiyear Program

Perhaps the most important lesson learned from the OSP experience, and certainly the one that now guides the OSP, is that effective professional development for pre-college (grades 7–12) science teachers is a long-term, continuous process. It must be accompanied by structure, in the form of curriculum materials, and support during the school year. Accordingly, a current goal is to integrate the SRIs and OSPNet into a coherent, long-term program for professional development. The formal program extends over three years, but our experience indicates that some teachers will remain connected to the OSP indefinitely if given the opportunity and incentive. (NSES Professional Development *More Emphasis* condition: *long-term, coherent plans*)

Curriculum

The OSP focuses on genes, mutations, and heredity. This choice is consistent with the NSES and *Benchmarks for Science Literacy* (AAAS 1993). *Benchmarks* listed what students should know in six areas related to biology (pp. 99–125). The terms *DNA*, *genes/genetic*, and *mutation(s)* appear 20 times in the sections "Diversity of Life," "Heredity," and "Cells" for grades 9–12, but only once for grades 6–8 (AAAS 1993). Clearly, a strong professional consensus endorses genes, mutation, and heredity as pedagogically suitable topics for the high school biology classroom.

The OSP curriculum focus rests also on other grounds. Our scientific understanding of genetics has informed a coherent view of life and its history on this planet. This view already ranks among humanity's fundamental intellectual achievements. It is implied constantly in articles about stem cells, emerging viral diseases, antibiotic-resistant bacteria, and so on. If students are to engage intelligently in public discourse about these matters and use the knowledge and understanding of scientifically literate persons in their careers, then surely they must be conversant with the structure and dynamics of the living world. Few would regard as educated someone who could not explain the difference between a star and a planet; the same judgment should apply to not knowing the difference between a gene and a chromosome (Kindfield 1991).

Remarkably, introductory high school biology courses generally fail to convey the enormity and significance of contemporary biology's achievements. Notwithstanding the NSES and similar calls for reform (AAAS 1993), too much pre-college classroom practice still relies upon massive textbooks that emphasize the diversity of life. Now life's diversity is certainly amazing. But the important principle is that all life, irrespective of form, is related by a common genetic chemistry, a common genetic code, and a common ancestry. Once this is understood, the diversity of life falls immediately into place as the formal manifestation of natural selection, which depends entirely on genetic inheritance. Without these central, simplifying concepts, life's diversity either remains a mystery or becomes another collection of details to memorize and quickly forget.

Because high school students' retention of classroom material is so limited, it makes sense to select for intensive study only those concepts and facts that are central to the subject. The NSES recognized the importance of content focus in calling for approaches that encourage a deeper understanding of a smaller number of general principles (NRC 1996, p. 181). Clearly, the professional development of pre-college science teachers should answer this call.

Outcomes: Is It Working?

Data from two sources suggest that the Oklahoma Science Project is effective in changing both teaching and learning behaviors. The first source is the academic science education community. Studies of the OSP published by Dr. Robbie McCarty of Southwestern Oklahoma State University and Dr. Jon Pedersen of the University of Oklahoma (McCarty and Pedersen 2002; McCarty 2003) provide qualitative evidence that the OSP increases teachers' content knowledge and transforms the way they view their role in the classroom. For example, McCarty (2003) found that "96% of the teachers added collaborative group learning to their classroom strategies and encouraged students to ask more complex questions than before their OSP experiences." (NSES Professional Development *More Emphasis* conditions: *teacher as producer of knowledge about teaching, teacher as leader, teacher as source and facilitator of change*)

Confirmatory evidence comes from the teachers themselves in the form of unsolicited e-mails. Individually, or even by twos or threes, these would be merely anecdotal. Collectively however, they constitute a consistent and impressive body of data covering an eight-year interval. These communications document change as a direct result of the OSP.

I have collected examples under three headings. These are teaching practices, motivation/confidence, and student performance.

Teaching Practices

As I learned last summer, true science is much more than just learning concepts and techniques. True science is solving problems and sometimes not solving problems. It is open-ended and frustrating and completely addictive. True science is something every science teacher should be trying to teach. Science is about the process and not just the content. (NSES Professional Development *More Emphasis* condition: *teacher as intellectual, reflective practitioner*)

He [a collaborator] and I have two hours during which we can link up and share labs…(we're both beginning biochem discussions next week…so we'll be ready to do the enzyme studies in the next couple of weeks. (NSES Professional Development *More Emphasis* condition: *collegial and collaborative learning;* note also that enzyme studies reflect a significant increment in content knowledge for this teacher)

I hope to spend more time in the lab than ever before. …we [referring to a collaborator; see previous quote] are working out a time to use the video [videoconferencing] to do some labs…we are going to do the enzyme lab together. (NSES Professional Development *More Emphasis* condition: *collegial and collaborative learning*)

Once you start teaching using OSP, you will never teach the same way again. (NSES Professional Development *More Emphasis* condition: *teacher as a source and facilitator of change*)

Motivation/Confidence

A very big part of this success [with student science fair projects] is the fact that I was motivated by the experience last summer and I have been more successful in motivating my students and colleagues. (NSES Professional Development *More Emphasis* condition: *teacher as leader*)

[The experiment] worked beautifully. Can you believe it?! It worked the first time! I guess it pays to do it over and over before you try it with students. We're going to discuss operons tomorrow. (NSES Professional Development *More Emphasis* conditions: *integration of science and teaching knowledge, learning science through investigation and inquiry;* note also that a discussion of operons based on experimental data instead of a textbook cartoon represents a significant increase in content and process knowledge for this teacher)

There is no substitute for hands-on experience. Since arriving home, I have been reading through notes I took during previous summer institutes. I was astounded to find information on diauxic curves, lac-operon, and antibiotic resistance. The concepts had been introduced in lectures but without practical experience, I had forgotten the terms and am certain I had little understanding at the time. (NSES Professional Development *More Emphasis* condition: *learning science through investigation and inquiry*)

Student Performance

Setting an ultimate goal of isolating, identifying and learning all we can about a local virus has given my students an incentive to fully understand the basic concepts and techniques required to accomplish this goal. Giving them a final direction, rather than what seems to be unrelated bits and pieces of data, has pulled them together.... I am elated!.... If you can change the perspective of ONE teacher..., you can stimulate the minds of MANY students.

I have some students working on the microbes for the past week or so and I thought I would give you an update. They are really having a GOOD TIME! One of the students brought in some water from his fish tank and we did the "selection" activity with Tet[racycline]. We had about a hundred [tet-resistant] colonies.... It turns out that they had been using tet in the tank to try to clear up an "epidemic" which had been killing their fish! So, my students are really excited!

My students experienced a new level of science instruction. I believe they sensed a new freedom to think outside the box.... I saw new levels of creativity with my students and myself.

In my level-one biology class, [the OSP approach] is a question and discussion generator.

I did not realize this would generate such interest and excitement with the students. I knew that it could be useful, but I think it will have an even bigger impact on my classes than I anticipated.

The students are very inquisitive! One student in particular had all of the "right" questions! You could certainly tell she was doing some critical thinking. And she wasn't the only one!

These data, fragmentary though they are, document that the OSP can change the way teachers think about themselves and their profession. Moreover, they document how these changes spill over into altered student attitudes about science. Since the OSP conforms so closely to the tenets of the NSES, the data validate the NSES as well as the OSP as such. We know these data are preliminary; controlled and quantitative evaluation of the OSP still lies ahead. We certainly need to know more about its effects on student performance and interest in science and how it affects students' appreciation and understanding of the nature and value of science and scientific knowledge. These studies will be a major challenge, but, as the NSES emphasize, we must *focus on what is most highly valued instead of what is easily measured*. So far, it appears that the NSES, critically applied in the context of the OSP and similar efforts, can make a substantive difference in pre-college science instruction.

Acknowledgments

I am indebted to the many colleagues who have brought life to the Oklahoma Science Project. I wish especially to thank Dr. William G. Thurman for encouragement at the beginning and Vernon Cook and Frank Merrick for enthusiasm and steadfast support ever since. I am indebted to the Howard Hughes Medical Institute, the Williams Companies, and generous foundations and individuals throughout Oklahoma for financial support. Finally, I will never be able to repay Oklahoma's public high school science teachers for what they taught me about commitment, dedication, and perseverance.

References

American Association for the Advancement of Science (AAAS). 1993. *Benchmarks for science literacy: Project 2061*. New York: Oxford University Press.

Carey, S. 1986. Cognitive science and science education. *American Psychologist* 41: 1123–1130.

Clough, E., and C. Wood-Robinson. 1985. Children's understanding of inheritance. *Journal of Biological Education* 19: 304–310.

Duschl, R. 1989. A framework for reapplying history and philosophy of science to science education. ERIC Document Reproduction Service No. ED 320 782.

Egan, K. 1997. *The educated mind: How cognitive tools shape our understanding*. Chicago, IL: University of Chicago Press.

Feynman, R. 1998. *The meaning of it all: Thoughts of a citizen-scientist*. Reading, MA: Addison-Wesley.

Kindfield, A. 1991. Confusing chromosome number and structure: A common student error. *Journal of Biological Education* 25: 193–200.

Leslie, M. 2001. Scientific outliers. *HHMI* [Howard Hughes Medical Institute] *Bulletin* 5: 26–29.

McCarty, R. 2003. Specified ignorance: A pedagogical and cognitive tool for learning the nature and process of science. *Teaching and Learning: The Journal of Natural Inquiry and Reflective Practice* 17: 113–132.

McCarty, R., and E. Marek. 1997. Natural selection in a petri dish. *The Science Teacher* 64: 37–39.

McCarty, R., and J. Pedersen. 2002. Making the invisible visible: The Oklahoma Science Project. *Science Education International* 13: 16–22.

Merton, R. 1987. Three fragments from a sociologist's notebook. *Annual Review of Sociology* 13: 1–28.

National Research Council (NRC). 1996. *National science education standards*. Washington, DC: National Academy Press.

Posner, G., K. Strike, P. Hewson, and W. Gertzog. 1982. Accommodation of a scientific conception: Toward a conceptual change. *Science Education* 66: 211–227.

Seago, J. 1992. The role of research in undergraduate education. *The American Biology Teacher* 54: 401–405.

Shamos, M. 1995. *The myth of scientific literacy*. New Brunswick, NJ: Rutgers University Press.

Silverman, P. 2003. The origins of molecular biology: A pedagogical tool for the professional development of pre-college science teachers. *Biochemistry and Molecular Biology Education* 31: 313–318.

Supovitz, J. 2003. Evidence of the influence of the national science education standards on the professional development system. *www.nap.edu/openbook/0309087430/html/64.html*.

Wheeler, G. 1998. The wake-up call we dare not ignore. *Science* 279: 1611.

Professional Development Based on Conceptual Change: Wyoming TRIAD Process

Joseph I. Stepans
University of Wyoming

Barbara Woodworth Saigo
Saiwood Biology Resources/Saiwood Publications

Joan Gaston
Wyoming Department of Education

School and Community Setting

The professional development program known as the Wyoming TRIAD (WyTRIAD) is a three-way partnership between a facilitator (usually a university faculty member), teachers in a school, and their administrator (usually a principal). It is research-based and includes an integrated core of professional components, including those shown in Figure 1.

The WyTRIAD was developed by Joseph Stepans at the University of Wyoming (Stepans 1989) and was first implemented in 1991 in Torrington, Wyoming, a rural school district in the eastern part of the state. It has been used successfully in several states and in schools of varying size and demographic composition (Figure 2). It has twice been used for National Science Foundation (NSF) Systemic Initiatives—in the state of Florida and the city of Detroit. The following examples were chosen to demonstrate distinctly different circumstances in which the process has been successful.

Osceola Magnet School (OMS), Indian River School District, Vero Beach, Florida. Vero Beach is a generally affluent coastal community with a low percentage of minority families. OMS is an elementary magnet school with unusually strong parent involvement. Science instruction and professional development for teachers were strongly supported by the administrator.

Detroit Public Schools, Michigan. In Detroit's urban, inner-city schools, most students are African American and many are eligible for Title I benefits. Instructional supplies and materials for

Figure 1. Some Professional Components Integrated Into the WyTRIAD Professional Development Process

- Learning from and about students
- Interviewing
- Modeling
- Assessment strategies
- Research on learning and teaching
- Peer coaching and sharing
- Questioning rationale
- Examining and developing curriculum
- Alignment: standards, curriculum, instruction, assessment

- Instructional strategies
- Constructivism and conceptual change
- Connecting and integrating disciplines
- Learning resources
- Collaborative sharing, communicating
- Developing and implementing new ideas
- Personal and professional reflections
- Conducting classroom research/inquiry
- Leadership development

science were extremely limited, but administrators and parents were strongly supportive of professional development.

A collaborative of three small Wyoming schools. To establish a critical mass for professional development, three communities joined together, with sessions rotating among them. Thermopolis (Hot Springs County) has about 4,000 residents and a generally lower middle-class socioeconomic status. Residents are predominantly white, and Hispanics are the largest minority group. Fort Washakie School is on the Arapahoe-Shoshone reservation where, although the socioeconomic status of families is low, the school facilities are modern and well-appointed, with computers, equipment, and supplies for science instruction. The University of Wyoming Laboratory School is preK–8, with the middle level (6–8) considered experimental, emphasizing interdisciplinary teaching. Its 200 students come from mainly professional families in Laramie, which has a population of about 30,000. Multiple ethnicities are present, but the majority of the population is white.

First in the World (FITW) Consortium, Chicago, Illinois. The consortium includes a group of successful suburban districts from the North Shore area of Chicago, with a combined enrollment of about 37,000 students. Encouraged by the outstanding performance of their students on TIMSS (the Trends in International Mathematics and Science Study), the districts formed the FITW Consortium in 1995 in order to build on and focus even more intensively on student achievement in science and mathematics. This is the only circumstance where WyTRIAD has been adapted to meet local needs for a summer experience.

Fremont County School District #25, Riverton, Wyoming. Riverton has a population of about 10,000, and is surrounded by Arapahoe-Shoshone reservation lands. Socioeconomically, the population is lower middle-class, engaged mainly in blue-collar employment. The students are primarily white, with American Indians as the largest minority group (about 20%). About 40% of the 2,500 K–12 students qualify for Title I benefits. Many teachers have participated in WyTRIAD from 1997 through 2004, the majority of them at the middle school level (39 of 51). Riverton provides the fullest longitudinal picture of how the WyTRIAD process engenders change from

Figure 2. Sites Where the WyTRIAD Professional Development Model Has Been Implemented, 1991–2004

*1991–1995	Goshen County, WY
1993	Uinta County, WY
*1993–1999	Indian River School District, FL
*1993–1996	Pontiac Elementary School, SC
1994	Henderson State University, AR
*1997–1999	University Lab School, WY
1994–1995	Albany County Schools, WY
1994–1995	Laramie County Schools, WY
*1994–2000	Ft. Myers Schools, FL
1995	Sweetwater County #2, WY
1995	Jensen Beach, FL
1996	Platte County, WY
*1996–present	Sweetwater County #1, WY
*1996–1997	Fort Washakie Schools, WY
*1995–1997	Hot Springs County, WY
*1996–2001	Campbell County Schools, WY
**1998–2000	First in the World Consortium, Chicago, IL
1996–1998	Johnson County, WY
*1997–1999	Detroit Public Schools, MI (NSF Urban Systemic Initiative)
*1999–2000	Cathedral Home, Laramie, WY
*1997–2004	Fremont County #25, WY
*1999–2004	Laramie County Junior High, WY
*1999–2004	Albany County Science Department, WY
*2002–2004	Goshen County, WY
*2002–2004	Colorado River County, AZ
*2003–2004	Teton County School District, WY

*Administrative involvement

**Summer professional development

within (Cantrell, Stepans, and Gaston 2002; Cantrell 2000; Berube, Gaston, and Stepans 2002; Stepans, Saigo, and Gaston 2004).

Alignment of WyTRIAD and the National Science Education Standards

The WyTRIAD was designed to explicitly incorporate (1) research knowledge about teaching, learning, and professional development and (2) the philosophy and recommendations of reform documents (Stepans 1989; Stepans, Saigo, and Ebert 1996, 1999; Darling-Hammond 1996; ACE 1999; Yager 2000). The program continues to develop, based on emerging research findings, including those of K–12 professionals. The *National Science Education Standards* (NRC 1996) and many other documents, including *Blueprints for Reform: Science, Mathematics, and Technology Education* (AAAS 1998), state that effective professional development is developmental and constructivist; is based on best practices; is informed and reflective; and is coherent, coordinated, integrated, relevant, and contextual. It builds on and expands the research base. WyTRIAD has all of these characteristics (Table 1). WyTRIAD also aligns with the National Staff Development Council standards for context, process, and content (NSDC 1995a, 1995b, 1996).

Teachers, Students, and Classrooms

Rather than fostering a few superstar teachers, the WyTRIAD develops cadres of exemplary *colleagues*, creating opportunities for all to benefit from the individual strengths of many. Students also become adept at a collegial approach to learning through sharing and testing ideas. After three years of participation, some teachers become facilitators. With sustained participa-

Table 1. Effective Professional Development: What the National Science Education Standards Call For and What the WyTRIAD Program Does

National Science Education Standards	WyTRIAD Program
Clear, shared goals	Goals, expectations, and commitments are mutually agreed on by partners (facilitator, teachers, administrators) and are linked to district needs
Integrated, coordinated components	Teaching, learning, content, and professional development components are fully integrated and coordinated in a coherent sequence; there is a discrete plan and schedule for topics, classroom implementation, evaluation, and peer collaboration
Developmental	Uses a constructivist approach that emphasizes discovery of existing conceptions and assumptions as a basis for conceptual change, understanding, and professional growth
Individual and group specific	Implementation is based on the needs of the school and teachers and is adaptable to diverse school and community settings and content areas
Collaborative	A genuine, interactive partnership exists throughout the process; multiple components engage teachers in collaborative sharing, peer coaching and mentoring, observing, developing and aligning curriculum, instruction, and assessment, planning, and research
Relevant to school site	Sessions are on-site, with modeling, implementation, and evaluation of strategies in teachers' own classrooms; classroom-based inquiry (action research) guides curriculum decisions; sessions are individualized based on teachers' present students and teacher-selected instructional topics
Continuous assessment	Uses immediate and ongoing action research, evaluation, and written reflection; reflective sharing occurs among all participants at the beginning of each session; organized studies and evaluation are carried out by researchers and districts regarding the program's impact on teachers, students, and schools

tion, the process builds a self-sustaining, continually renewing, systemic culture—changing the classroom from within.

WyTRIAD has been implemented with grades K–12, with regular and special education students, in science and other content areas, and in content-specific interdisciplinary curricula. Participating teachers have varied widely in a number of respects: experience (years of teaching, extent of professional development, leadership roles, use of classroom-based inquiry instruction); science content knowledge and teaching-and-learning preferences/styles; flexibility and willingness to experience change; confidence in understanding of and ability to teach science; views about and experience with peer collaboration; and attitudes toward administrators, students, and school culture.

As noted earlier, participating schools have been rural, suburban, and urban. Most schools have had mixed racial and ethnic diversity, some with high numbers of American Indians and some predominantly African American.

Commitment and participation on the part of administrators have varied. Because the WyTRIAD is a true three-way partnership, the administrator *must* participate fully by attending sessions as well as providing assistance to the teachers between sessions. A strong, direct correlation has been demonstrated between administrator involvement and teacher enthusiasm, attitudes, and effectiveness in bringing about reform-based strategies, collegiality, and leadership.

Challenging Assumptions, Fostering Conceptual Change

Science education today is grounded in a constructivist philosophy (Duit and Treagust 1998), the view that individuals construct meaning from their own experiences and that learning progresses through conceptual change, from naive ideas to more mature conceptions (Bell 1995). As learners develop and have new experiences their mental frameworks are altered to accommodate these experiences—adding new ideas and rearranging or replacing existing views.

The preconceptions and assumptions of students, teachers, and administrators exert a collective impact on what transpires in the classroom. Students have preconceptions about

Figure 3. Some Common Assumptions Held by Teachers

- Students come to class ready to learn.
- Inattentive students are unmotivated and do not want to learn.
- I can't teach products of a poor home environment.
- Learning starts where the last teaching stopped.
- My students "got it" because they performed acceptably on the test.
- I know what is best for students.
- I don't have time/I'm already teaching as fast as I can to get through the curriculum.
- I have to do something with all the topics.
- The next teaching strategy will be the "silver bullet" that solves my students' problems in learning.
- My classroom is my own domain, and the same is true of my colleagues.

science concepts. Teachers have assumptions about students, the teaching-and-learning process, science concepts, learning resources, and instructional strategies (Figure 3). Teachers' assumptions about their professional roles determine their teaching philosophy and practices, classroom atmosphere, and comfort level with new ideas and expectations. Administrators have assumptions about how students and teachers should interact in the classroom; about teaching, learning, curriculum, and teacher professional development; and about how to balance being an administrator, disciplinarian, advocate, educational leader, and liaison with the district, school board, and community.

Just as there are consequences to not challenging students' science preconceptions and misconceptions, there also are consequences to not challenging teachers' and administrators' assumptions. Unchallenged, these assumptions can be barriers to change, to the understanding of new strategies, to teacher development, and to the ability to generalize and extend new knowledge. Unfortunately, most professional development does not truly challenge assumptions.

If meaningful learning involves conceptual change, it follows that meaningful teaching should explicitly identify, challenge, and test existing views. Synthesizing numerous research-based recommendations, Stepans developed his Conceptual Change Model (CCM), a six-part instructional strategy (Stepans 1994, 1996, 2003; Stepans, Saigo, and Ebert 1996, 1999). An essential feature of the model is that students and teachers deliberately identify preconceptions as a basis for "helping students to develop their own ideas and understanding" (Bell 1995) through instructional challenges to these preconceptions.

In the CCM, the learner begins (1) by privately thinking about, and committing to, an explanation concerning a concept, problem, or situation. (2) Ideas then are shared (exposed), first in small groups and then with the entire group. This part of the CCM uncovers existing ideas in the classroom more thoroughly and with less individual risk than whole-group brainstorming and questioning. (3) Learners then challenge their preconceptions and those of their classmates through activities and other experiences, followed by (4) a facilitated process of accommodating

Table 2. Parallels Between Steps of the Conceptual Change Model (CCM)/Instructional Strategy and Effective Professional Development

Students are constructing meaning about a concept when they are...	Teachers are constructing meaning about teaching and learning when they are...
Becoming aware of their own views (preconceptions).	Becoming aware of their own views about their students' ideas.
Becoming aware of the views of others.	Becoming aware of the views of others.
Confronting (testing) their ideas.	Confronting their assumptions about their students' ideas.
Going through the process of making sense of observations (resolving conflicts).	Examining how new ideas fit into existing beliefs (philosophy).
Applying concept to other situations.	Applying a new idea or strategy to other situations.
Going beyond by posing new questions/problems.	Going beyond by posing new questions about teaching, learning, and curriculum.

new ideas and resolving cognitive conflict. Students are encouraged to express what they have learned in *their own words* and actions. (5) Students are then given the opportunity to extend and test new ideas through application and (6) go on to pose new questions and problems for investigation. The CCM incorporates components of the traditional and popular learning cycle strategy but differs significantly by requiring explicit identification of individual student preconceptions as a component of lesson design and by asking students to pose new problems. The CCM allows a teacher to identify more precisely whether or not conceptual change actually has occurred within students, as emphasized by Bell (1995) and others.

WyTRIAD professional development closely parallels this instructional strategy (Table 2), fostering conceptual change and causing teachers to become "constructivists of the teaching-and-learning process" (Stepans, Saigo, and Ebert 1996, 1999).

This is an active, challenging, and at times uncomfortable process, unlike most traditional professional development experiences. As Ball (1996) discusses, lack of conflict in staff development sessions can be a disservice. Presenting participants with enthusiastically delivered tips, tricks, guidelines, and handouts is not enough. "Such an approach offers participants an enormous assortment of resources, but their potential is restricted by the lack of critical discussion. Seeking to make participants comfortable, staff development leaders rarely challenge teachers' assumptions or intentionally provoke disequilibrium or conflict." By contrast, Ball recommends a process that puts teachers in "a stance of critique and inquiry toward practice." The WyTRIAD process deliberately invokes disequilibrium (Table 3).

The Structure of WyTRIAD

Prior to creating a partnership, university and district representatives participate in an informational meeting to discuss the process and the expectations of teachers, administrators, and other

Table 3. Parallel Learning Through Disequilibrium as It Occurs With Both the Conceptual Change Model for Instruction and the WyTRIAD Professional Development Process for Teachers and Administrators

Stages of the Process		
Initial equilibrium →	Disequilibrium →	New equilibrium
Teaching for Conceptual Change Model		
Preconceptions based on prior experiences →	Active challenge of experiences that don't match predictions →	More appropriate understanding of concept
WyTRIAD Professional Development Experience		
Comfortable habits and assumptions about students, teaching, and learning →	Unexpected data from students; experience with new ideas and strategies, classroom inquiry, collegial sharing, and professional expectations →	New understanding, ideas, and skills; comfort through implementation and results

Table 4. Typical WyTRIAD Schedule, Showing Agendas for the Sessions as Well as Activities That Take Place in Classrooms Between Sessions*

Session I: Two days, on-site	**Between Sessions I and II: Four to six weeks**
Facilitator, teachers, administrators:	**Teachers:**
• Experience a constructive-based lesson to stimulate thinking and frame discussion	• Interview students about selected concept
• *Topic: Parallels—Applying what we know about learning to teaching students and to effective professional development*	• Compare student views with expectations and assumptions, curriculum, books
	• Journal—Observations, ideas, reflections
• *Topic: Philosophy and components of WyTRIAD*	**Administrators:**
• *Topic: Roles of partners*	• Make all arrangements to enable teacher activities
• *Topic: Learning from and about students via interviews*	• Observe, reflect
• Model interviewing with students	
• Share observations and implications about interviewing	
• Each teacher selects a concept that is planned for teaching and prepares to interview students about the concept	
• Journal—Teachers and administrators reflect on session and activities	
Parent session	

Session II: Two days, on-site	**Between Sessions II and III: Four to six weeks**
Facilitator, teachers, administrators:	**Teachers:**
• Share what was learned from interviewing students	• Implement CCM lessons
• *Topic: Constructive-based strategy (Conceptual Change Model [CCM])*	• Observe and record observations
	• Get involved with peer coaching
• Model CCM lesson with teachers and administrators	• Journal—Observations, ideas; reflect on changes in students and selves
• Model CCM lesson with students while teachers and administrators observe	**Administrators:**
• *Topic: Peer coaching*	• Make all arrangements to enable teacher activities
• Teachers prepare lesson materials using constructive strategy	• Observe, reflect
• Share plans	
Parent session	*(**Table 4** continues on next page)*

partners. This meeting emphasizes that WyTRIAD is an open-ended, developmental *process* to improve learning and teaching, not a content-specific set of workshops or classes. If the terms are agreed upon, the partners sign a contract.

One WyTRIAD sequence occurs over the course of a semester and consists of four to five formal sessions separated by blocks of time when teachers implement and assess what they are learning (Table 4). Most teachers and their administrators participate for a least one or two semesters. Preservice teachers also may be involved.

(Table 4 continued)

Session III: Two days, on-site
Facilitator, teachers, administrators:
- Share experiences, observations, insights
- Discuss implications
- Model CCM with different topic, first with participants, then in classroom
- Develop lessons, materials
- *Topic: Collecting classroom data (planned, organized classroom inquiry/research)*

Parent session

Between Sessions III and IV: Four to six weeks
Teachers:
- Continue using interviews
- Implement lessons, materials
- Continue collaboration and peer coaching
- Collect classroom data
- Journal—Observations, ideas; reflect on changes in students and selves

Administrators:
- Make all arrangements to enable teacher activities
- Observe, reflect

Session IV: One day, on-site
Facilitator, teachers, administrators:
- Share experiences, observations, insights, implications
- *Topic: Teaching integrated materials using constructive approach*
- *Topic: Alignment of standards, expectations, instruction, assessment*
- Based on experiences of students and colleagues during the process, reflect on appropriateness of expectations of students, instructional experiences, and assessments
- Discuss future plans, strategies, and grant opportunities to continue and expand the process
- Agree to share WyTRIAD experiences with other teachers and administrators considering participation

After last formal session
Teachers and administrators:
- Continue using and developing Year One components, including interviewing, developing conceptual change lessons, peer coaching, peer sharing, examination of curriculum, alignment, etc.
- Share experiences and encourage participation of other teachers and administrators
- Engage in professional presentations based on what they learned from their own experiences

Facilitator:
- Provide ongoing advice, including through the use of e-mail and telephone
- Evaluate
- Initiate arrangements for another go-round

*For full details of the process, see J. Stepans, B. W. Saigo, and C. Ebert. 1996, 1999. *Changing the classroom from within: Partnership, collegiality, constructivism*. 1st and 2nd eds. Montgomery, AL: Saiwood Publications.

   Many teachers and administrators elect to continue this ongoing process for a second year (Table 5). After two years, teachers often report that they are fully comfortable with the instructional strategies and have expanded their use. Ideally, districts are involved for three to four years, leading to the development of some teachers as facilitators who continue and institutionalize the process during Year Three. As some teachers become facilitators, the process becomes fully resident in the local district. At this point, the university facilitator transitions to being a consultant instead of convener and instructor.

Table 5. Overview of Second- and Third-Year Participation in WyTRIAD	
Second-year (and beyond) participants:	**Third-year participants who plan to become facilitators:**
• Continue developing and implementing Year One components • New topics introduced • New strategies modeled, explained, implemented, evaluated • Classroom research (action research by teachers) • Mentor new Year One participants	• Observe Year One or Year Two sessions • Meet with facilitators • Plan own activities and schedules • Confirm agreements between teachers, administrators, district

WyTRIAD and NSES *More Emphasis* Conditions

The following paragraphs demonstrate how the WyTRIAD is consistent with the NSES *More Emphasis* conditions for professional development (NRC 1996, p. 72).

More emphasis on inquiry into teaching and learning. WyTRIAD participants are challenged from the beginning to inquire into their assumptions and practices. They learn from and about students through interviews, observation, classroom research, journals, reflection, and collegial sharing.

More emphasis on learning science through investigation and inquiry. Instructional strategies such as the Conceptual Change Model promote increased mastery of science content; better understanding of the nature of science; skills in scientific inquiry and ways of thinking; and abilities to apply and extend knowledge.

More emphasis on integration of science and teaching knowledge; integration of theory and practice in school settings. Participants simultaneously learn about and apply current research in science education through the multiple components of the process. Strategies such as interviewing students and teaching with the CCM are modeled with participants and with students in the teachers' own classrooms. Teachers then implement, evaluate, reflect on, and share their experiences with colleagues.

More emphasis on collegial and collaborative learning. Collegial sharing, peer coaching, mentoring, and collaborative curriculum evaluation and development are fundamental to the process. The facilitator, teachers, and administrators are active participants in all sessions.

More emphasis on long-term coherent plans; a variety of professional development activities; a mix of internal and external expertise; staff developers as facilitators, consultants, and planners; teacher as intellectual, reflective practitioner; teacher as producer of knowledge about teaching; teacher as leader; teacher as a member of a collegial professional community; teacher as source and facilitator of change. The WyTRIAD is a full, committed partnership of teachers, administrators, and professional development facilitators that integrates all of the above emphases. The facilitators share knowledge, model strategies, and facilitate the process; teachers implement new ideas in the classroom, collect information, reflect, share, and learn from their students and one another. A coherent sequence of integrated components improves science teaching and also nurtures local leadership. Teachers' inquiry is a centerpiece of the process, as they implement changes based on their own organized inquiry and keep track of meaningful changes in students and themselves. They make decisions about curriculum and learning resources based on what they are learning, and align curriculum, instruction, and assessment with standards. They develop habits of collegial practice, including sharing, classroom observing and modeling, peer coaching, and collaborative lesson development. Even lunchroom chat becomes professional.

In Addition...

WyTRIAD has important features in addition to those mentioned above. It commonly results in success for a broader array of students, not just those with an aptitude for science or for traditional, reading-based approaches. It encourages connecting and integrating disciplines, which is especially important for teachers at elementary and middle levels. Moreover, as teachers develop and implement new ideas, parents become excited about their children's improved attitudes toward (and success with) science.

Evidence of Impact

Impact on Students

In WyTRIAD, teachers learn to critically analyze their work, including its impact on their students, their colleagues, and themselves. Teachers report significant results with students, as in the following examples.

Student Attitudes and Abilities to Make Connections Improve

Especially as a result of using the Conceptual Change Model, my students started synthesizing, talking about science. They looked on their own for science materials and books outside the classroom. They brought questions to [middle school] class.

Through the strategies, experiences, and questions, my [fifth-grade] students are beginning to think, to make connections and ask questions. Another result is promotion of curiosity—they are looking for new ideas.

Student Collegiality and Enthusiasm Increase

I observe [fifth-graders] when they are working on tasks. They go to the computer and to books for more information. They pick each other's brains. They ask, "I wonder if ...?" They are excited and enthusiastic.

The so-called "book-smart" students were not necessarily the ones who came up with the best ideas. But those who were ignored by the others before suddenly became very important. Other [middle school] students began paying attention to and respecting them.

Concept Retention Is Improved

Teachers often commented that their students developed a deeper and more persistent understanding of science concepts:

> *I noticed long-term [middle school] learning, which helped make later connections with other concepts.*

Concept retention was tested in a collaborative study by a researcher and five high school biology teachers (Saigo 1999), using alternative forms of a week-long instructional unit dealing with biosystematics. Six sections of the introductory biology course were involved in the study. Three sections experienced the traditional format, emphasizing lectures, worksheets, and confirmatory activities ($n = 42$). Three sections experienced the constructivist format, emphasizing questioning and teacher facilitation of collaborative, conceptual change activities ($n = 42$). Because of concern about whether or not results of the second kind of instruction could be detected on traditional testing formats (e.g., district tests), the researcher developed a multiple-choice content test. The test was administered preinstruction, immediately postinstruction, and a month after instruction. Students in both groups showed significant initial gains, but those who experienced the constructivist-based format had greater retention of gain after one month.

A Florida middle school teacher also reported an indication of impact. About 45% of her students were learning disabled. After she implemented interviewing, the conceptual change strategy, and other WyTRIAD components, her students scored the highest in the district on state standardized tests in science.

A Change in How Students Approach Their Own Learning Is Evident

> *There is a tremendous difference in the way students approach learning, based on the kind of teacher they had. It is very clear that students of the teachers who have embraced the process are far more comfortable, and approach things from a constructive learning base compared to students of [high school] teachers who have not.*

After three years of WyTRIAD partnership in Riverton, the district administrator observed that students are comfortable with and now expect conceptual change instruction. They complain when teachers do not provide them with what has become known as a "TRIAD" classroom atmosphere. During sign-up for classes, student lines for WyTRIAD teachers are the longest.

Impact on Teachers

A two-year study looked at teacher change over time in regard to six WyTRIAD components and compared first-year WyTRIAD teachers with nonparticipating colleagues in terms of teacher efficacy (Cantrell 2000). WyTRIAD teachers made significant gains in all six areas, especially in use of the Conceptual Change Model. Teacher efficacy (beliefs about oneself as a teacher) was chosen for study because of its positive relationship to student achievement. Bandura (1997) has identified four sources of teacher efficacy: physiological and emotional arousal, mastery experiences (such as a successful teaching episode), vicarious experiences (such as seeing a lesson modeled or hearing or reading the experiences of others), and social persuasion—especially verbal persuasion such as course work, encouragement, feedback, and peer coaching. Mastery experiences are especially powerful. WyTRIAD teachers showed significant gains in personal teaching efficacy (PTE) "beyond any increase in PTE otherwise gained simply by teaching an additional year" (Cantrell 2000).

Perhaps the most compelling evidence of impact has come from written reflections, evaluations, and structured interviews of participants over the years (Stepans and Saigo 1993; Kleinsasser and Miller 1994; Stepans, Saigo, and Ebert 1996, 1999; Galloway 2000; Cantrell, Stepans, and Gaston 2002). Comments of teachers and administrators demonstrate three consistent themes: Teachers' commitment to and active engagement in the process (1) lead to change in the way participants view their students and themselves, in the ways they teach and assess, and in the ways they interact with colleagues; (2) increase their knowledge of and effectiveness in teaching science; and (3) increase their ability to share what they know and do with others, so they become mentors and/or leaders in their schools.

Further, every evaluation of the process has underscored one seemingly absolute requirement: The administrator must be actively engaged in the process, not just by providing time and substitute teachers so teachers can participate, but also by attending and learning with them. The administrator must understand, encourage, and facilitate the new strategies and teamwork the teachers are implementing and become an intermediary and advocate for building and district change, based on what is being learned in the process. At the request of the teachers, effective administrators in some districts revised their evaluation of teachers to reflect components of the WyTRIAD.

Teachers have strong feelings about the value of specific components of the process, as demonstrated by representative comments provided here.

Interviewing

It is absolutely crucial to interview [fifth-grade] students because otherwise there is no way of knowing what they think and why they think it.

Interviewing is one of the most useful components. For example, I interviewed some students about the water cycle and found they knew the right terminology, but didn't really understand the loop. I assumed the water cycle was covered in middle school, but through interviews I discovered some major gaps. Interviewing not only helps the teachers, but thinking about the questions also helps the [high school] students.

Conceptual Change Strategy

Using the conceptual change model was like a miracle. I found I could use it for anything and felt comfortable about doing it. Seeing kids make connections was incredible. The conceptual change strategy is powerful—things happen [in middle school] in ways that aren't planned.

Classroom Inquiry

Observing students as they approach investigations has been very helpful to me in creating an environment to allow for these different approaches. Some kids start by sketching, some just sit and look at material and think about it, some play with the materials and jot down ideas, some talk to colleagues. Just because a kid is sitting there and not doing anything doesn't mean the [fifth-grade] student isn't thinking.

I have become a more cerebral teacher. I ask, "What am I really trying to convey and what should my [middle school] kids walk away with? What depth of understanding is necessary to make new connections?"

Collegial Sharing

Sharing was one of the most beneficial aspects of the whole process. It was our first opportunity to be involved in in-depth, serious discussions on important questions. It was invigorating and mentally stimulating.

[Sharing] validates what I do. I feel more professional in my career. I have [middle school] student results to support my decisions and feel very comfortable sharing with others. As I share, it provides me an opportunity to reflect even more deeply into the process.

One of the most important results of collegial sharing is building trust. It is okay to make mistakes. It's an opportunity to build trust. This is very powerful.

Reflecting

The act of writing things down and reflecting is very helpful to make sense of the whole process in depth. It helps in putting the pieces together, formulating new questions, and thinking about where to go next.

You really cannot internalize unless you reflect. When I go back and read reflections from past years I can see that I may have created some misconceptions for my [fifth-grade] students and I don't want to do that again.

I am more aware of the bigger picture of where [middle school] kids are when they come to me and where I need to take them before they leave me.

I am more honest with myself as a teacher. I look more closely at what I want from [middle school] students and what is really happening with them, and what I need to do to get what I expect of them.

Aligning Standards, Expectations, Instructional Experiences, Assessment, Evaluation

Alignment has had one of the biggest impacts on me. It has encouraged us to teach with a purpose, to really look and plan, and to understand that the way you teach [fifth grade] is the way you should assess. It is helpful to bring together and truly align with the standards.

I came to realize that in spite of good teaching, [middle school] kids did not synthesize, think about things because the district had not paid attention to the message of the standards. The alignment helped.

Impact on School and School Culture

I am more willing to share what works with other teachers. I once thought that teaching was a very private experience, that what works for me may not work for others. WyTRIAD has worked for all teachers in all grade levels. I am interested in what other [middle school] teachers do who are thoughtful, not the tricks or gimmicks we so often mistake for teaching. I read more professional journals now—I never did that before.

One of the most exciting things is that my colleagues see my enthusiasm and how excited my [fifth-grade] students are and ask if they can observe my class. I am opening doors to other teachers, modeling not preaching.

The fullest long-term story of WyTRIAD has been in Riverton, Wyoming (Fremont County District #25). Cantrell, Stepans, and Gaston (2002) report that over several years of participation, teachers have progressed from "looking only at what they expected from students toward improving their own skills and attitudes as well, and then to what they could do to help colleagues." Teachers have taken leadership and the school culture has changed. "Teachers are more communicative, open, helping, and caring.... Classrooms are more student-centered, and [teachers] have more trust in and respect for their colleagues. For the first time, communication is free-flowing and not contrived. Teachers celebrate successes—and share failures." The WyTRIAD process encourages "trust, confidence, respect, and understanding between teachers and administrators" as they "focus on students" and share their observations and understandings.

It seems fitting to close this section with a quotation from a veteran teacher—one who has been through all manner of professional development experiences.

I have participated in staff development for over 30 years. This is the only sustainable staff development I have ever participated in. Before, there was little continuity between what I had as staff development and what I should do if what was given did not work for me, and therefore as a [middle school] teacher I had little professional growth.

Summary

The WyTRIAD is a three-way partnership, a constructivist-based professional development process that is long-term, on-site, and job-embedded. It takes place over several months, with four to five structured sessions, separated by intervals during which teachers implement research-based and standards-supported strategies. In the WyTRIAD, teachers and administrators examine their assumptions; their roles and students' roles; the number and appropriateness of concepts to teach; textbooks and other materials; alignment of standards, expectations, experiences, and assessments; and how to increase the accessibility of their courses to diverse learners. They learn to use their students as barometers to understand what is working and what is not working. They question everything that comes to bear on their classrooms and students, conducting organized, reflective inquiry. They create informed, mutually supportive, professional teams.

References

American Association for the Advancement of Science (AAAS). 1998. *Blueprints for reform: Science, mathematics, and technology education.* New York: Oxford University Press.

American Council on Education (ACE). 1999. *To touch the future: Transforming the way teachers are taught. An action agenda for college and university presidents.* Washington, DC: American Council on Education.

Ball, D. L. 1996. Teacher learning and the mathematics reforms: What we think we know and what we need to know. *Phi Delta Kappan* 77(7): 500–508.

Bandura, A. 1997. *Self-efficacy: The exercise of control.* New York: W. H. Freeman.

Bell, B. 1995. Interviewing: A technique for assessing science knowledge. In *Learning science in the schools: Research reforming practice*, eds. S. M. Glynn and R. Duit. Hillsdale, NJ: Lawrence Erlbaum Associates.

Berube, W., J. Gaston, and J. I. Stepans. 2002. The role of the principal in teacher professional development. Presentation at Northern Rocky Mt. Educational Research Association, Annual Conference, Estes Park, CO, October.

Cantrell, P. 2000. The effects of selected components of the WyTRIAD professional development model on teacher efficacy. Doctoral diss., University of Wyoming, Laramie.

Cantrell, P., J. I. Stepans, and J. Gaston. 2002. Create a three-way partnership. *Journal of Staff Development* (Summer): 35–38.

Darling-Hammond, L. 1996. The quiet revolution: Rethinking teacher development. *Educational Leadership* 53(6): 4–10.

Duit, R., and D. F. Treagust. 1998. Learning in science—From behaviourism towards social constructivism and beyond. In *International Handbook of Science Education, Part One*, eds. B. J. Fraser and K. G. Tobin. Dordrecht, The Netherlands: Kluwer.

Galloway, D. 2000. The impact of WyTRIAD professional development on teacher change. Doctoral diss., University of Wyoming, Laramie.

Kleinsasser, A., and P. Miller. 1994. *An evaluation of the TRIAD.* University of Wyoming monograph. Laramie: University of Wyoming.

National Research Council (NRC). 1996. *National science education standards.* Washington, DC: National Academy Press.

National Staff Development Council (NSDC). 1995a. *Standards for staff development: Elementary school edition.* Oxford, OH: NSDC.

National Staff Development Council (NSDC). 1995b. *Standards for staff development: High school edition.* Oxford, OH: NSDC

National Staff Development Council (NSDC). 1996. *Standards for staff development: Middle school edition.* Oxford, OH: NSDC.

Saigo, B. W. 1999. A study to compare traditional and constructivism-based instruction of a high school biology unit on biosystematics. Doctoral diss., University of Iowa.

Stepans, J. I. 1989. A partnership for making research work in the classroom. *Researcher* 6(1): 3–5. (A publication of the Northern Rocky Mountain Educational Research Association.)

Stepans, J. I. 1994, 1996. *Targeting students' physical science misconceptions: Physical science activities using the conceptual change model.* 1st and 2nd eds. Riverview, FL: The Idea Factory.

Stepans, J. I. 2003. *Targeting students' science misconceptions: Physical science concepts using the conceptual change model.* Tampa, FL: Showboard.

Stepans, J. I., and B. W. Saigo. 1993. Barriers which may keep teachers from implementing what we know about identifying and dealing with students' science and mathematics misconceptions. In *Third International Seminar on Misconceptions and Educational Strategies in Science and Mathematics*, ed. J. Novak. Ithaca, NY: Cornell University.

Stepans, J., B. W. Saigo, and C. Ebert. 1996, 1999. *Changing the classroom from within: Partnership, collegiality, constructivism.* 1st and 2nd eds. Montgomery, AL: Saiwood.

Stepans, J. I., B. W. Saigo, and J. Gaston. 2004. Students' science misconceptions and teachers' misconceptions about students, learning, and teaching: Parallels for professional development. Presentation at the Association for the Education of Teachers of Science, 2004 Annual International Conference, Nashville, TN (Jan.).

Yager, R. E. 2000. The history and future of science education reform. *The Clearing House* 74(1): 51-54.

Hey! What're Ya Thinkin'? Developing Teachers as Reflective Practitioners

Barbara S. Spector
University of South Florida

Ruth Burkett
Central Missouri State University

Cyndy Leard
University of South Florida

Setting

The College of Education at the University of South Florida in west-central Florida is home to one of the largest urban colleges of education in the country, producing almost 1,800 new teachers over the academic years 2000–2001 and 2001–2002. Twenty undergraduate programs and 10 master's degree programs leading to initial teacher certification are offered. The median age of the undergraduates is 26. Eighty-five percent of the undergraduates are female. Of the 18% minority undergraduate population, 8% are African American and 7.3% are Hispanic. Most university students work 20 or more hours per week to support their academic pursuits.

National Science Education Standards *More Emphasis* Conditions and Goals of Science Education

The ongoing program described here—the Science/Technology/Society Program for Middle Grades Education—focuses on specific *More Emphasis* conditions from both the Professional Development Standards and the Assessment Standards of the National Science Education Standards (NSES) (NRC 1996). There is a secondary focus on the Teaching Standards and a tertiary focus on the Content and

Inquiry Standards. The *More Emphasis* conditions targeting K–12 students are included to give university learners the chance to walk in the shoes of youngsters who learn science in a way that is aligned with the NSES. For example, program participants make their own decisions during their inquiry into teaching and learning and they have "Ah ha!" moments in which they experience the excitement of coming to a new understanding of events in the natural world and in science teaching. By generating their own questions and gathering data to answer the questions, the participants are sensitized to the idea that science is part of their everyday lives. As the participants engage in discourse, both in class and on the electronic bulletin board, they develop skills in posing arguments and providing support for their positions. Becoming scientifically literate and comfortable with the application of the *More Emphasis* conditions in the classroom lays a foundation for teachers to obtain certification from the Interstate New Teacher Assessment and Support Consortium (INTASC) and subsequently from the National Board for Professional Teaching Standards (NBPTS), accomplishments that lead to both personal and monetary rewards in their careers.

The program embodies the *More Emphasis* conditions of the Professional Development Standards through the use of the following unique course features: "Organizing a Course as an Inquiry," "Using Yourself as a Learning Laboratory," "Creating Community Through Metacognitive Processes," and "Nature of Learning Opportunities." The "Nature of Learning Opportunities" feature also embodies the *More Emphasis* conditions described under the Assessment Standards, as does "Self-Assessment and Self-Evaluation." The *More Emphasis* conditions of the Teaching and Content Standards and the Changing Emphases to Promote Inquiry (NRC 1996, p. 113) are enacted through "Flexibility and Teachable Moments" and "Nature of Learning Opportunities." Table 1 indicates the relationships between *More Emphasis* conditions and the unique program features that enable the conditions.

While this chapter deals with the conditions named in the preceding paragraph, the program itself incorporates all of the NSES *More Emphasis* conditions in a coherent whole. The program designer's intention was for participants to live and learn through the paradigm engendered in the NSES in order to become willing and able to teach secondary school students within this paradigm. The program involves a methods course as well as a science/technology/society interaction (STS) course.

The Instructor, the Student Body, and the Nature of the Classroom

The instructor for this program was a science education professor with 18 years experience in higher education and more than a decade of teaching in secondary schools. She has been at the forefront of the reform movement and a leader in many national and state science education organizations. The teachers her program produces are committed to learning and teaching according to the holistic model of the NSES *More Emphasis* conditions.

Required for all secondary science education graduates, the program consisted of two courses—a middle grades science methods course and a science/technology/society interaction course. One section of each course was offered during the academic year, with a total of between 10 and 20 participants per course section. About 25% of the participants were already teaching, although uncertified. Participants ranged in age from 19 to 50+. The classroom for the methods course included both the Museum of Science and Industry (MOSI) adjacent to the university's campus and the virtual classroom on the university's Web CT server. The classroom for the STS course consisted of the university classroom and another virtual classroom on the university's Web CT server.

Museum Classroom

MOSI was used for face-to-face meetings and as a curriculum resource in response to an earlier study that suggested using a novel setting could mitigate learners' resistance and encourage them to explore new ways of thinking and learning (Spector and Strong 2001). Learners investigated a wide variety of exhibits in which they studied the interaction of science, technology, and society, and they participated in special events such as the Challenger Learning Center Mission to Mars role play (Spector and Burkett 2002).

Virtual Classrooms

Each of the virtual classrooms consisted of a website divided into four areas: (1) syllabus and study guide, (2) virtual resource center (VRC), (3) student headquarters, and (4) communication center. The syllabi and study guides were extensive interactive documents that provided learners with an overview and objectives for each course, together with basic directions and definitions related to general use of the website (Spector 2003). The VRC allowed learners to design their own plans for accessing the provided resources, which included multimedia materials such as videos (including views of model classroom teaching), slide presentations, music, and artwork, as well as links to additional relevant websites. The student headquarters offered links to the university library, necessary software, and other resources helpful in completing assignments. The communication center contained an asynchronous bulletin board for weekly reflective journals and subsequent discourse and an e-mail program for one-to-one communications.

Unique Features of the Program

The unique features of the program are briefly described in this section. Following each description is a statement indicating which of the *More Emphasis* conditions are developed and enhanced through the implementation of this feature.

Organizing a Course as an Inquiry

Each course was organized as a semester-long inquiry. The methods course focus question was, "What are the characteristics of science teaching in the middle grades that are consistent with the National Science Education Standards?" Four shorter inquiries accompanied the overall course focus question. Students gathered data from the VRC, explorations in the museum, debriefings (reflections immediately following a learning opportunity), and wide-ranging discussions during weekly face-to-face class meetings. They generated, planned, and executed additional inquiries focusing on science content and science teaching.

The STS course focus question was, "What is STS and how does it relate to science teaching?" Students gathered data from their VRC, from site explorations in business and industry,

Table 1. NSES *More Emphasis* Conditions and Unique Features of the Science/Technology/Society Program for Middle Grades Education

More Emphasis Conditions	Unique Program Features and Tasks
Professional Development Standards	
• Inquiry into teaching and learning	• Organizing a Course as an Inquiry • Nature of Learning Opportunities • Task: Journals and Scientific Discourse
• Collegial and collaborative learning	• Creating Community Through Metacognitive Processes • Nature of Learning Opportunities • Tasks: Journals and Scientific Discourse; Electronic Project
• Teacher as intellectual, reflective practitioner	• Using Yourself as a Learning Laboratory • Nature of Learning Opportunities • Task: Journals and Scientific Discourse
• Integration of theory and practice in school settings	• Nature of Learning Opportunities • Task: Journals and Scientific Discourse
• Teacher as producer of knowledge about teaching	• Nature of Learning Opportunities • Tasks: Journals and Scientific Discourse; Concept Maps; STS Issue
• Teacher as a member of a collegial professional community	• Creating Community Through Metacognitive Processes • Tasks: Journals and Scientific Discourse; Biography; Electronic Project
• Integration of science and teaching knowledge	• Nature of Learning Opportunities • Task: Journals and Scientific Discourse
• Mix of internal (students) and external (website resources, instructor) expertise	• Nature of Learning Opportunities • Task: Journals and Scientific Discourse
• Long-term coherent plans	• Task: Study Plan
• A variety of professional activities	• Nature of Learning Opportunities
Assessment Standards	
• Assessing what is most highly valued	• Task: Exit Memos
• Assessing rich, well-structured knowledge	• Self-Assessment and Self-Evaluation • Task: Concept Maps
• Assessing scientific understanding and reasoning	• Self-Assessment and Self-Evaluation • Task: Concept Maps
• Assessing to learn what students do understand	• Tasks: Concept Maps; Final Task
• Assessing achievement and opportunity to learn	• Nature of Learning Opportunities • Task: Journals and Scientific Discourse
• Students engaged in ongoing assessment of their work and that of others	• Self-Assessment and Self-Evaluation • Task: Concept Maps

(*Table 1* continues on next page)

(Table 1 continued)

More Emphasis Conditions	Unique Program Features and Tasks
Teaching Standards	
• Selecting and adapting curriculum	• Flexibility and Teachable Moments • Task: Complete Learning Opportunity
• Providing opportunities for scientific discussion and debate among students	• Creating Community Through Metacognitive Processes • Task: Journals and Scientific Discourse
• Supporting a classroom community with cooperation, shared responsibility, and respect	• Nature of Learning Opportunities
• Understanding and responding to individual students' interests, strengths, experiences, and needs	• Self-Assessment and Self-Evaluation • Tasks: Study Plan; Final Task
• Focusing on student understanding and use of scientific knowledge, ideas, and inquiry processes	• Self-Assessment and Self-Evaluation • Task: Unifying Themes
• Guiding students in active and extended scientific inquiry	• Nature of Learning Opportunities • Task: Journals and Scientific Discourse
Content and Inquiry Standards	
• Studying a few fundamental science concepts	• Tasks: Content Standard; Unifying Themes
• Understanding scientific concepts and developing abilities of inquiry	• Tasks: Content Standard; Unifying Themes
• Learning subject matter disciplines in the context of inquiry, technology and science in personal and social perspectives, and history and nature of science	• Tasks: Content Standard; Unifying Themes; Media Watches; STS Issue; Site Visits; Electronic Project; Complete Learning Opportunities
• Activities that investigate and analyze science questions	• Tasks: Content Standard; Unifying Themes
• Public communication of student ideas and work to classmates	• All Learning Opportunities

Note: The unique features and tasks listed in the right-hand column enabled the learners to experience the *More Emphasis* conditions listed in the left-hand column. For a discussion of the unique features, see pages 191–196. For a description of the tasks, see pages 196–198.

from informal education agencies and local schools, and from a variety of public media sources of their choosing, as well as debriefings and discussions during five face-to-face class meetings. The students generated, planned, and executed their own inquiries, focusing on the interactions among science, technology, and society and the relationship of STS to science teaching. The program structure of inquiry facilitated the NSES Professional Development Standards, placing more emphasis on "inquiry into teaching and learning" (NRC 1996, p. 72) This approach stands in contrast to the traditional emphasis on "transmission of teaching knowledge and skills by lecture" (NRC 1996, p. 72).

Using Yourself as a Learning Laboratory

Throughout the program, all learners were encouraged to use the strategy of "using yourself as a learning laboratory," whether involved in exploration of MOSI, in the community, on the website, or in class (Burkett, Leard, and Spector 2003). Learners reflected on their experiences, noting their emotional responses and the development of their understanding of science pedagogical content knowledge. They reported in class and in their journals on how they were "making their own meaning" from the experiences by integrating thinking, feeling, and acting (Novak and Gowin 1994). The program was iterative and recursive. Learners chose resources and other experiences, explored and read to gather, organize, and analyze data, created and shared interpretations and reflections in journals, received comments from the community of learners, explored, read more, and revised interpretations. Thus, they engaged in the steps in Kolb's (1984) experiential learning cycle.

The "using yourself as a learning laboratory" strategy placed more emphasis on the "teacher as intellectual, reflective practitioner," rather than on the teacher as "technician" (NRC 1996, p. 72).

Creating Community Through Metacognitive Processes

Learners were encouraged to use metacognitive processes and tools to analyze what science content and teaching they learned from each experience, how they learned it, and the relationships among the experiences. Learners posted analyses in the form of weekly journals and periodic concept maps. Responses included combinations of critiques, multiple perspectives, and questioning of evidence and reasoning—creating enthusiastic interchanges in which everyone contributed to the discussion. By understanding their peers' experiences with making meaning, learners gained insights into some of the ways their K–12 students might make connections when learning.

In-class debriefings provided spontaneous reflections for the learners, and weekly journal entries gave learners time for more considered reflections. The combination of synchronous dialogue during face-to-face classes and asynchronous dialogue responding to each other's journal entries in Web CT created a professional, collegial community of learners. Learners perceived the community as a safe environment inviting intellectual risk taking. Taking intellectual risks became highly valued by learners as a necessary step in facilitating their growth.

The metacognitive processes and tools facilitated the Professional Development *More Emphasis* conditions for "teachers as intellectual, reflective practitioners," "the teacher as a member of a collegial professional community," and "collegial and collaborative learning" (NRC 1996, p. 72). In addition, the subsequent discussions regarding these reflections facilitated a *More Emphasis* condition of the Teaching Standards: "providing opportunities for scientific discussion and debate among students," in contrast to the more traditional "asking for recitation of acquired knowledge" (NRC 1996, p. 52).

Self-Assessment and Self-Evaluation

Learners were required to complete a self-assessment and self-evaluation twice during each course, using the same tool in both the midterm and final sessions. The tool incorporated a research-based rubric assessing the maturity of learners' understanding (Wiggins and McTighe

1998). The form included a series of questions requiring learners to conduct a systematic inquiry into their own learning and provide evidence of knowledge constructed during the learning opportunities (exit memos, journals, scientific discourse, concept maps, site explorations, media watches, STS issues, electronic projects). The data they analyzed were the ideas and comments they had expressed throughout each course. Learners placed a value, indicated by a grade, on their own assessments of the data and explained the evidence used to arrive at that grade. For example, comparing their own and others' successive concept maps, journals, and responses enabled learners to illustrate the increasing complexity of their cognitive structures.

The self-assessment and self-evaluation task facilitates the Assessment Standards *More Emphasis* condition of "assessing rich, well-structured knowledge" (NRC 1996, p. 100). This task also carries out the Teaching Standards *More Emphasis* condition of "understanding and responding to individual student's interests, strengths, experiences and needs" (NRC 1996, p. 52).

Flexibility and Teachable Moments

The process of creating a need to know and just-on-time delivery of responses required the professor to be flexible. She did not plan a specific sequence of course topics. Instead, she consistently sought teachable moments, as evidenced by her students' need to know a particular topic, made explicit through their actions, words, or body language. In a traditionally structured course in which topics are selected and sequenced up front by the instructor, responding to teachable moments may be interpreted as being off-task. Even in a traditionally structured classroom, however, Reinsmith (1993) reported, "Time wasted, tangents pursued and side-lines which are followed up encourage learning" (p. 7).

The Teaching Standards point to a change from "rigidly following curriculum" to placing more emphasis on "selecting and adapting curriculum" (NRC 1996, p. 52). The instructor's flexibility in sequencing topics, seeking out teachable moments, and following the seemingly off-task tangents illustrates this *More Emphasis* condition.

Nature of Learning Opportunities

Instead of traditional assignments in which learners execute a teacher-specified task to demonstrate what they have previously learned by meeting teacher-established criteria, "assignments" in each course were open-ended, inquiry-driven, scaffolded learning opportunities. Learners interpreted teacher-generated and learner-negotiated general statements describing each task and then shared their products, resulting in dramatically varied individual products that enabled learners to see the value that multiple perspectives contribute to learning. The outcomes of the discussion of each product resulted in class-formulated criteria for success with the task. Individuals then revised their products to meet the group's criteria. Participants were consistently amazed that so many different approaches to a task could be meaningful and therefore considered to be "correct." Establishing criteria for their own course products also provided insight into what must be considered in creating criteria for their K–12 students' assignments.

Products were designed to facilitate many of the *More Emphasis* conditions of the Professional Development Standards, including inquiry into teaching and learning, integration of science and teaching knowledge, teacher as intellectual, reflective practitioner, collegial and collaborative learning, a variety of professional development activities, mix of internal and external expertise, and integration of theory and practice in school settings (NRC 1996, p. 72).

Description of Tasks

Following are brief descriptions of the learning opportunities, the professor's intended purpose for the assigned task, and links to *More Emphasis* conditions. Although each of these learning opportunities is linked to a particular *More Emphasis* statement here, each is part of a complex whole, integrated in the way pieces of tile placed in mortar create a mosaic masterpiece.

Autobiography. The autobiography, posted on the bulletin board, provided introductions shared among class members. This first step in developing the community of learners facilitated the Professional Development Standards *More Emphasis* condition for the "teacher as a member of collegial professional community" (p. 72).

Study Plan. Learners created a plan, indicating the tentative path they would follow and a time line. This task was intended to build on learners' personal prior knowledge and provide practice in designing learning pathways. The task promotes the Professional Development Standards *More Emphasis* condition for "long-term coherent plans" (p. 72), as well as the Teaching Standards *More Emphasis* condition for "understanding and responding to individual student's interests, strengths, experiences, and needs" (p. 52).

Exit Memos. At the end of each face-to-face class meeting, learners wrote exit memos describing their reactions. These spontaneous responses gave insight into how learners experienced each class. This task provided learners with an opportunity to assess what they most valued in each class meeting, a *More Emphasis* condition under the Assessment Standards.

Journals and Scientific Discourse. The weekly journal posted on the bulletin board was intended to provide an opportunity for written reflection and a stimulus for sharing how learners were making sense of experiences. The discussion fostered by responses to journal writings contributed to the development of scientific discourse. Participation in the journaling task places more emphasis on the Professional Development Standards, including these conditions: "inquiry into teaching and learning, collegial and collaborative learning, integration of theory and practice in school settings, teacher as producer of knowledge about teaching, teacher as intellectual, reflective practitioner, and teacher as a member of a collegial professional community" (p. 72). This task also directly facilitates the Teaching Standards *More Emphasis* condition for "providing opportunities for scientific discussion and debate among students" (p. 52).

Concept Maps. Learners mapped their vision for middle school science teaching three times during the semester in the course of the methods class. In the STS class they mapped their increasing understandings of the complexities of STS interactions every three weeks to generate their own, grounded theory of STS. Completion of these tasks helped learners organize their own, idiosyncratic cognitive frameworks, incorporate the unifying themes and content standards, and generate grounded theory. This task particularly stresses the Professional Development Standards condition for the "teacher as producer of knowledge about teaching" (p. 72). More importantly, the Assessment Standards *More Emphasis* statements on "assessing rich, well-structured knowledge, assessing scientific understanding and reasoning, assessing to learn what students do understand, and students engaged in ongoing assessment of their work and that of others" (p. 100) are also evident in this task.

Content Standard *(methods course only)*. For this task, learners selected one content standard from the NSES or the state standards and created a concept map and a narrative identifying the prerequisite concepts. This activity developed learners' abilities to diagnose and remediate K–12 students' understanding of a content standard. This task includes aspects of each of the conditions of the NSES Content and Inquiry Standards.

Unifying Themes *(methods course only)*. During the exploration of the museum exhibits, learners looked for evidence of unifying themes, as identified in the NSES or in *Benchmarks for Science Literacy* (AAAS 1993). They described examples of the theme and noted the disciplines in which they were framed. This task was intended to give learners experience in analyzing an event and sensitizing them to the pervasiveness of the themes in real-world events. All of the *More Emphasis* conditions of the NSES Content Standards are addressed by this task. Additionally, this task provides more emphasis on the Teaching Standard for "focusing on student understanding and use of scientific knowledge, ideas, and inquiry processes" (p. 52).

Complete Learning Opportunity. Learners developed and presented a nine-week unit for middle or high school students, using a community site exploration as the centerpiece. They identified specific standards to which this unit contributed and indicated pathways to disciplines other than science. This open-ended task encouraged learners to be creative as they analyzed a real-world event and incorporated it into a coherent, long-term unit. This task reflects the Teaching Standard condition for "selecting and adapting curriculum" (p. 52).

Media Watch *(STS course only)*. Weekly, each student posted in Web CT a report about one STS event found in the media. Students were asked to include a broad variety of media sources. The postings to the website included the name and a brief description of the event, a minimum of one basic science concept and one technology concept inherent in the event, and an explanation of why it was perceived to be an example of STS interaction.

This task led to students developing perceptual screens that enabled them to recognize STS in all aspects of their lives and to recognize the basic science and technology understanding needed to make reasoned decisions related to real-life events.. This database of media watches became a resource from which participants could design learning opportunities to help youngsters understand the relevance of specific basic science concepts. This task develops the *More Emphasis* condition in the NSES Content and Inquiry Standard, "Learning subject matter disciplines in the context of inquiry, technology, science in personal and social perspective, and history and nature of science" (p. 113).

Site Visits *(STS course only)*. Learners selected one business, industry, or government organization in the community from which they expected to learn about STS interaction. They visited the site and shared what they learned in a presentation. This assignment increased their awareness of STS in the world of work and of the richness of the community as a resource for teaching STS to any audience. The learners also conducted site visits to local schools; some of the schools modeled STS and others did not. This task contributes to the *More Emphasis* NSES Content and Inquiry Standard, "Learning subject matter disciplines in the context of inquiry, technology, science in personal and social perspective, and history and nature of science" (p. 113).

STS Issue (STS course only). Each student selected a controversial STS issue to investigate and constructed a presentation that explicated multiple dimensions of the science, technology, and societal aspects of the issue and their connections to each other. The task involved selecting the salient points about the issue, interpreting them, and presenting a coherent story. The complexities involved in the STS issue were to be articulated thoroughly enough to inspire the listener to experience self-efficacy regarding teaching that issue to future audiences. This task reflects the NSES Content and Inquiry Standard *More Emphasis* condition "Learning subject matter disciplines in the context of inquiry, technology, science in personal and social perspective, and history and nature of science" (p. 113). It also supports the Professional Development Standard *More Emphasis* condition "Teacher as producer of knowledge about teaching, inquiry into teaching and learning, and collegial and collaborative learning" (p. 72).

Electronic Project (STS course only). Program participants worked in teams of four or five to identify and compile a collection of various genres of electronic resources related to an STS issue of their choosing. The collection compiled by each team became a resource that others would use to determine their own understanding of the subject and create their own stories about that particular STS issue. The NSES Professional Development Standards *More Emphasis* conditions enhanced by this task include "Teacher as a member of a collegial professional community and collegial and collaborative learning" (p. 72).

Final Task. In each course learners developed an original format to showcase the degree to which they had integrated information from the experiences in this program into their own conceptual frameworks. By allowing learners total freedom in completing this task, the instructor supported the NSES Teaching Standards *More Emphasis* condition "Understanding and responding to individual student's interests, strengths, experiences, and needs" (p. 52) as well as the NSES Assessment Standards' "Assessing to learn what students do understand" (p. 100).

Evidence of Learning

An anonymous survey using *Less Emphasis/More Emphasis* charts from the NSES was distributed to learners. They were asked to use a four-point Likert scale to identify the degree to which they perceived this program provided opportunities to move from each *Less Emphasis* to *More Emphasis* description. The 371 item responses indicated learners clearly perceived they had opportunities to accomplish the desired learning.

This emphasis on student-centered learning was also seen in open-table discussions in which learners identified where they had experienced *More Emphasis* conditions. Learners highlighted the extensive opportunities they had throughout the program to exercise choice. In their journals, most learners agreed that given the opportunity to do so, they would be inclined to teach to the *More Emphasis* items. The triangulated data from the journals, class discussion, and end-of-semester surveys were consistent and supported each other. It appeared that the more opportunities learners perceived they had to exercise freedom of choice, the more they learned to function in, and come to understand the meanings of, the *More Emphasis* conditions and the more inclined they were to incorporate these emphases in their own teaching.

Statements below exemplify the evidence of learning. These quotations were made by learners on the bulletin board, in e-mail, or in face-to-face class meetings. They provide evidence of learners' perceptions of the *More Emphasis* conditions.

Professional Development Standards

Integration of Theory and Practice in School Settings

All the practical information the professor shared was extremely valuable.

This assignment [the final task] was a real eye-opener for me. I realized that having it in my head does not mean that I can put it into action. Even great ideas are only great to a particular audience under a particular circumstance. I realized that as a teacher everything you do has to take into consideration your students' abilities, interests, and limitations. What works for one teacher may not work when put into practice by another teacher with her students.

Collegial and Collaborative Learning

I am more comfortable in this class than I have ever been in a class. We are able to say anything and discuss anything. The structure of the course encourages students to speak their mind on any issue they feel is important. Everyone contributes.

A Variety of Professional Development Activities

I have never been in a class where I was able to contribute to decision making. Here I got to make decisions about how to do assignments and all sorts of things. It made learning work for me.

Teacher as Intellectual, Reflective Practitioner

[From a learner's final self-assessment]: *This course taught us inquiry through inquiry. It made us think about what we were doing and why we were doing it; to analyze outcomes; and if we came across inconsistencies compared to our classmates, then we went back to investigate how we differed. This process of evaluation and reevaluation of our data sources is scientific inquiry and science as process.... We developed a community and a safe environment to speak our minds in this class, a community where I believe everyone contributed their thoughts without too much reservation.*

Teacher as Producer of Knowledge About Teaching

I was thrilled with the idea of having such an open-ended assignment [on unifying themes]. But I admit I was also a little nervous. I wanted to do something no one else would; but I was afraid to venture there alone. . . . In the following class, we shared our thinking processes and why we did our projects the way we did. . . . Now, looking back at the Unifying Themes assignment, I can't help but think how important it is for students to not be afraid to take risks in their learning process.

Teacher as Member of Collegial Professional Community

Now looking back, I realize that the biography assignment was vital in creating a community of learners. Getting to know a little bit about each other allowed us to accept each other. If someone had an idea far from ours, we could easily take a look at their biographies and say, "Yeah, they came into this class with a different box of tools than I did." If we thought maybe some didn't understand something, we wanted to help them because we felt as though we knew them. And, they were part of our team.

Teaching Standards

I personally have chosen to see this class as a big research paper and the instructor has been kind enough to go to the library and do the research for me. All I have to do is read, watch, absorb, shake it around in my brain and state what has happened to me on the computer. This becomes valuable when I make a big "Ah-ha" and realize a few things: What makes me think, not think, why do I think, and what am I going to do with this new thinking.

Science, technology, and society are happening around me everyday. My problem is I never paid any attention to it. Now I am inclined to inquire and learn more about it.

Content and Inquiry Standards

Everything I look at lately I try, not intentionally, to link to STS. Everything from TV shows, to road construction, to pregnant moms. They all have connection to STS. . . . Everything has a connection!

I had an STS moment while fishing with [my father] last night. Well, you never know when and where you are going to learn something valuable.

I suddenly realized the technology I take for granted.

It's amazing how much the media affects our lives. With information available to us nowadays it's hard to imagine what it would be like without it.

Summary

This chapter highlights the *More Emphasis* conditions for the Professional Development Standards and Assessment Standards by analyzing an inquiry based, web-enhanced program conducted in a novel setting. Through the professor's modeling of the *More Emphasis* conditions of the NSES, learners came to recognize the paradigms within which they had previously functioned and the NSES program paradigm. Successive concept mapping emphasized participants' learning and bolstered their self-efficacy and belief in the NSES paradigm.

The learners perceived this program was significantly different from any they had encountered in the College of Education or the College of Arts and Sciences. Unique program features included the following: Organizing a course as an inquiry, using yourself as a learning laboratory, creating community through metacognitive processes, self-assessment and self-evaluation, flexibility and teachable moments, and the nature of learning opportunities. The open-ended tasks designed with a reflection component helped participants to become autonomous learners who continually evaluated their own learning and revised their plans to achieve desired goals. They often sought resources beyond those found in the VRC to pursue self-initiated inquiries. They learned the impact of prior knowledge and ways to honor and build on it. They developed attitudes toward the teaching and learning of science that projected into their future as teachers. As one participant said,

I came into this class as a bud full of potential and plenty of room for growth. Then the learning process began. With each learning opportunity, I progressed (blossoming a little more and more). This final assignment is like the distribution of the pollen and the forming of the seeds. I hope to take these seeds with me and plant them in my teaching methods. Maybe then, I can watch my students sprout and grow. And so the learning process is spread and continues on.

References

American Association for the Advancement of Science (AAAS). 1993. *Benchmarks for science literacy.* www.project2061.org/tools/benchol/bolframe.html

Burkett, R. S., C. Leard, and B. S. Spector. 2003. *Using yourself as a learning laboratory: A strategy to mitigate preservice elementary teachers' resistance to teaching through inquiry.* Paper presented at the Association for the Education of Science Teachers, St. Louis, Jan. 29–Feb. 2.

Kolb, D. 1984. *Experiential learning: Experience as a source of learning and development.* Englewood Cliffs, NJ: Prentice-Hall.

National Research Council (NRC). 1996. *National science education standards.* Washington, DC: National Academy Press.

Novak, J. D., and D. B. Gowin. 1994. *Learning how to learn.* New York: Cambridge University Press.

Reinsmith, W. A. 1993. Ten fundamental truths about learning. *National Teaching and Learning Forum* 2 (4): 7–8.

Spector, B. S. 2003. *Science in the middle grades.* Retrieved May 3, 2003, from *http://webct.acomp.usf.edu/ sce4320/syllabus.htm*

Spector, B. S., and R. S. Burkett. 2002. *Using the science museum to mitigate preservice teachers' resistance to inquiry.* Paper presented at the National Association for Research in Science Teaching, New Orleans, April 7–10.

Spector, B. S., and P. Strong. 2001. *The 3 C's of inquiry learning and teaching: Culture, context and cues.* Paper presented at the Association for the Education of Teachers in Science, Costa Mesa, CA, Jan. 18–21.

Wiggins, G. P., and J. McTighe. 1998. *Understanding by design.* Alexandria, VA: Association for Supervision and Curriculum Development.

Rethinking the Continuing Education of Science Teachers:
An Example of Transformative, Curriculum-Based Professional Development

Joseph A. Taylor and Janet Carlson Powell
Center for Professional Development
at Biological Sciences Curriculum Study (BSCS)

David R. Van Dusen, Bill Pearson,
Kim Bess, Bonnie Schindler, and Danine Ezell
San Diego City Schools

Setting

In the fall of 2001, the science leaders at San Diego City Schools (SDCS) faced a complex challenge in curriculum implementation. The challenge stemmed in part from SDCS having recently adopted a "physics first" high school science sequence. Now, instead of a relatively small number of elite students taking physics (1,200 annually), physics was a required course for all freshmen in 23 schools (10,000 students annually). As a result of this dramatic increase in physics enrollment, SDCS needed to augment its existing physics faculty (~40 teachers) by asking an additional 40 district science teachers, who held credentials in science disciplines other than physics, to teach ninth-grade physics.

Another aspect of the implementation challenge centered on curriculum materials. Most SDCS teachers were unfamiliar with *Active Physics*, the program selected for use in ninth-grade physics, and had never taught physics to ninth-graders. Consequently, SDCS was charged with the task of designing meaningful professional development for *all* (more than 80) ninth-grade physics teachers, who would focus on a specific set of curriculum materials. (This professional development program continues to be offered each year before school starts and during the school year.)

San Diego City Schools is the second largest district in California with a total of 26 high schools (traditional, atypical, charter). The population served by SDCS is ethnically diverse: 38.8% Hispanic, 26.6% Caucasian, 17.6% Asian, and 16.6% African American. In addition, 64 languages other than English are reported as the primary language in the home; 29.4% of all students are English Language Learners.

Program Overview

The professional development program designed and implemented by SDCS exhibits many of the changing emphases described in the *National Science Education Standards* (NRC 1996). As the Standards recommend, the program provides ongoing support for the implementation of inquiry-based physics materials by helping teachers develop and integrate understandings of science and teaching. It is structured to build a community of reflective practitioners. This design has fostered the growth of a community of physics teachers who share expertise and support one another toward a common goal: maximizing student learning through effective instruction and quality curriculum materials.

To design and conduct the professional development, SDCS formed a team of administrators and physics teacher-leaders. As a result of their work with the professional development program, team members developed deep understandings of physics content, pedagogy, student learning, curriculum materials, and the change process. These understandings have been essential in assisting colleagues with implementing the new curriculum.

A major emphasis of the professional development program is to prepare teachers to use inquiry-based curriculum materials by engaging them in inquiry from the learner's perspective. Specifically, teachers formulate their own questions, design and conduct their own experiments, and develop, defend, and revise explanations about scientific phenomenon. The emphasis on inquiry that is foremost in SDCS's professional development program is consistent with the primary goals of science education (NRC 1996, p. 13). Specifically, if students are to develop knowledge of science content and processes that can inform decisions and allow them to engage meaningfully in science-related discourse, they must be given the opportunity to develop this knowledge under the guidance of a teacher who understands the nature of scientific inquiry.

Curriculum

San Diego City Schools has developed an ongoing professional development program for more than 80 physics teachers to support the implementation of new, inquiry-based curriculum materials. In this program, teachers are prepared by physics lead-teachers and district-level science personnel to implement inquiry-based curriculum materials by engaging in their own inquiries into scientific phenomena and reflecting on the basic tenets of constructivist learning and teaching. Each year, the program provides teachers with opportunities to collaboratively "try out" and discuss activities directly from the curriculum materials. In addition, teachers are encouraged to discuss the quality of their students' work as well as issues that arise from everyday use of the curriculum materials. By helping their colleagues learn about and implement the new curriculum, teacher-leaders in the district have developed the skills necessary to facilitate curriculum reform.

Program Components

The SDCS program consists of five major components: (1) summer institutes supported by monthly follow-up workshops, (2) content courses for out-of-field teachers, (3) common planning periods to promote collaboration, (4) curriculum support materials, and (5) support from behind the scenes. Each component is discussed in more detail in this section.

Summer Institutes and Monthly Follow-Up Meetings

The summer institute, usually held in August, kicks off the professional development program each academic year in SDCS. The broad purpose of the intensive summer institutes is to prepare teachers to begin implementing *Active Physics* by helping them understand the instructional approach used in the curriculum as well as broader issues, such as inquiry-based and constructivist learning and teaching. The strategies used in the summer institutes are consistent with recommendations in the professional development literature. For example, the facilitators model exemplary teaching (NRC 1996, p. 62), use the curriculum materials to engage teachers as *learners* of physics and of physics pedagogy (Loucks-Horsley et al. 2003), and challenge teachers' existing beliefs about learning and teaching (Thompson and Zeuli 1999).

In the past, the institutes varied in length from one to two weeks, depending on the participants' needs. Held in 2001, the first summer institute featured a two-week program for new and out-of-discipline teachers, who worked together in the second week with returning physics teachers. The focus of the first week was building physics content knowledge and familiarizing the first group of teachers with the *Active Physics* materials, as well as increasing their understanding of inquiry and the BSCS 5E Instructional Model (Bybee 1997; Bybee and Landes 1990). The second week of the institute focused on inquiry and the need for changing instructional practices to meet the needs of a diverse and changing student population. Experts in inquiry and *Active Physics* collaborated in the instruction. During the second week, school-site teams planned and presented to other teachers a unit from the *Active*

Teachers taking part in an SDCS summer science institute.

Physics curriculum. This task helped build professional teams at school sites and further developed an understanding of the curriculum.

In the summer of 2002, an expanded summer institute was established, which all physics teachers attended for the full two weeks. In the course of the program, each participant's time was divided between large-group meetings, covering such topics as physics pedagogy and scientific inquiry, and smaller-group meetings, including a meeting specifically for returning physics teachers and one specifically for new and out-of-discipline teachers. The customized meetings better met the needs of teachers with a wide range of experience and expertise.

The new-teacher group focused on basic teaching strategies, becoming comfortable with the curriculum and materials, classroom management, cooperative grouping, and physics content knowledge relevant to that addressed in the curriculum. These topics were all identified the previous year by teachers as those they would like to know more about. The veteran teachers completed an entire unit from *Active Physics* in the role of the learner while stepping back at critical points to discuss the process from the teacher's point of view. In doing so they were able to experience what inquiry instruction looks and feels like, learn different strategies for dealing with cooperative groups, learn questioning techniques, and gain relevant content knowledge.

A desire on the part of SDCS to provide relevant instruction, enabling teachers to be more effective in their classrooms, guided the design of the institutes. The sequence of the individual professional development sessions followed the BSCS 5E Instructional Model as a way to model exemplary (and expected) classroom practices. Continual feedback throughout the institutes and during the school year helped shape the program to meet the needs of the teachers, while maintaining a commitment to reforming science teaching in the SDCS.

These goals and strategies applied to the monthly meetings, bringing 80-plus colleagues together on a regular basis throughout the academic year to address implementation issues in a timely fashion (Thompson and Zeuli 1999). With implementation under way in the classrooms, the monthly meetings allowed time for reflection on student learning, current teaching practices (Sparks 2002), and implementation experiences. The ongoing nature of the monthly meetings also allowed the facilitators—that is, the physics lead-teachers and district-level science personnel—to engage teachers in extended activities and discussions that might span one or more meetings. Such extended activities are conducive to helping teachers develop deep understandings of content and pedagogy (NRC 1996, p. 70).

Content Courses for Out-of-Discipline Teachers

The district's desire to design professional development that is sensitive to the range in teachers' physics knowledge and teaching expertise (NRC 1996, p. 70) influenced the development of the course sequence: *Physics for Educators* (Physics 496 I-IV). This course sequence, for which San Diego University grants credit, was approved as a means for SDCS teachers to obtain a supplemental authorization in physics by the California Commission on Teacher Credentialing. The four-semester sequence augments the content preparation provided in the summer institutes and monthly meetings, and it models inquiry-based teaching strategies and engages teachers as learners of physics content. Since activities from *Active Physics* were not designed to fully engage adult learners in the study of physics, course instructors often use materials from *Physics by Inquiry* (McDermott 1996), a course designed for preservice and practicing teachers.

Common Planning Periods at the Building Level

To assist in the implementation of the new ways of thinking and learning, as well as the new curriculum, the district offered a common planning period for the first two years of implementation, in addition to the teacher's regular planning period. The goals of the common planning period were to maintain the community developed at the monthly meetings and summer institutes and to promote professional growth and the sharing of expertise at the site level. During that period, teachers addressed implementation issues that were specific to their sites, such as organization of lab materials, distribution of supplies, and storage. They also planned upcoming lessons by working through the activities and using the strategies developed during the summer institute and monthly meetings. The integration of this professional development experience into the *normal workday* made such planning possible. This sort of integration is also a strong signal of the district's belief that professional development is a valued and worthwhile use of district resources (Sparks 2002). Today, although the district has not been able to continue funding the additional planning periods, individual schools have continued the spirit of this program component by devising other ways to help teachers work together.

Curriculum Support Materials

SDCS has developed a support guide for each module of *Active Physics* to assist teachers in the pacing, planning, implementation, and evaluation of instruction. In addition, SDCS maintains a comprehensive website to support teachers who are implementing *Active Physics*. The site contains resources and materials such as lesson plans, assessments, and scoring rubrics that can be downloaded. It also contains archived discussion threads related to implementation issues, as well as contact information for district support personnel.

Support From Behind the Scenes

Implementing the program at SDCS required fundamental changes in how professional development was structured. These changes included a transformation from often disconnected, one-day-and-done professional development options to an ongoing, coherent, districtwide program that coordinated teacher release time, compensated teachers for their time, adjusted teachers' workdays, and promoted collaboration. Resounding administrative support made such a transformation possible.

The implementation of the program was facilitated by the emergence of district-level leadership and expertise, as well as the influence of external catalysts. Specifically, the professional development model described here was, to some extent, influenced by what physics teacher-leaders learned at the National Academy for Curriculum Leadership (NACL) at twice-yearly meetings. NACL is funded through a National Science Foundation (NSF) grant housed at Biological Sciences Curriculum Study (BSCS) and developed jointly by the Science Curriculum Implementation (SCI) Center at BSCS and WestEd. At the academy, the SDCS leadership team developed understandings about inquiry, the characteristics of quality curriculum materials for physics, well-designed professional development to support curriculum implementation, leadership, and the change process. Many of the physics teacher-leaders involved with the professional development program have transitioned into site-based science administrator roles in which they now, in addition to their districtwide duties, promote reform and provide site-based professional development. The development of this "in-house" leadership capacity (NRC 1996, p. 68) and expertise has been most influential in the success of the professional development program.

Evidence of Growth from the SDCS Professional Development Program

One of the major advantages of curriculum-focused professional development is its usefulness in developing an understanding of physics teaching that integrates knowledge of physics and physics pedagogy. Evidence that a teacher is developing rich, integrated understandings of physics teaching can be found in his or her implementation of curriculum materials. SDCS and BSCS examined two aspects of this evidence. Specifically, data regarding the *scope* (i.e., what parts of the curriculum program are being used) and *fidelity* (i.e., alignment with developer's intent) of the implementation were collected.

Implementation Scope

A teacher's choice of whether to use a particular program component can be a strong indicator of his or her comfort level and skill in using that part of the curriculum materials. An anonymous

Table 1. Implementation Scope: *Active Physics* Core Components Used by New Physics Teachers, 2001–2002.

Active Physics Core Component	Brief Description	% of Teachers Indicating Their Frequency of Use as *Often* or *Always*	# of Respondents
"Chapter Challenge"	Drives student activity and thinking throughout the module	66%	56
"What Do You Think?"	Intended to elicit students' prior knowledge before beginning an activity	75%	55
"For You to Do"	Hands-on activities related to the chapter challenge	98%	58
"Physics Talk/ For You to Read"	Summarizes physics principles addressed in each activity and introduces new terminology and equations where appropriate	69%	58
"Reflecting on the Activity and the Challenge"	Relates each activity to the larger chapter challenge	51%	57
"Physics to Go"	Generally a homework assignment where students apply concepts learned during the activity	80%	55

survey was administered at the end of the 2001–2002 school year to determine the degree to which each core component of *Active Physics* was being used by teachers in the district. A subset of the survey data is summarized in Table 1.

The data indicate that, in general, the core components of the curriculum were being used. However, the data also suggest that areas of future professional development work include helping teachers understand the value of the *Active Physics* "Chapter Challenges" as a way to motivate students and to establish a need on the students' part to learn the physics concepts developed in the chapter. Similarly, future professional development should focus on teaching strategies for helping students reflect on how each activity's core concepts connect to the "Chapter Challenge."

Implementation Fidelity

Evidence that a teacher is developing deep, integrated understandings of physics and physics pedagogy can also be found by examining the quality and *fidelity* of his or her implementation of curriculum materials. This preliminary analysis of teachers' fidelity of use is based on a set of interviews and observations conducted by BSCS and SDCS in the fall of 2001 and spring of 2002 (see Table 2). Again, in general the interview data suggest that teachers are using *Active Physics* with fidelity. Some teachers, however, although staying true to the curriculum, were implementing at a mechanical level. In other words, these teachers were staying true to the basic design of each module and using the various components in the intended order, but the connections among and transitions between ideas were sometimes unclear to the students. It is important to note that some of these same teachers, through continued implementation participation in the professional development program, became very skilled at strengthening the connections between activities to make the flow of ideas more cohesive.

Table 2. Implementation Fidelity: General Observations From Classroom Visits

September 2001	April 2002
Many teachers are sticking closely to program as written. Some teachers are not using all program components effectively.	Many teachers are still sticking closely to the program as written.
Teachers who are modifying and supplementing activities are doing so with varying effectiveness.	Most modification and supplementation of the program is being done in a more informed manner. That is, the changes are more consistent with the conceptual flow and instructional design intended by the developer.

The comments made by many teachers during the interviews were quite compelling in support both for the adoption of curriculum materials that include strong teacher support materials (e.g., teacher guides) and for professional development that is tightly linked to the adopted curriculum. A number of teachers indicated they could not imagine teaching without this combined support. Their conviction that the curriculum and professional development together were vital to their survival in the classroom seems to have had a positive influence on teaching with fidelity. Many of the out-of-discipline teachers did not trust their ability to teach physics, so they put their trust in the curriculum. Then, because they had strong support from the physics lead-teachers, district science personnel, and other colleagues in the program for learning to use *Active Physics*, they were able to stick with the curriculum at times when they were struggling. This support increased their familiarity with the program and consequently their willingness to teach it with fidelity. Here is a summary of the comments made during interviews that indicate high fidelity.

I like having a curriculum to give direction to the course.

I liked having a curriculum selected because it helped balance what teachers like to teach with what students should know. That is, the teachers were forced to teach topics that they did not necessarily like or excel at.

The teacher support materials helped me develop background knowledge.

This curriculum has the same constructivist teaching strategies used by our [pd] instructor.

The tight link between the curriculum and the professional development made this possible.

I would not teach without it [the established curriculum] *and would not have accepted the position if it were not in place.*

Without the curriculum in place, I would have stuck strictly to the outline of some text and that would not have been best for the kids.

All teachers should have to learn about how the curriculum is organized.

Professional development that helps teachers understand the structure of the program (such as the instructional model) is worthwhile.

Professional development should engage teachers with actual activities from the program.

Summary

San Diego City Schools' comprehensive professional development program for its physics teachers includes intensive summer institutes, monthly meetings, common planning periods, content courses for out-of-discipline teachers, and both print and web-based support materials. These components have been effective in promoting the growth of a learning community of physics teachers. In addition, the program's curriculum focus has provided teachers with opportunities to develop the relevant scientific and pedagogical knowledge necessary to implement the curriculum effectively. The initial successes of the professional development program are small but important steps toward the vision of professional development described in the *National Science Education Standards* (NRC 1996), whereby teachers lead and engage in long-term experiences that promote reflection, collaboration, inquiry, and the development of integrated understandings of science and teaching.

References

Bybee, R. W. 1997. *Achieving scientific literacy: From purposes to practices*. Portsmouth, NH: Heinemann.

Bybee, R. W., and N. M. Landes. 1990. Science for life and living: An elementary school science program from Biological Sciences Curriculum Study. *The American Biology Teacher* 52 (2).

Loucks-Horsley, S., N. Love, K. Stiles, S. Mundry, and P. Hewson. 2003. *Designing professional development for teachers of science and mathematics*. 2nd ed. Thousand Oaks, CA: Corwin Press.

McDermott, L. C., and The Physics Education Group at the University of Washington. 1996. *Physics by inquiry*. Volumes 1 and 2. New York: Wiley.

National Research Council (NRC). 1996. *National science education standards*. Washington, DC: National Academy Press.

Sparks, D. 2002. *Designing powerful professional development for teachers and principals*. Oxford, OH: National Staff Development Council.

Thompson, C. L., and J. S. Zeuli. 1999. The frame and the tapestry. In *Teaching as the learning profession: Handbook of policy and practice,* eds. L. Darling-Hammond and G. Sykes. San Francisco: Jossey-Bass.

Successes and Continuing Challenges:
Meeting the NSES Visions for Professional Development

Robert E. Yager
University of Iowa

The 16 exemplary programs described in this book illustrate the progress that science education has made in meeting the Professional Development Standards of the National Science Education Standards (NRC 1996). In addition, descriptions of these programs for teachers in training and teachers in the field demonstrate how well the *More Emphasis* conditions of the Teaching Standards, Assessment Standards, and Content Standards have been met. In this Postscript, I outline the *More Emphasis* conditions that are being fulfilled successfully and those where more attention is needed. (For a complete listing of the *More Emphasis* conditions, see Appendix 1.)

Of particular interest is that the 16 programs our Advisory Board selected for publication have addressed all the professional development *More Emphasis* conditions in an exemplary fashion. Only one of these conditions fell below a 75% success rate. This one condition—casting the teacher in the role of a "producer of knowledge about teaching"—is arguably an issue we should work harder toward achieving. Perhaps more attention should be paid to the Lesson Study initiative (developed and practiced in Japan) that is being used in many regions across the United States.

The professional development *More Emphasis* conditions with the greatest, most focused implementation are (1) "collegial and collaborative learning," (2) "teacher as a member of a collegial and professional community," (3) developing "long-term, coherent plans," and (4) "teacher as an intellectual, reflective practitioner."

An analysis of the implementation of *More Emphasis* conditions for the Teaching Standards gives clear, positive evidence of change. Of the nine *More Emphasis* conditions concerning teaching, the only one that was not approached by at least 60% of the programs was the teacher's role in "selecting and adapting curriculum." Conversely, the most success was reported in "supporting a classroom community with cooperation, shared responsibility, and respect." It is certainly significant that the exemplary programs in professional development are so successful in changing teaching in ways that the Standards envision.

The exemplary programs for professional development were also successful in meeting the Assessment Standards. The seven *More Emphasis* conditions of the Assessment Standards were met in a positive fashion, resulting in teachers who understood and used these new guidelines and who understood their value in ensuring student learning. Just as was the case with the teaching *More Emphasis* conditions, the one weakness in the assessment area for the professional development providers discussed in this book was in developing teachers who could either be involved in preparing external assessments or be invited to assist with such assessments. This is one issue where more work must be done. We need to increase the involvement of teachers committed to the visions of the Standards in the preparation of external assessments. Too often in the past, those who produce such assessments have assumed that their job was to devise tests that reflect what teachers are doing in their classrooms—not what teachers should be doing if they are implementing the National Science Education Standards.

Most of the exemplary professional development programs also focused on the definition and description of science content (including a focus on inquiry) found in the Standards. The authors used the general content descriptions and reported major successes. We do need to note, however, the lack of success with four *More Emphasis* conditions from the Content Standards. These were not even in evidence for a third of our exemplars. These areas of continuing weakness are

- *using evidence and strategies for developing or revising an explanation;*
- *science as argument and explanation;*
- *doing more investigations in order to develop understanding, ability, values of inquiry, and knowledge of science content; and*
- *applying the results of experiments to scientific arguments and explanations.* (NRC 1996, p. 113)

Failure to focus on and emphasize these four conditions suggests a need for more attention to the meaning, history, sociology, and psychology of science. Lack of attention to these areas has been a weakness in teacher education programs, where there has been almost total emphasis on content knowledge (almost exclusively in a disciplinary context) and on learning theory and pedagogy.

Furthermore, too many educators think of *science* only as life, physical, and Earth/space—and pay little or no attention to the other four facets of content as defined in the National Science Education Standards (inquiry, technology and its relation to science, science as a means of meeting social challenges, and the history and philosophy of science). There is too little indication that the exemplary professional development programs discussed here have moved far enough toward this broader view of science content.

An analysis of how well the *More Emphasis* conditions have been met by the 16 programs produces exciting results: an 80% success rate. Perhaps programs such as these will succeed in the next two years, with more showing up in the remaining 20%.

Many of the teachers involved with the production of the Standards suggested that it would take at least 10 years to achieve the visions that inform the document. Two years remain, and our 16 exemplars are nearly there! The hope is that other educators will take the ideas described here and develop other programs for teacher candidates and inservice teachers that include a mechanism for collecting evidence of change with respect to all the *More Emphasis* conditions.

More effort is needed when one considers that there are nearly 1,300 colleges and universities with preparatory programs for science teachers. One cannot help but wonder if some of these programs should not combine, so that the numbers enrolled justify a program with all the features demanded by the Standards. It is also apparent that most of the funding for professional development of inservice teachers must be directed more toward the full visions of national standards (including the standards of the National Council of Teachers of Mathematics and the International Technology Education Association) if we are going to be as successful as we need to be in the next decade.

Reference
National Research Council (NRC). 1996. *National science education standards.* Washington, DC: National Academy Press.

Less Emphasis/More Emphasis Conditions of the National Science Education Standards

The National Science Education Standards envision change throughout the system. The **Science Teaching Standards** advocate the following changes in emphases:

LESS EMPHASIS ON	MORE EMPHASIS ON
Treating all students alike and responding to the group as a whole	Understanding and responding to individual student's interests, strengths, experiences, and needs
Rigidly following curriculum	Selecting and adapting curriculum
Focusing on student acquisition of information	Focusing on student understanding and use of scientific knowledge, ideas, and inquiry processes
Presenting scientific knowledge through lecture, text, and demonstration	Guiding students in active and extended scientific inquiry
Asking for recitation of acquired knowledge	Providing opportunities for scientific discussion and debate among students
Testing students for factual information at the end of the unit or chapter	Continuously assessing student understanding
Maintaining responsibility and authority	Sharing responsibility for learning with students
Supporting competition	Supporting a classroom community with cooperation, shared responsibility, and respect
Working alone	Working with other teachers to enhance the science program

Source: National Research Council (NRC). 1996. *National science education standards.* Washington, DC: National Academy Press, p. 52. Reprinted with permission.

The National Science Education Standards envision change throughout the system. The **Professional Development Standards** advocate the following changes in emphases:

LESS EMPHASIS ON	MORE EMPHASIS ON
Transmission of teaching knowledge and skills by lectures	Inquiry into teaching and learning
Learning science by lecture and reading	Learning science through investigation and inquiry
Separation of science and teaching knowledge	Integration of science and teaching knowledge
Separation of theory and practice	Integration of theory and practice in school settings
Individual learning	Collegial and collaborative learning
Fragmented, one-shot sessions	Long-term coherent plans
Courses and workshops	A variety of professional development activities
Reliance on external expertise	Mix of internal and external expertise
Staff developers as educators	Staff developers as facilitators, consultants, and planners
Teacher as technician	Teacher as intellectual, reflective practitioner
Teacher as consumer of knowledge about teaching	Teacher as producer of knowledge about teaching
Teacher as follower	Teacher as leader
Teacher as an individual based in a classroom	Teacher as a member of a collegial professional community
Teacher as target of change	Teacher as source and facilitator of change

Source: National Research Council (NRC). 1996. *National science education standards.* Washington, DC:
National Academy Press, p. 72. Reprinted with permission.

National Science Teachers Association

The National Science Education Standards envision change throughout the system. The **Assessment Standards** advocate the following changes in emphases:

LESS EMPHASIS ON	MORE EMPHASIS ON
Assessing what is easily measured	Assessing what is most highly valued
Assessing discrete knowledge	Assessing rich, well-structured knowledge
Assessing scientific knowledge	Assessing scientific understanding and reasoning
Assessing to learn what students do not know	Assessing to learn what students do understand
Assessing only achievement	Assessing achievement and opportunity to learn
End of term assessments by teachers	Students engaged in ongoing assessment of their work and that of others
Development of external assessessments by measurement experts alone	Teachers involved in the development of external assessments

Source: National Research Council (NRC). 1996. *National science education standards.* Washington, DC:
National Academy Press, p. 100. Reprinted with permission.

The National Science Education Standards envision change through-out the system. The **Science Content Standards** advocate the following changes in emphases:

LESS EMPHASIS ON	MORE EMPHASIS ON
Knowing scientific facts and information	Understanding scientific concepts and developing abilities of inquiry
Studying subject matter disciplines (physical, life, earth sciences) for their own sake	Learning subject matter disciplines in the context of inquiry, technology, science in personal and social perspectives, and history and nature of science
Separating science knowledge and science process	Integrating all aspects of science content
Covering many science topics	Studying a few fundamental science concepts
Implementing inquiry as a set of processes	Implementing inquiry as instructional strategies, abilities, and ideas to be learned

CHANGING EMPHASES TO PROMOTE INQUIRY

LESS EMPHASIS ON	MORE EMPHASIS ON
Activities that demonstrate and verify science content	Activities that investigate and analyze science questions
Investigations confined to one class period	Investigations over extended periods of time
Process skills out of context	Process skills in context
Emphasis on individual process skills such as observation or inference	Using multiple process skills—manipulation, cognitive, procedural
Getting an answer	Using evidence and strategies for developing or revising an explanation
Science as exploration and experiment	Science as argument and explanation

LESS EMPHASIS ON	MORE EMPHASIS ON
Providing answers to questions about science content	Communicating science explanations
Individuals and groups of students analyzing and synthesizing data without defending a conclusion	Groups of students often analyzing and synthesizing data after defending conclusions
Doing few investigations in order to leave time to cover large amounts of content	Doing more investigations in order to develop understanding, ability, values of inquiry, and knowledge of science content
Concluding inquiries with the result of the experiment	Applying the results of experiments to scientific arguments and explanations
Management of materials and equipment	Management of ideas and information
Private communication of student ideas and conclusions to teacher	Public communication of student ideas and work to classmates

Source: National Research Council (NRC). 1996. *National science education standards.* Washington, DC: National Academy Press, p. 113. Reprinted with permission.

The National Science Education Standards envision change throughout the system. The **Science Education Program Standards** advocate the following changes in emphases:

LESS EMPHASIS ON	MORE EMPHASIS ON
Developing science programs at different grade levels independently of one another	Coordinating the development of the K–12 science program across grade levels
Using assessments unrelated to curriculum and teaching	Aligning curriculum, teaching, and assessment
Maintaining current resource allocations for books	Allocating resources necessary for hands-on inquiry teaching aligned with the *Standards*
Textbook- and lecture-driven curriculum	Curriculum that supports the Standards, and includes a variety of components, such as laboratories emphasizing inquiry and field trips
Broad coverage of unconnected factual information	Curriculum that includes natural phenomena and science-related social issues that students encounter in everyday life
Treating science as a subject isolated from other school subjects	Connecting science to other school subjects, such as mathematics and social studies
Science learning opportunities that favor one group of students	Providing challenging opportunities for all students to learn science
Limiting hiring decisions to the administration	Involving successful teachers of science in the hiring process
Maintaining the isolation of teachers	Treating teachers as professionals whose work requires opportunities for continual learning and networking
Supporting competition	Promoting collegiality among teachers as a team to improve the school
Teachers as followers	Teachers as decision makers

Source: National Research Council (NRC). 1996. *National science education standards.* Washington, DC: National Academy Press, p. 224. Reprinted with permission.

The emphasis charts for the **Science Education System Standards** are organized around shifting the emphases at three levels of organization within the education system—district, state, and federal. The three levels of the system selected for these charts are only representative of the many components of the science education system that need to change to promote the vision of science education described in the National Science Education Standards.

FEDERAL SYSTEM

LESS EMPHASIS ON	MORE EMPHASIS ON
Financial support for developing new curriculum materials not aligned with the Standards	Financial support for developing new curriculum materials aligned with the Standards
Support by federal agencies for professional development activities that affect only a few teachers	Support for professional development activities that are aligned with the Standards and promote systemwide changes
Agencies working independently on various components of science education	Coordination among agencies responsible for science education
Support for activities and programs that are unrelated to Standards-based reform	Support for activities and programs that successfully implement the Standards at state and district levels
Federal efforts that are independent of state and local levels	Coordination of reform efforts at federal, state, and local levels
Short-term projects	Long-term commitment of resources to improving science education

STATE SYSTEM

LESS EMPHASIS ON	MORE EMPHASIS ON
Independent initiatives to reform components of science education	Partnerships and coordination of reform efforts
Funds for workshops and programs having little connection to the Standards	Funds to improve curriculum and instruction based on the Standards
Frameworks, textbooks, and materials based on activities only marginally related to the Standards	Frameworks, textbooks, and materials adoption criteria aligned with national and state standards
Assessments aligned with the traditional content of science	Assessments aligned with the Standards and the expanded education view of science content

Current approaches to teacher education	University/college reform of teacher education to include science-specific pedagogy aligned with the Standards
Teacher certification based on formal, historically based requirements	Teacher certification that is based on understanding and abilities in science and science teaching

DISTRICT SYSTEM

LESS EMPHASIS ON	MORE EMPHASIS ON
Technical, short-term, inservice workshops	Ongoing professional development to support teachers
Policies unrelated to Standards-based reform	Policies designed to support changes called for in the Standards
Purchase of textbooks based on traditional topics	Purchase or adoption of curriculum aligned with the Standards and on a conceptual approach to science teaching, including support for hands-on science materials
Standardized tests and assessments unrelated to Standards-based program and practices	Assessments aligned with the Standards
Administration determining what will be involved in improving science education	Teacher leadership in improvement of science science education
Authority at upper levels of educational system	Authority for decisions at level of implementation
School board ignorance of science education program	School board support of improvements aligned with the Standards
Local union contracts that ignore changes in curriculum, instruction, and assessment	Local union contracts that support improvements indicated by the Standards

Source: National Research Council (NRC). 1996. *National science education standards.* Washington, DC: National Academy Press, pp. 239–240. Reprinted with permission.

List of Contributors

Valarie L. Akerson, co-author of "A Collaborative Endeavor to Teach the Nature of Scientific Inquiry: There's More to Science Than Meets the I,'" is an associate professor of science education at Indiana University, Bloomington.

Sondra Akins, author of "Bringing School Science to College: Modeling Inquiry in the Elementary Science Methods Course," is a professor of science education at William Paterson University, Wayne, New Jersey.

Dale Baker, co-author of "TEAMS: Working Together to Improve Teacher Education," is a professor of science education at Arizona State University, Tempe.

Kim Bess, co-author of "Rethinking the Continuing Education of Science Teachers: An Example of Transformative, Curriculum-Based Professional Development," is director of science and educational technology, San Diego City Schools, San Diego, California.

Ruth Burkett, co-author of "Hey!What're Ya Thinkin'? Developing Teachers as Reflective Practitioners," is an assistant professor of science education at Central Missouri State University, Warrensburg.

Douglas Clark, co-author of "TEAMS: Working Together to Improve Teacher Education," is an assistant professor in the College of Education at Arizona State University, Tempe.

Timothy Cooney, co-author of "Exemplary Science: Best Practice in Science Teaching Today," is a professor of Earth science and science education at the University of Northern Iowa, Cedar Falls.

Pradeep M. Dass, author of "Facilitating Improvement Through Professional Development: Teachers Rising to the Occasion," is an associate professor of science education and biology at Appalachian State University, Boone, North Carolina.

Danine Ezell, co-author of "Rethinking the Continuing Education of Science Teachers: An Example of Transformative, Curriculum-Based Professional Development," is science program manager, San Diego City Schools, San Diego, California.

Joan Gaston, co-author of "Professional Development Based on Conceptual Change: Wyoming TRIAD Process," is director of special initiatives in the Wyoming Department of Education.

Shawn M. Glynn, co-author of "The Contextual Teaching and Learning Instructional Approach," is a professor in and interim head of the Department of Mathematics and Science Education, University of Georgia, Athens.

Leslie S. Gordon, co-author of "Applying the National Science Education Standards in Alaska: Weaving Native Knowledge Into Teaching and Learning Environmental Science Through Inquiry," is co-principal investigator of Global Change Education Using Western Science and Native Observations at the University of Alaska, Fairbanks.

Deborah L. Hanuscin, co-author of "A Collaborative Endeavor to Teach the Nature of Scientific Inquiry: There's More to Science than Meets the I,'" is an assistant professor in the Southwestern Bell Science Education Center at the University of Missouri, Columbia.

Leslie G. Hickok, co-author of "Knowing and Teaching Science: Just Do It," is a professor of botany at the University of Tennessee, Knoxville.

Paul Kelter, co-author of "Operation Chemistry: Where the Clocks Run by Orange Juice and the T-Shirts Are Never Bare," is University Distinguished Teacher/Scholar and a professor of chemistry at the University of Illinois, Urbana-Champaign.

Raymond Kessel, co-author of "Emphasizing Inquiry, Collaboration, and Leadership in K–12 Professional Development," is a co-director of the Wisconsin Teacher Enhancement Program in the Department of Medical Genetics (where he is also a professor) at the University of Wisconsin, Madison.

Susan B. Koba, co-author of "Community of Excellence: More Emphasis on Teacher Quality," is project director of the Urban Systemic Program for the Omaha Public Schools, Omaha, Nebraska.

Thomas R. Koballa, Jr., co-author of "The Contextual Teaching and Learning Instructional Approach," is a professor of science education at the University of Georgia, Athens.

Cyndy Leard, co-author of "Hey! What're Ya Thinkin'? Developing Teachers as Reflective Practitioners," is an education specialist in the Center for Ocean Sciences Education, College of Marine Science, University of South Florida, St. Petersburg.

Cherin Lee, co-author of "Exemplary Science: Best Practice in Science Teaching Today," is an associate professor of biology and science education at the University of Northern Iowa, Cedar Falls.

Julie A. Luft, co-author of "Filling the Void in the Professional Development Continuum: Assisting Beginning Secondary Teachers," is an associate professor of science education at the University of Texas at Austin.

Eddie Lunsford, co-author of "Knowing and Teaching Science: Just Do It," is an instructor of biology at Southwestern Community College, Sylva, North Carolina.

C. W. McLaughlin, co-author of "Operation Chemistry: Where the Clocks Run by Orange Juice and the T-Shirts Are Never Bare," is a senior lecturer at the University of Nebraska, Lincoln.

National Science Teachers Association

Claudia T. Melear, co-author of "Knowing and Teaching Science: Just Do It," is an associate professor of science education at the University of Tennessee, Knoxville.

Carol T. Taylor Mitchell, co-author of "Community of Excellence: More Emphasis on Teacher Quality," is an associate professor of science education at the University of Nebraska, Omaha.

Michael Patrick, co-author of "Emphasizing Inquiry, Collaboration, and Leadership in K–12 Professional Development," is co-director of the Wisconsin Teacher Enhancement Program in the Department of Medical Genetics at the University of Wisconsin, Madison, and co-director of the Center for BioMolecular Modeling and adjunct professor of chemistry and physics at the Milwaukee School of Engineering.

Nancy C. Patterson, co-author of "Filling the Void in the Professional Development Continuum: Assisting Beginning Secondary Science Teachers," is an assistant professor of secondary social studies education at Bowling Green State University, Bowling Green, Ohio.

Bill Pearson, co-author of "Rethinking the Continuing Education of Science Teachers: An Example of Transformative, Curriculum-Based Professional Development," is a physics lead teacher in the San Diego City Schools, San Diego, California.

Andrew J. Petto, co-author of "Emphasizing Inquiry, Collaboration, and Leadership in K–12 Professional Development, " is editor of Reports of the National Center for Science Education in Berkeley, California, and a lecturer in anatomy and physiology in the Department of Biological Sciences at the University of Wisconsin, Milwaukee.

Michael Piburn, co-author of "TEAMS: Working Together to Improve Teacher Education," is a professor of science education at Arizona State University, Tempe.

Janet Carlson Powell, co-author of "Rethinking the Continuing Education of Science Teachers: An Example of Transformative, Curriculum-Based Professional Development," is associate director, Biological Sciences Curriculum Study (BSCS) Center for Professional Development, Colorado Springs, Colorado.

Gillian H. Roehrig, co-author of "Filling the Void in the Professional Development Continuum: Assisting Beginning Secondary Science Teachers," is an assistant professor in the Department of Curriculum and Instruction at the University of Minnesota, Minneapolis.

Barbara Woodworth Saigo, co-author of "Professional Development Based on Conceptual Change: Wyoming TRIAD Process," is president of Saiwood Biology Resources/Saiwood Publications in St. Cloud, Minnesota.

Bonnie Schindler, co-author of "Rethinking the Continuing Education of Science Teachers: An Example of Transformative, Curriculum-Based Professional Development," is science program director, San Diego City Schools, San Diego, California.

Philip M. Silverman, author of "The Oklahoma Science Project for Professional Development: A Road Taken," is a member of the Program in Molecular, Cell, and Developmental Biology, Oklahoma Medical Research Foundation, Oklahoma City, Oklahoma.

Elena B. Sparrow, co-author of "Applying the National Science Education Standards in Alaska: Weaving Native Knowledge Into Teaching and Learning Environmental Science Through Inquiry," is a research associate professor of soil microbiology and science education in the School of Natural Resources and Agricultural Sciences at the University of Alaska, Fairbanks.

Barbara S. Spector, co-author of "Hey!What're Ya Thinkin'? Developing Teachers as Reflective Practitioners," is a professor of science education at the University of South Florida, Tampa, Florida. She is also director of the Center for Ocean Sciences Education, College of Marine Science, University of South Florida, St. Petersburg, Florida.

Joseph I. Stepans, co-author of "Professional Development Based on Conceptual Change: Wyoming TRIAD Process," is a professor of science and mathematics education at the University of Wyoming, Laramie.

Sidney Stephens, co-author of "Applying the National Science Education Standards in Alaska: Weaving Native Knowledge Into Teaching and Learning Environmental Science Through Inquiry," is a science educator in the School of Natural Resources and Agricultural Sciences at the University of Alaska, Fairbanks.

Joseph A. Taylor, co-author of "Rethinking the Continuing Education of Science Teachers: An Example of Transformative, Curriculum-Based Professional Development," is a science educator at Biological Sciences Curriculum Study (BSCS), Colorado Springs, Colorado.

David R. Van Dusen, co-author of "Rethinking the Continuing Education of Science Teachers: An Example of Transformative, Curriculum-Based Professional Development," is a science administrator with the San Diego City Schools, San Diego, California.

Jerry Walsh, co-author of "Operation Chemistry: Where the Clocks Run by Orange Juice and the T-Shirts Are Never Bare," is a professor of chemistry at the University of North Carolina, Greensboro.

Robert E. Yager, author of the Introduction and the Postscript, is a professor of science education at the University of Iowa, Iowa City.

Index

Page numbers printed in **boldface** type indicate tables or figures.

Professional development: and Alternative Support for Induction Science Teachers, 123–130; and Basic Science Minor at University of Northern Iowa, 45–52; challenges and solutions of, xi–xii; and Collier Chautauqua Program, 55–73; and Community of Excellence in Mathematics and Science, 111–120; and Contextual Teaching and Learning approach, 75–83; definition of, xi; and Inquiry-Based Teaching and Learning Model for Science Methods, 13–32; and Knowing and Teaching Science: Just Do It program, 133–145; and Learning Science by Inquiry program, 1–11; and Observing Locally, Connecting Globally program, 85–98; and Oklahoma Science Project, 161–169; and Operation Chemistry, 99–110; and San Diego City Schools program for continuing education, 203–211; and Science/Technology/Society Program for Middle Grades Education, 189–201; successes in and continuing challenges for, 213–215; and TEAMS (Teacher Education in Arizona for Mathematics and Science), 35–43; and Wisconsin Teacher Enhancement Program, 147–159; and Wyoming TRIAD process, 171–186. *See also* National Science Education Standards; Teachers

Professional Development Schools (PDSs), and Wisconsin Teacher Enhancement Program, 159

Professional development specialist (PDS), and Community of Excellence in Mathematics and Science, 112, 115

Profiler (online instrument), 113, 118

Project Jukebox, and Observing Locally, Connecting Globally program, 88, 89

Public policy, and Op Chem program, 106

R

Reflection: and Inquiry-Based Teaching and Learning Model for Science Methods, 24–

26, 30–32; and Observing Locally, Connecting Globally program, 90, 93, 94–95; and Science/Technology/Society Program for Middle Grades Education, 189–201; and Wisconsin Teacher Enhancement Program, 152; and Wyoming TRIAD process, 184

Reformed Teaching Observation Protocol (RTOP) (Piburn et al. 2000), 42–43

Reinsmith, W. A., 195

Return to Science, and Oklahoma Science Project, 165

Reuss–Ianni, E., 63

Rocks, and Inquiry-Based Teaching and Learning Model for Science Methods, 15–16, 22–23. *See also* Earth science

Roehrig, G. H., 126

Rubrics, and Knowing and Teaching Science: Just Do It program, **138**, 139, **140**, 141

S

Saigo, B. W., 177

Salad Bowl course module, and Wisconsin Teacher Enhancement Program, 151

Salish I Research Project, Secondary Teaching Analysis Matrix (STAM), 144

San Diego City Schools (SDCS) program for continuing education of science teachers, 203–211

School culture, and Wyoming TRIAD process, 185

Schoolwide Path, and Community of Excellence in Mathematics and Science, 112, 117–120

Science: Basic Science Minor at University of Northern Iowa and methods of, 50; and common views of elementary children about scientists, 14, 21; definition of, x; Inquiry-Based Teaching and Learning Model for Science Methods and literacy in, 20–21, 26–27, 32; need for more attention to meaning, history, sociology, and psychology of, 214; students and misinformation or precon-